# ARCHER'S DIGEST

## 3rd Edition

## By Cheri Elliott

### Edited by Jack Lewis

**DBI BOOKS INC., NORTHFIELD, ILLINOIS**

**About the Cover**
A colorful assemblage of archery gear typifies today's state of the art. Featured is Bear's Delta-V compound which is billed as the "world's fastest bow." The bow, arrows, accessories and targets are from Chicago Archery Center, Chicago, Ill. Photo by John Hanusin.

# EDITORIAL DIRECTOR
## Jack Lewis

# PRODUCTION DIRECTOR
## Sonya Kaiser

# ART DIRECTORS
## Dana Silzle
## Denise Hegert

# PRODUCTION COORDINATOR
## Betty Burris

# COPY EDITOR
## Dorine Imbach

# CONTRIBUTING EDITORS
## Roger Combs
## Sam Fadala
## C.R. Learn

# PUBLISHER
## Sheldon Factor

**Produced by**

*Charger Productions*

ISBN: 0-910676-40-2

Library of Congress Catalog Card Number 77-148722

# CONTENTS

# INTRODUCTION

Although your only intention when picking up this book may have been to satisfy your curiosity about archery, the seeds of participation are already there. The interest is also there, needing only a belief in your ability to prompt you to give archery a try. Whether or not you know it, the ability is also there, for *anyone* can shoot a bow, and *anyone* can become skilled at it. It only takes some basic knowledge of the sport and the desire to achieve.

Within these pages you will find all you need to know about what you need and how to go about becoming an archer. All that remains is for you to provide the desire.

*Cheri Elliott*

Cheri Elliott
Burton, South Carolina

# Chapter 1

# ARCHERY THROUGH THE AGES

## From Caveman To Soldier To The Sportsman Of Today, No Other Invention Has Remained So Useful For So Long

Archery has been a force in civilization since time began, as evidenced by the legendary Colossus of Rhodes statue.

ONCE CONSIDERED the primary military weapon, the bow today rarely affects the growth or existence of civilizations. And yet, it once did. It is doubtful that the average person will recognize the effect archery has had on mankind; it is true that it once played a vital role in the development or destruction of entire nations and societies of people. So important was the contribution of the bow that men were given special honors if they could master its use, sons were forced by law to learn how to use it, and great statues were erected featuring it.

One of the seven wonders of the world indicates that archery was a prominent force in civilization as early as 260 B.C. That wonder is known as the Colossus of Rhodes, the Fifth Wonder of the World. Erected to honor the sun god Helios, the people of Rhodes are said to have spent some twelve years building the Colossus, which stood more than one hundred feet high and was said to span the city's harbor, one foot perched atop each side of a wall surrounding either side of the harbor. So huge was the Colossus that ships were said to have sailed between its legs.

In his right hand the bronzed Helios held the flame of light, and in his left, his bow.

In Greek mythology we also hear of the great powers and effectiveness of the bow and arrow. Who has not heard of the great Achilles, the mythical hero of ancient Greece, famed for his great strength and courage. He was considered perfect, or nearly so, and impervious to the weapons of that date, for his mother is said to have dipped him into the River Styx when he was but an infant, thus protecting him from any and all of mortal man's assaults. As fable tells us, it was the one small spot from which Achilles' mother had suspended him over the water that proved his undoing — shot by a poisoned arrow into his heel.

And finally, there is the mythical being to which men of today still refer; the Roman god of love, Cupid. In representations of Cupid we see a cherubic child with bow and arrow, ready to pierce the heart of any unwary man with his load of love.

As with all mythical events, there was reason to honor

the archer, for the prowess of the bow and arrow have been recorded throughout ancient history.

Today we may think of the bow and arrow as primitive, archaic, perhaps even primeval. And all of these adjectives are correct. Although we do not know precisely when archery first came into being, it is reasonable to assume that it began shortly after man learned how to design and build its more primitive brothers, the spear and dagger. Were you to trace its development through the centuries you might be surprised to discover how great a role archery really has played in history and in the lifestyles of mankind.

References are made to the use and importance of the bow in nearly all known ancient civilizations. From hieroglyphics and crude records we can prove its existence not only as a weapon, but as the primary weapon and harvester of meat for early man.

In 400 B.C. we are told of a great military struggle referred to in history books as the March of the Ten Thousand. In actual numbers the Athenian soldiers probably numbered closer to 13,000 men who, deceived into the loss of most of their leadership, were forced to retreat to their homeland in Cyrus. Throughout their journey home they were attacked unmercifully by slingers and mounted bowmen. When the Greeks finally reached their homeland their numbers had been reduced to but about six thousand soldiers, the remainder having fallen victim to the devastation of the bowmen's arrows and the persistent onslaught of mother nature.

About that same period of time, 490 B.C., it was the established tradition of military leaders to plan their attacks with reliance on their archers to rout the advancing enemy. Each army would approach the other with bowmen lofting

*Stone Age artifacts that were laboriously chipped from flint and obsidian are included in the Fred Bear Museum, which presents the history of archery down through the ages. Included in this part of the collection are an arrowhead, spear point, adze, skinning knife, fish hooks. In spite of crudeness, note care of design, workmanship.*

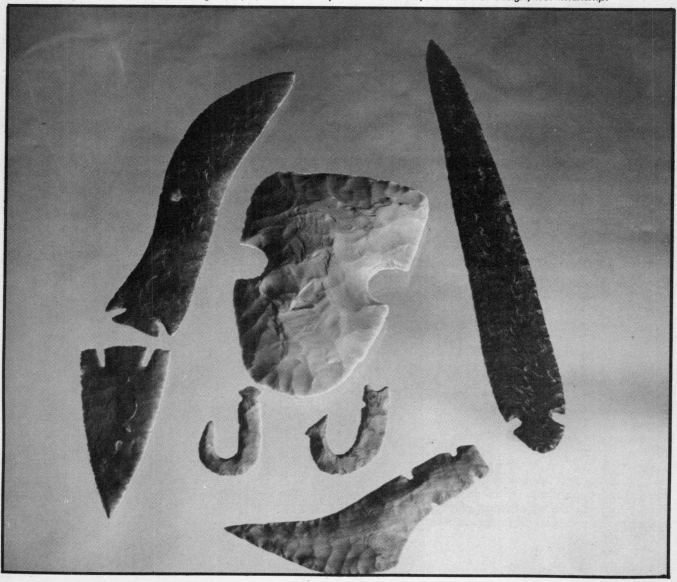

*The so-called March of the Ten Thousand has been depicted by many artists; in each instance, archery tackle of era is featured.*

arrows as they went. Each time it was the same. The archers carrying their aerial attack, followed by the ever forward advance of the foot soldiers. The effectiveness of the archers was so expected that the military leaders grew to rely heavily on it.

In 490 B.C. it was this expected effectiveness of the bowmen that proved the undoing of the master archers of Persia. The Persian army, intent on overcoming Greece, relied heavily on the effectiveness of its bowmen. Their quest was to overwhelm the citizens of Athens, who were armed only with spears. The plan should have worked, and probably would have, had the people of Athens waited out the attack as previous opponents had done. But the Greeks chose, instead, to rush the surprised Persians. Coming so quickly and unexpectedly their attack left the Persian arrows striking empty ground behind the Greeks, soon resulting in the hand-to-hand combat so appropriate to the Greeks. Having lost untold numbers of soldiers, the Persians felt no other option available except to retreat.

References are found frequently in the Latin writings of

the famed Roman ruler and soldier Julius Caesar and his rise to power. We know, for instance, that when Caesar conquered "all of Gaul" he did so with the wise use of bowmen, which he used as an advance army, to clear the way for his foot soldiers. A cloud of arrows was far from exaggeration in 40 B.C. It was fact!

It probably did not matter how accurate the archer of that day might be — only how many arrows he could loft into the sky in a given period of time. By sheer law of averages some of these arrows were bound to hit enemy troops, especially since it was the habit of troops of that time to remain in tight clusters as they advanced.

In every nation of that time there were archers. The Turks were renowned for their bowmanship, as were the Chinese. But perhaps no greater fame was earned than that of the English bowman. In his quest to rule England, William, Duke of Normandy, counted on the skills of his archers to overcome Harold, a Saxon who'd had himself crowned King of England in 1066.

In a fierce battle, lasting some nine hours, the forces of William and Harold fought, but the skill of the Norman archers, sending waves of arrows through the sky succeeded in swinging the victory to William, earning him the title we know him by today, William the Conqueror.

Youngsters tell of Robin Hood and his Merry Men, said to be master archers excelling all others during the Middle Ages. Robin symbolized the common man; a fair comparison since most archers of that day were in fact

This old print concerning the Battle of Crecy in 1346 illustrates the fact that the English, with the longbows, proved far superior to French archers, who were armed with crossbows; the English won the hard, bloody battle.

commoners. Although we hear a great deal about the romance of the English knight, there were, in reality, very few knights and noblemen in the English forces. The bulk of the forces were commoners, professional fighters who hired out in return for a pay scale twice what they could expect as a laborer. As an added incentive there was the possibility of obtaining booty from successful raids on enemy towns.

Because the bow was the most important weapon of that day, families were encouraged to practice archery. It is said to have been the only sport permitted to be practiced on Sundays. Another law, supposedly, required that all male sons be given lessons with the bow and arrow until such time as they could prove themselves proficient with it.

The English bow of that day was a massive thing, measuring some five feet in length. It was shot by lugging the string back as far as possible, raising the bow to give the arrow length in its cast. The arrow, itself, was known as a "cloth-yard" shaft, which referred to its length of exactly one yard. All bowmen shot the same length arrow, there were no allowances for differences in arm length, nor in physical strength.

It was in the famed Hundred Year's War (1337-1453) that the English bowman had his finest hour. The English were largely outnumbered in nearly all of the battles they fought and yet they won most of those battles. Of special note were the battles of Crecy and Poitiers (1346 and 1356). The French came by the score, armed with crossbows. Against them stood the English longbowmen. Even though the English are said to have included the use of cannons in both of these battles, it was the longbow that proved the greatest influence. It should also be noted, in fairness to the French, that their forces contained a large number of knights and noblemen who, although possessing great authority, lacked greatly in training and the ability to follow orders. It was the desire of the French knight to meet in hand-to-hand battle. The English had only to gauge the progress of the advancing Frenchmen as they marched forward and knock them down as they came.

With the advent of the gun and gunpowder the influence

*This display in the National Museum illustrates the use of the bow by American Indians before white man's arrival.*

of the bow and arrow gradually ebbed in "civilized" countries. The bow was relegated to the status of primitive weapon. The effectiveness it offered was all but forgotten.

Forgotten, perhaps, until settlers landed on Plymouth Rock and were introduced to the American Indian. While we may picture the Englishman as many things, we seldom picture him as an archer. Indians, however, are always seen as such. And they were, in fact, excellent archers. As soon as a lad could hold a bow he was taught to shoot it. He used that bow not only for defense, but for obtaining food. And he became extremely proficient with it.

Until the arrival of the white man, Indians fought exclusively with bow and arrow, spear and tomahawk. But it took very little time for them to realize that the rifle was a better weapon for them. It could far outdistance their arrow range, and eventually could fire many more shots within a given time. Still some continued to use their bows and their skill made history. They could shoot from nearly any position, standing or riding horses. Sometimes the arrows were poisoned. Always they were effective.

Today men seldom fight with bows and arrows and there are no bowmen within military ranks. Only in the remote, so-called uncivilized areas of the world is the bow still a valued tool of war or food supply. From the tool of necessity to the tool of war, it has grown to the tool of leisure. Archery is now a sport, but it remains the sport of the common people.

The bow plays an important role in Greek mythology and was invariably carried by Diana, goddess of the hunt. (Below) In this painting displayed in the Pantheon in Paris, bowmen attempt to capture immortal Joan of Arc.

*The immediate thrill of an introduction to archery is in hitting the target, as these young archers in South Carolina have discovered. In spite of their youth, a bit of practice soon will have them centering target's gold.*

## Chapter 2

# IS ARCHERY FOR YOU?

*Thousands Of Men, Women And Children Are Finding Archery Challenging, Rewarding*

A 7-YEAR-OLD child struggles briefly with his recurve bow as he attempts to sight in on the gold, releases his arrow, then watches the shaft as it sails not into the ten-point gold, but settles in the white ring of a two. And he smiles! That huge, ear to ear smile that tells anyone around that he has really accomplished something. He is an archer!

Is archery for you? You bet it's for you, regardless of

At 7 years of age, Brian Cormier may experience a little difficulty in positioning his armguard, but he handles a bow with increasing success at ranges up to twenty yards.

Championship form is obvious in this young El Monte, California, archer. As a member of the Junior Olympic Archery Development Program, he hopes one day to shoot for Olympic medals, representing U.S. in competition.

your age or physical condition, regardless of your mental or physical limitations! A 60-year-old gentleman can shoot a bow with as much skill and expertise as does his 31-year-old son. A 10-year-old boy can outshoot a 20-year-old man. A teenage girl can place six arrows within a three-inch circle at twenty yards in one target while her mother does the same in another target.

You can shoot a bow regardless of your age, provided you can draw it back, and there are excellent bows requiring draw weights of as little as fifteen pounds.

You also can shoot a bow regardless of your physical condition or handicap. There are archers who are confined to wheelchairs, others who shoot with artificial limbs and still others who shoot even though they are legally blind. Admittedly it takes special archery equipment to outfit these fine archers, an added amount of determination, but the equipment is available and it is being used by numbers of archers who otherwise could only watch from the sidelines.

There is a romantic draw to archery, allowing us to travel back to the days of the Wild West and "California or Bust." In busting balloons at forty yards we can see ourselves as skilled Indians on the plains or as members of Robin Hood's Merry Men, though of course we probably will not admit it.

Children still play cowboys and Indians today, even though they share their enthusiasm with space and *Star Wars*. Give a child a few minutes, along with a branch from a tree and some twine, and he still will build himself a bow.

Why do we bother with a sport that non-shooters tell us is archaic; a once-was? There are no crowds clamoring for seats in stadiums where they might watch the final ends of an archery tournament. In fact, to the average spectator, even to many of us involved in archery, watching an archery tournament is a lot like watching grass grow. There is no sudden burst of enthusiasm, no conquest of one man over another. It's just you — the archer — and your target.

Perhaps that is what makes archery so interesting to more than 200,000 people. While shooting your bow you have no one to please but yourself. You can set goals for yourself or not set them; it doesn't matter to anyone but you. There is no great urge to prove yourself.

Does that mean that archery is boring to the archer? Hardly. Place your first arrow into the center of a target and feel the surge of adrenaline — the total feeling of accomplishment. Watch the light in a child's eyes when he finally creeps his arrow along the grass to the target and places that first arrow in the scoring rings. Talk about pride in oneself; it's doubtful that any one thing can make you

*Children can participate in archery, regardless of size or strength, as bow weights are simply matched to strength of the child; techniques of draw are the same. From left: Mike Elliott, Adam Neidig, Rob Hard, Christie Neidig.*

feel any more contented with your abilities.

The fact is that, although you will not see it prescribed in medical journals, archery is a highly therapeutic sport. As a method of unwinding, it's hard to beat, for it allows you to concentrate on one object (your target) while you expend some of that bottled up energy that is making stomach muscles tighten, and head throb. If you like, you can even pretend for a brief time that the target you are shooting is the object of your pent-up anger or fears. It can, for a time, take on the images of the typewriter that continuously spelled incorrectly, the computer that gave incorrect feedback, the jackhammer that jarred your aching back all day long. And it does all this without ever really changing form. Because you need only to concentrate on one spot, and can call the spot anything you wish; you can see that 10-gold as a silver dollar or as the flat tire on your automobile and nothing is harmed. Yet with each cast arrow, your anger and frustrations ebb away until you can

*With only two weeks of training, these determined young archers have mastered the basic techniques, including the provision for elevation, even though draw weight and physical strength are in short supply for somewhat distant target.*

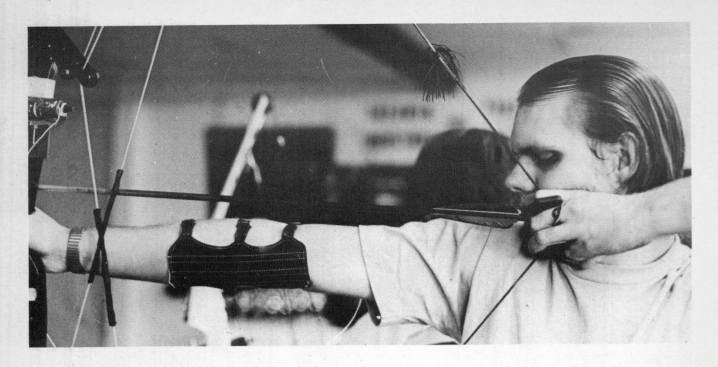

Archery can be pursued by anyone, regardless of handicap, as evidenced by this archer who is legally blind. He uses his ears to sight, utilizing a specially adapted sight on his bow, which provides a tone for him to react upon when he is sighted in on the bull's-eye of the target. This type of program is enjoying increased success among handicapped.

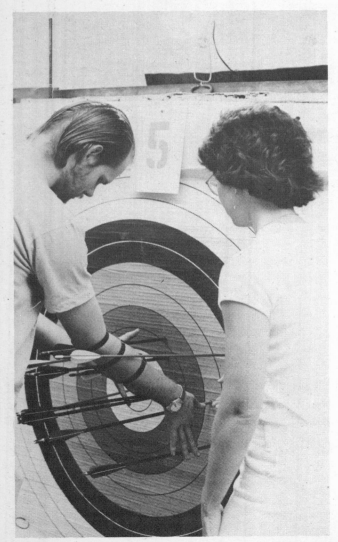

As much a thrill as the actual shooting is the scoring of a round. A competitor in the first national blind archery tournament, Skeeter Revard, feels placement of his arrows.

admit that that tire had been in need of replacing for some time, or that it wasn't really the typewriter that spelled incorrectly, but the typist operating the typewriter.

Archery also is an individualized sport, for the most part, which means that when you have a bad day — and eventually you will have one or more — you are letting no one down. There are no teammates counting on your score. Even when you shoot in competition, whether as a professional archer or as an amateur in one of the national archery programs, you do not have to place yourself in a position where others are counting on your performance.

If you enjoy the competition between other participants, you can have that as well. You can join an archery team, particularly one of the college teams, if you are a student. You can join a local club, and compete with your club against other clubs. Or you can compete against your neighbor, your wife, your child. If you want to compete, the options are there for the taking. Few recognized sports offer such liberty.

Archery is open to nearly all economic levels. It is not uncommon to hear archery referred to as "a depression sport," a pastime that becomes most inviting when funds

Championship archery can begin at any age, with most major tournaments open to all age levels. Archers such as Annette Popoff begin earning medals while still at the grade school level.

If you're looking for competition on the team level, college archery teams earn funds for schools, with medals for individual members of the team.

are in short supply. It is a title it shares with such other sports as fishing and baseball. Why would archery be more interesting to the average individual during a depression status than in the more lucrative eras? Because, in reality it costs little to participate. It's true that you can spend several hundred dollars on archery tackle if you so desire. But you can also limit your expenditures to less than $100 and give yourself years of enjoyment and participation.

For the archer who wishes to shoot just for the enjoyment of it, the more economical bows are just as suitable as are the highly effective and efficient deluxe models. You can even trade up, using your old bow as a trade-in on a newer model, much like many of us trade-in our used cars for later models.

In order to shoot archery, you must have a bow, arrows and a safe shooting zone. You do not have to have a quiver. You can simply lay your arrows on the ground or build a makeshift quiver out of odds and ends from around the house. You do not have to have an armguard, but if you can't afford a purchased one yet still desire one, you can make your own out of a section of denim and a piece of cardboard. Even the cutoff end of a sock will do to hold the cardboard to your arm for a period of time. Obviously the length of time the makeshift armguard will prove effective will be short, but when the sock wears out, there's always the mate to that sock to convert.

Beginning bow kits can be purchased for as little as $10 for a set, complete with fiberglass bow, three arrows and an

*In archery, the opportunities for junior competitors to shoot alongside skilled experts is not unusual. Lynnette Johnson of the United States Archery Team is quick to show junior archers from California the techniques she favors.*

*If your interest is financial reward, famed Las Vegas shoots, an annual affair, draw the finest archers from across the nation. Competition is fierce, scores often close, but a winning series of rounds can pay off big.*

*A basic need for young archers is good coaching so they do not pick up poor habits before they really get into the sport. An experienced target shooter can catch problems early and help the youngster develop proper techniques.*

armguard. You also can spend up to $500 for a bow alone. The $100 figure probably will be more sensible, at least initially.

Whatever price range you decide on, you can have fun. You also can make many of your items. Unique to archery is the opportunity to make many of your equipment items if you so desire: quivers, armguards, targets, bowstrings, arrows. Even compound bows can be made today from kits available through several of the major archery manufacturers. Thus archery can be not only one of your favorite sports, but one of your favorite hobbies as well.

How much time you need to spend on it will be totally up to you. In archery there are no established minimums, unless you are competing in a tournament. You can spend fifteen minutes or five hours, provided your arms don't give out. Although you need a safe backstop, you can shoot at that backstop from any distance, in rain or in sunshine. There is no need for a specialized court, or net. A hillside

will do nicely for a backstop, if you have not the traditional backstop available to you. It is difficult to substitute something else for a basketball net, although business executives have been known to use their wastebaskets for free throw shots. But nearly anything will do for an archery target, from a printed animal target to a wild flower growing in a clearing.

What can you expect to get out of archery? Enjoyment; as well as plenty of exercise for the back and leg, arm and chest muscles. You'll be surprised at how quickly you'll be able to handle the heavier bows.

You'll also find challenge, in getting that wood or aluminum or fiberglass shaft to the target with any degree of consistency, and accomplishment, when it does finally get there.

And you'll be doing it all at your own pace, when you want to, because you want to.

# Chapter 3
# SELECTING EQUIPMENT
## *How Does The Novice Make These Choices Wisely?*

*Determining which eye is dominant is relatively simple. With someone providing an aiming point for you, place your hands in front of your face, then extend your arms fully, hands overlapping to form an aiming triangle.*

**Y**OU'VE DECIDED *to give archery a try. Excellent! That's the first step toward learning and enjoying one of America's most personally rewarding but little publicized sports. But making that decision will give you no real enjoyment — participation will. How then does the novice archer obtain equipment? Where does he go? And how can he know if the equipment he is purchasing will work well for him?*

Whatever the equipment item might be that you are purchasing, your first step must be to locate a source. Where do you buy archery supplies?

A quick look through your telephone book probably will tell you that archery pro shops in your neighborhood are few and far between — perhaps even non-existent if you live in a small, rural area. Yet, the pro shop is probably your best source of not only equipment but expertise; as the pro shop deals only in archery supplies it must rely on its ability to retain you as a regular customer in order to survive. It's retention capabilities more than likely will depend on the service it supplies, rather than on the equipment itself.

More often than not the pro shop owner is an archer, perhaps a tournament archer, but more than likely a bowhunter. Thus he not only knows how the equipment is supposed to work, he knows how to use it and, perhaps more importantly, what to do if it should fail to work properly.

*Keeping your hands in the position described in adjoining photo, quickly draw your hands to your face. Repeat this several times, while your assistant records to which eye your hands are drawn. This is your dominant eye. As you'll note the archer's right eye has been completely blocked by his right hand and he is sighting through left dominant eye.*

Generally speaking, pro shop owners are eager to assure that you have the proper equipment. On occasion you might even think them too eager, especially when, after agonizing moments spent deciding exactly which item to purchase, you finally make up your mind, only to find them trying to sway your thinking to another selection. Their recommendation probably will have nothing to do with the cost of that item. In fact, their selection may cost less than yours. Why, then, do they seemingly interfere? Because they want you to be satisfied with your final selection for years to come. They *need* for you to be happy in order to keep you as an archer, thus as a customer.

But, as mentioned, archery pro shops are few in number and, for a large percentage of the would-be archers, the pro shop is nothing more than a dream or, at best, a lengthy drive. For the archer devoid of a pro shop there are still several sources of gear: the local sporting goods store, including major department stores with archery lines; the mail-order warehouses; the archery manufacturers. Of the three, the local sporting goods store will serve you well providing you know what you want *before* you go there. If you are a novice archer, and choose to shop at such a store, try to find an experienced archer to shop with you — someone who will know what you need and why.

What about mail-order businesses? Can you get what you want from them? Are there guarantees with the products they sell? Will service be reasonably quick, and can adjustments be made if the product is not what you really wanted?

Generally speaking, mail-order businesses that specialize in archery equipment offer an excellent alternative to the

*Test the effect of changing your aiming eye by sighting in on a target while closing one eye. In this case, archer has closed his right eye and is sighting through his left eye. (Below) Now switch eyes and note where your finger points. The target seems to have moved to the right, but in reality, it has not moved at all, aim is affected.*

pro shop. Like the pro shop dealer, the mail-order retailer is probably an archer. Often he has established his mail-order business because, like you, he had some difficulty in obtaining archery supplies locally and decided to be his own source of supplies.

The major advantage to the mail-order shop is that it generally carries a much larger inventory of supplies than does the average pro shop. Consequently you are offered a greater choice of equipment. Like the pro shop owner, the mail-order dealer is eager to meet your needs, but to do so he must rely on your knowing what you want, or at least being able to provide the basic information necessary to allow him to meet your needs. The same is true of the individual who purchases his equipment directly from the manufacturer.

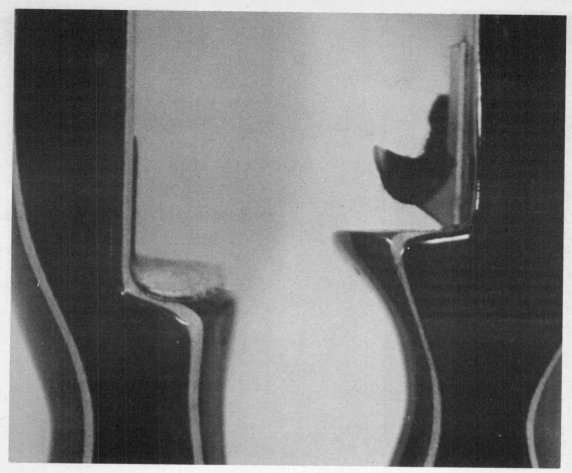

When looking over bows from major manufacturers, you will note that most of them produce models for either the left or right-handed archer. Most custom bowyers also offer the buyer this option.

Whether purchasing through the manufacturer or the mail-order dealer, you can expect service to be as quick as is possible. Since they do not rely on personal service as a selling point, these organizations rely instead on the appeal of the merchandise itself and on their ability to get it to you swiftly and to fill your order accurately.

Although you cannot get personal service on a one-to-one, face-to-face basis, both organizations will offer you a service department whose function is to answer your queries, and to handle any possible complaints or performance problems in their equipment.

Usually, if the item you order does not fit you — is perhaps too heavy or too short in draw length — they will offer an exchange program that allows you to swap the item for one that fits your needs more closely. Neither organization wants you outfitted with a bow, for instance, that doesn't "fit," because they know that you will be more likely to stick with that particular brand of bow, or that particular source of equipment, even when you decide to move up a line, if you have been initially satisfied by it. However, in both cases they will be relying on you to give them the basic information needed to fit you properly. Fit, then, becomes your first major area of concern when selecting equipment.

The legend that appears on the lower limb of all bows offers most of the information one needs to know about that bow, including draw length, weight, compound let-off.

## DOES IT FIT?

When you buy a new shirt or pair of hunting boots, you try them on to see if they fit. The same should be true of your archery equipment. This is especially true in the case of your bow, as it is generally the most expensive single item of equipment you will purchase. How do you determine whether or not a bow fits you? You try it on!

The fit of a bow involves several factors: draw length, draw weight, mass weight, design, whether right or left-handed.

Most archers purchase their initial bow in the left or right-hand model that accommodates their normal use. If they write right-handed, then they generally shoot right-handed, even though they could possibly shoot much better left-handed. Whether to shoot left or right-handed has nothing to do with writing techniques. Which you should use becomes dependent on your vision, not your habits. Many excellent archers shoot left-handed, and yet do "everything else" right-handed. The reverse is equally true. Determining whether or not to shoot right or left-handed should be dependent on your "dominant eye."

What is a dominant eye, and how can you quickly decide which of your eyes is dominant? In laymen's terms, a dominant eye is that eye which tends to "take over" your vision, especially when you become tired. Everyone has one eye that is dominant over the other, though to some people the difference might be more readily recognized than in others. You want to shoot to that dominant eye because it is apt to take over your shooting eventually, even though you would rather that it didn't.

The mass weight of a bow can be just as important as the draw weight, if you intend shooting for long periods.

How much a bow weighs can be important in the field, too, if you plan on carrying it long distances on the hunt.

The photos above show that recurve bows weigh in vicinity of two pounds each, while the compounds weighed by the author ranged in weight from four to six pounds each.

How can you tell which eye is dominant? A simple test involves the use of a second person to score your results. Standing directly in front of you, he places one finger in front of you. Place your arms outstretched, hands overlapping one another to form a triangle with which to "aim" through with both eyes open onto that single finger. The finger is your aiming point. Continuing to sight in on that extended finger, draw your arms quickly to your face, hands remaining in an overlapping position. Do this several times before making your determination. Your dominant eye will pull your hands to it as you draw them toward your face, and with your hands directly in front of your face you will find yourself looking through only one eye.

If you do not have someone to assist you in this simple test, you can obtain reasonably accurate results by sighting in on a stationary object, such as a chair leg, or door knob. When your hands touch your face, hold them still while you force yourself to determine which eye is dominating the other.

Do you have to shoot to your dominant eye? No, you do not. But be prepared to experience some sighting inconsistencies if you do not. During the first few minutes of shooting, you may be able to keep that dominant eye in check simply by closing it, or concentrating on the use of your other eye. But more than likely it eventually will overcome that eye — especially as your practice sessions wear on and you begin to tire. Having spent a good deal of effort and time in adjusting your bowsights until you finally have your arrows hitting gold, you may be suddenly surprised and not a little bit irritated to find yourself shooting wild to the right or left. Why? The cause may be any number of things, from a slipping arrow rest to a poor release. But more than likely it will be due to the change of eyesight.

To realize just how much of a difference a change of eye can make in your shooting, point the finger of your right hand at a given spot on a target — say the bull's-eye. Close your left eye and, sighting down your arm, place that finger directly in the center of the target. Now, without moving your arm, switch eyes. What has happened to your point of aim? Instead of being on target you'll notice that the end of your finger is instead pointing some distance to the right of the bull's-eye. Use your left eye to sight in, and then change eyes, and the target seems to move to the left, even though you have not moved either your aiming finger or the target. The difference is in the sightline between left and right eye, and is apparent in every archer. Consequently you should determine which eye to shoot with and stick to that eye.

There was a time when shooting left-handed placed you at an extreme handicap — not because right-handed archers

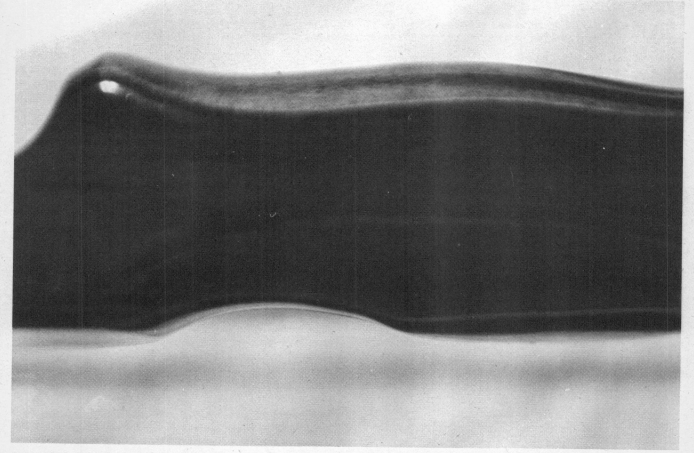

*Styles and sizes of bow handles vary greatly, depending upon the design favored by the individual manufacturer.*

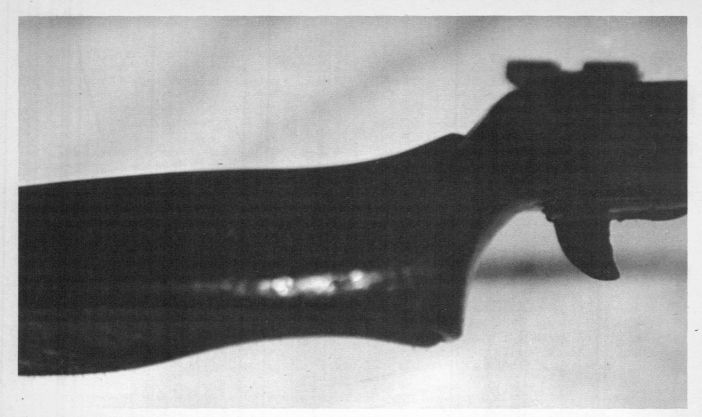

The handle of every bow is supposed to be functional and some makers have several different sizes, styles, which is an effort to offer a variety that will fit everyone. Some archers rework the handles to individual requirements.

could shoot any better than left-handed archers, but because they could find gear much more easily than could the left-hander. To a great extent that is no longer true, for even though local shops may carry mostly right-handed models, they can easily obtain a left-handed version for you if needed. All major manufacturers offer their bows in both right- and left-hand models. Accessories are designed to be used either way. There is no difference in either quantity or quality of bows whether left or right handed.

Usually a right-handed person's right eye is dominant; if left-handed, it is the left eye.

Once you know which hand you will be using to shoot, you can then turn your attention to which style of bow you will need. Basically, bows come in two styles: either target or hunting model. Both bows can be used for either activity, but each is more appropriate to only one. One quick glance generally will tell you the difference between the two. The target bow is usually the ornate one, often finished in a bright color, with plenty of shiny metal to accent its lines. The hunting bow is apt to be far more subtle in color — perhaps even drab. You should see no shine in its finish and any metal probably will be painted over with a dull, non-reflective paint. The reason for this is obvious: the brightness that attracts your attention also attracts the attention of the game animals.

Once you have decided on a right or left-hand style — and the type of bow you desire — you must now consider weight: both draw weight and mass weight.

Bow weight refers to the amount of pull necessary to draw the bowstring to full draw, normally to the corner of your mouth with your bow arm fully extended. If you intend to limit your shooting to backyard tournaments or indoor shooting, you probably will want a lightweight bow, that gives limited distance, yet is every bit as accurate for closer shots.

If you intend on doing some long-distance shooting or bowhunting, you will want a heavier, more effective, faster bow. The minimum weight bow for bowhunting generally is set at forty-five pounds for deer, thirty-five pounds for small game. That same thirty-five pounds is probably all you will need for indoor range shooting, although twenty-five pounds is equally effective, as evidenced by the skill of the young junior archers. In some states, in order to obtain a bowhunting license, you will be required to cast your arrow a given minimum distance. Your twenty-five-pound bow probably will not meet that minimum requirement.

Does that mean you must have two separate bows if you wish to do both bowhunting and target archery, or that you must overbow for tournament shooting to meet the minimum requirements of bowhunting? Not necessarily. Many of the bows on the market today offer weight range adjustments, of as much as fifteen pounds, which means that you may set your bow weight at twenty-five pounds for tournament shooting, but tune it up to forty pounds for small-game hunting. You'll find this capability common among compound bows. For recurve bowmen, the same option is available in the takedown bow, which allows you to purchase separate weight bowlimbs for the same bow handle.

We've mentioned bow weight, and each time we were referring to the draw weight of the bow. There is another

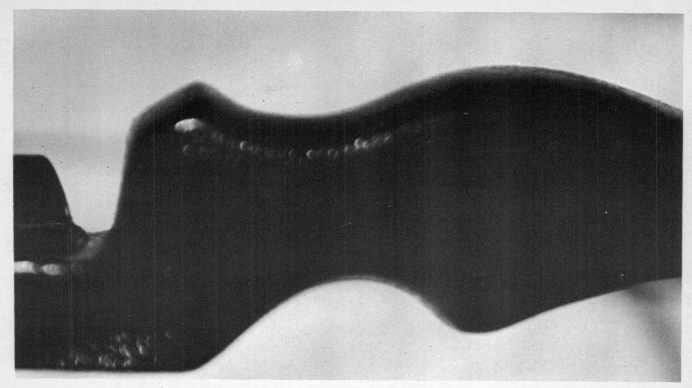

The wooden handle of this Proline bow is somewhat chunky, affording the archer a good handful when he exerts grip.

bow weight to consider, however — mass weight. All bows are *not* created equal. There can be a wide range of differences in the mass weight of one bow as compared to another, dependent on the physical makeup of that bow. Generally speaking, recurve bows will weigh a good deal less than compounds. The more accessory capabilities are built into the bow, the more it will weigh. If the bow has a magnesium handle, it will weigh more than a comparable bow with an all-wood handle. You may like the feel of a heavy bow in your hands, the solidity it projects and, if you are not intent on shooting for long periods of time, the heavier bow should serve you well. Its weight can actually function as a stabilizing factor for a brief time span. However, if you intend on shooting half the day or toting your bow over miles of hunting terrain, you may prefer a lighter weight version. Several dozen arrows after you begin shooting, even the lightweight bow begins to "gain weight" as muscles tire and concentration ebbs.

Now you are ready to consider draw length: the distance you will be drawing the bow back when at full draw. This distance should be measured, not guessed. A dowel with a nock placed on the end of it works well as a measuring device. A measuring stick also will work, although not quite as efficiently. Drawing the bow to the corner of your mouth, have someone mark the point at which the measuring device rests over the arrowrest. Then calculate that distance from the indentation of the nock to the rest. That is your draw length, and should be considered in even inches. Do not shorten the length of your draw. If your measurement is, for example, 29½ inches, use thirty inches

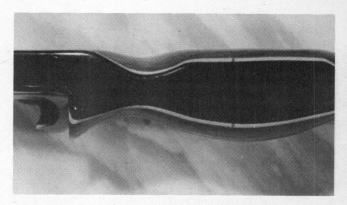

Combining clean lines with the practical requirements of grip that meets everyone's needs is design problem.

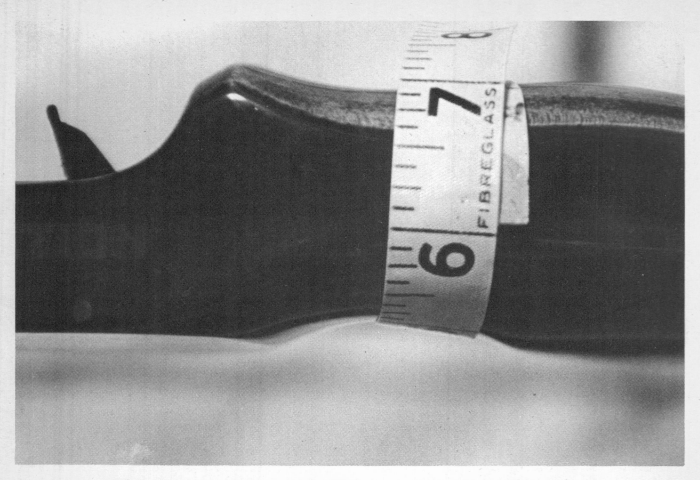

If you have a small-size hand, you may experience some difficulty in gripping this wide-handled bow properly.

as your determining factor, not twenty-nine inches. This is especially true for the archer new to archery and uncertain as to where his actual anchor point might be. As you practice you will find yourself increasing your draw length, as muscles become accustomed to the draw weight and you begin to form your shooting style. Consequently, you may find that the bow you thought fit perfectly at twenty-nine inches is now an inch or so too short.

For those who shoot recurve bows, draw length is not of great importance, since there are no eccentrics to limit the draw. Here, draw length is only of concern if you are requiring a specific *draw weight*. On the bottom limb of the bow will be the given draw weight at a specific draw length. The draw length is usually twenty-eight inches.

If your draw length is, however, thirty inches you can still shoot the same recurve bow. Your draw weight will increase an estimated four pounds for each inch you increase your draw length beyond the given twenty-eight inches.

## COSMETICS AND ADJUSTABILITY

If this is your first bow, you should expect to upgrade your equipment in the near future. You will be surprised at how quickly you will learn the basics of archery, and how rapidly you will find yourself wishing you could add or change your gear. A twenty-five-pound draw weight is a handful for a beginning young adult or female archer, but a few months of practice and both will wish the bow weight could be increased to thirty pounds or so. Consequently, if the bow you are purchasing offers adjustability in draw weight, either by adjustable turn bolts as used in compounds, or by changing bow limbs as in the takedown recurves, you're apt to be happier with the bow for a longer period of time.

Consider also how the bow feels in your hand. Does the grip fit you? Bowgrips come in a variety of sizes, from extremely thin, streamlined models to the chunky, more solid styles, often of wood. If you've a small hand, a wide handle can be difficult for you to control. If you've a large hand, you'll probably not want a handle so small that your

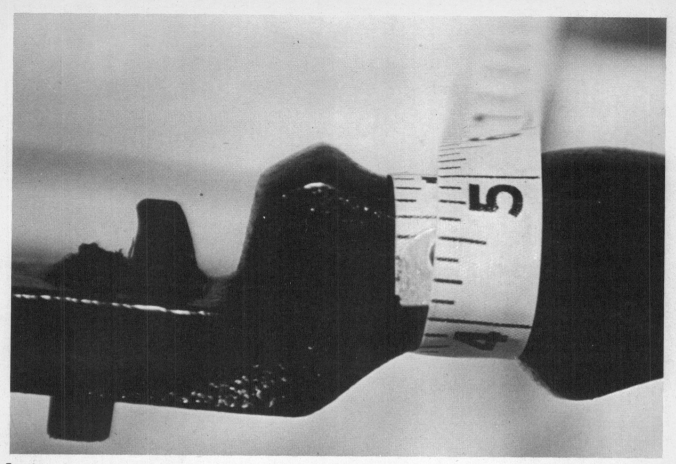

*For the archer who has large hands, he will find that a bow with a small handle such as this is not best choice.*

fingers entirely encircle the handle. Having held a few styles of bows, you will soon know which handle fits you best.

As a final consideration, you will want to look at the overall cosmetic effect of the bow. Although appearance has little or nothing to do with the performance of a bow, it is probably what drew you to a particular style of bow initially, and it does matter. If you like the appearance of your bow, you are apt to care for it more conscientiously, and apt to use it more often. You must also consider where you will be shooting it, whether indoors under protected weather conditions, or outdoors, possibly in poor, wet weather.

Once you have determined the bow that is right for you, many other decisions you will make regarding equipment will fall somewhat into place. The type of arrow you will use, discussed at great length in another chapter, will depend on the type and weight of bow you have chosen and what uses you will make of your bow. Whether or not you will need extras such as sights, weights, stabilizers, special rests, will depend on where and why you want to shoot as well as the type of bow you have chosen. You'll

not need to be in any particular hurry to acquire accessories once you have your basics: the bow, arrows and target. The remainder of the equipment, if indeed you choose to increase your tackle, can be purchased as needs dictate.

The most difficult decision you will have to make is in which type of bow to buy. In making your decision, provided the opportunity is there, shoot them all. Ask your friends. Ask members of the local archery clubs. Do not be afraid to ask as many questions as you possibly can. But keep in mind when you are asking that there is no one more prejudiced in favor of a particular type of bow than is the bowman who is using that bow. Every archer can give you a handful of reasons why his bow is better than someone else's, because it is *his* bow. It fits him, he knows how to use it, and he enjoys the effects of his shooting when he uses it.

Once you have found the bow for you, you'll find that you also have become opinionated. It will be *your* bow that shoots best, or the fastest, or the most comfortably. For it is your bow. You chose it. It has become your personal archery tool. And after all, bows *are* very personal things.

*Archery production equipment has come a long way since several pioneers started making bows in garages and home workshops. The factory above is the new Bear Archery facility in Gainesville, Florida; modern in every way.*

## Chapter 4

# SELECTING A BOW

*Longbow, Recurve, Compound: How Does The Novice Determine Which Is Right For Him?*

The legendary Howard Hill and his longbow skills were the subject of and used in numerous films of several decades ago. Many of his feats cannot be matched by today's archers.

## LONGBOW

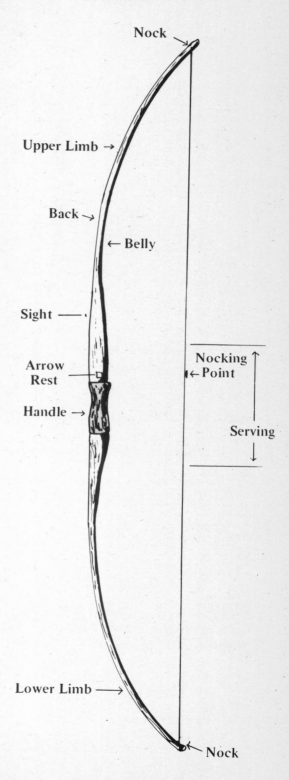

Nock

Upper Limb →

Back →

← Belly

Sight —

Arrow Rest

Handle →

Nocking
← Point

Serving

Lower Limb →

Nock

**L**ONGBOW? RECURVE? Compound? Place them side by side and what do you see? Two brothers and a step-child? Most individuals can see the relationship between the longbow and the recurve, but that compound bow is a horse of a different color; or, more accurately, a bow of a different generation.

For the majority of new archers, especially those choosing to bowhunt, the compound bow is *the* bow to shoot — the Bow of Today — symbolic, perhaps, of the advances of modern technology that created it. Yet there are countless archers who prefer to shoot the older, more traditional bows, the recurve and longbow. What, then do

*The recurve bow took over popularity in the Fifties, more forgiving of a bad release. Close up Big Five bow, below, shows shelf arrangement and leather insert at riser and handle. Shelf is brief; bow cant prevents arrow slip-off.*

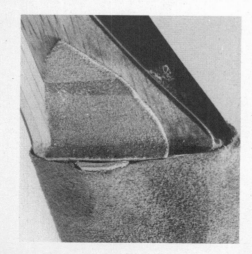

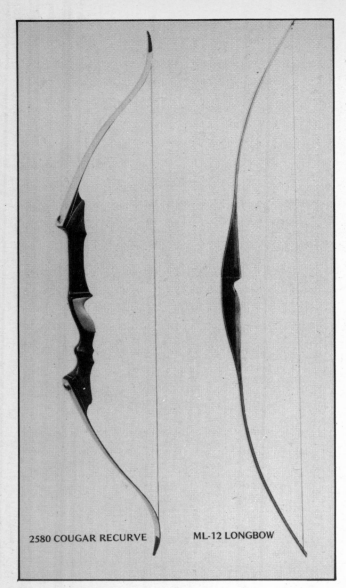

2580 COUGAR RECURVE          ML-12 LONGBOW

*Longbows and recurves have not lost all popularity; each still has its fans. These two by Martin are examples.*

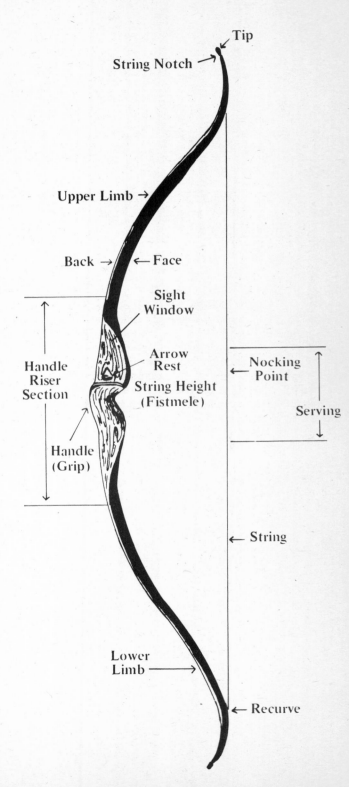

## RECURVE

Tip

String Notch

Upper Limb →

Back →   ← Face

Sight Window

Handle Riser Section

Arrow Rest

String Height (Fistmele)

Handle (Grip)

Nocking Point

Serving

String

Lower Limb →

Recurve

these three basic categories of bow offer to the new archer? How are they different? In what ways can they be compared?

## LONGBOWS

If you enjoy reliving the past, or perhaps simply testing your character against the challenge of ages past, you're apt to choose a longbow as your preferred style of bow. In terms of simplicity, nothing beats the longbow, whose basic design involves a straight stick-and-string composition. It is

*Fred Bear, at right, has perhaps done more to increase the popularity of archery than any other. He has dedicated his life to archery and game conservation.*

*The only bow acceptable for world and Olympic competition is the recurve. Modern bow handles are drilled and tapped to accept all accessories, adjustable rests, stabilizers, and sights, used by the tournament archer.*

this straight-limb design that gives the longbow its nickname, the stick bow. If you are like many of us, placing a longbow in your hands will bring back memories of decades past, when you whittled a branch from a fruit tree into a makeshift longbow, then set about stalking targets and squirrels with your branch-made arrows.

How simple it was to make your tree-limbed bow and how well it worked. After all, it was patterned after that famed English longbow of the Middle Ages; and the skill of those archers and their bent sticks will live throughout history.

The longbow of today is just as simple as was the design of its ancestors. There are no arrow rests and plungers to contend with, no stabilizers or peep sights; not even a bowquiver to hold your arrows. In fact, there are no accessories for the longbow whatsoever; just a string and the bow stave.

It's possible to add a rest to a longbow, if you like, and many archers do just that. But for the natural archer, the

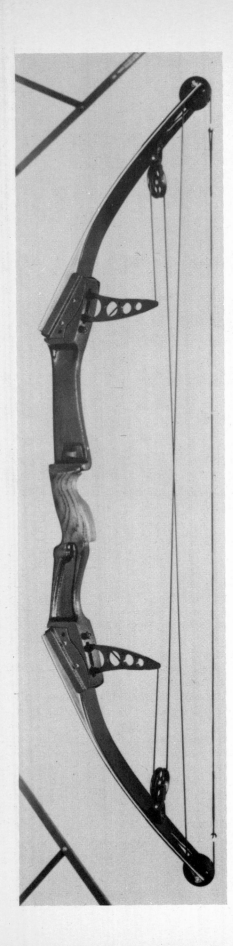

way to shoot the longbow is the way it's been shot for decades: straight off the bowshelf. Generally it's a pretty small shelf at that, and many a longbow archer has found himself shooting more off the top of his hand than off the shelf.

If simplicity is a major attraction of the longbow, it certainly is not the only attraction. One of the primary reasons the longbow is making a gradual comeback in archery circles is because of the reputation it holds as being a more forgiving bow.

The term *forgiving* means that an archer with a less-than-perfect release can get away with slight flaws and still hit his target. Of the three major styles of bows, the longbow is the most forgiving of errors in shooting form.

Howard Hill, the most famous of modern longbow shooters, once said that he shot a longbow exclusively because he felt he was not good enough to shoot the then-newer-styled recurves. Anyone who ever watched Hill shoot, whether in person or at their local movie houses during those shorts between feature films, would have found Hill's evaluation of his abilities somewhat difficult to

*Holless W. Allen, above, is credited with and holds the patent for development of the modern compound bow design.*

*Left: The modern four-wheel compound bow is a mass of cables, eccentric wheels, engineering and production skills.*

Bow manufacturer Tom Jennings utilized the compound bow theory to derive a quality product which is a leader in its field. Once known as a mechanical monster, the design is now accepted and used by 75 percent of all archers.

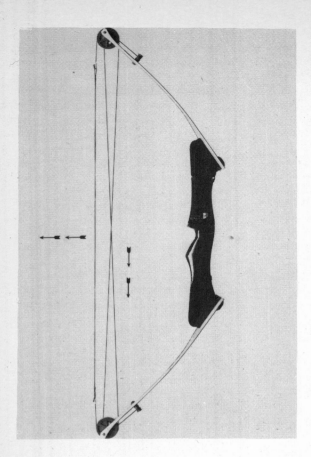

Browning's Nomad compound demonstrates the change in force direction from archers' draw on the string to the vertical cables. Pulley system permits archer to pull and hold greater draw weight at less effort than otherwise possible. Flexing limbs add additional force to arrow.

accept. Here was a man who could shoot arrow after arrow with amazing accuracy, who could entertain people of all walks of life with his skill, who could shoot a silver dollar out of the air. Hill knew what to expect from his longbow and how to make it perform well for him. He knew every inch of it by heart, for he had made it himself.

Today, we think of the individual who makes his own bow as a hobbyist, a garage craftsman. And the term *craftsman* is certainly correct, just as it was back in the Forties and Fifties when *most* archers made their own bows or had someone else make one for them. There were no mass-produced archery outlets. Bows were carved from wood, usually Osage orange, yew, hickory or lemonwood. They were usually long in length and heavy in draw weight. The bow that Hill used in his famed African hunt that yielded him the Big Five, including three elephants, provided a draw weight of 115 pounds, a heavyweight by anyone's standards.

Other than the cables, a primary feature of compound bows is the eccentric wheel. The term refers to the design of the axle holes, which are placed off-center, as indicated by arrows in photo above, so that the wheel actually rolls in an oval ring upon draw. A sharp curve is created on initial draw when resistance from the bow is less, but it swings to a wider arc at midpoint of draw, offsetting the increased resistance of the flexing bow limbs.

Today, the novice archer still can shoot a Howard Hill longbow, patterned after Hill's famous African model, the Sweetheart bow. Although mass-produced, they are nearly perfect in match to the original Hill bow.

Should you purchase such a bow, what can you expect, and how do you select the right bow for you? Your bow will be sixty to seventy inches in overall length, from tip to tip, far longer than the average compound. Your bow probably will be made of bubinga hardwood with heat-treated bamboo limbs backed by a form of fiberglass called Bow-Tuff. Although the bubinga may not be as attractive as Osage orange wood, it is a strong, sturdy material that serves well as a bow riser or handle.

Do not look for fancy grips or additions for your longbow. You'll find none. Generally, the only addition to the riser to mark the grip is a strip of leather wrapped around to serve as an aid in gripping the bow. At the uppermost end of that wrapping, you'll find an added piece of hard leather, shaped like an "L" laying on its side, which

has been woven into the strip to form a simple rest. Expect this rest to be extremely abbreviated, causing some archers to cant their longbow when they shoot it, slanting it slightly to prevent the arrow from falling off.

As you draw your longbow, you undoubtably will notice a rapid increase in resistance to your draw. This is termed *stacking* and is caused by the resistance being offered against the bending of the bow limbs. At twenty-eight inches in draw length, you will feel the full weight of that fifty-pound longbow, so be certain that is the weight you want to shoot before you purchase the bow.

It is this stacking of the longbow that caused some archers to look toward a bow that would be easier to draw. From their search came the recurve bow.

## RECURVE BOWS

The recurve bow gets its name from the shape of its limb tips. Relaxed and unstrung, the limbs seem to curve gradually toward the archer, then suddenly sweep out and

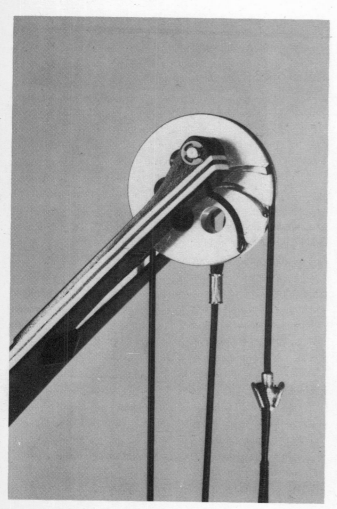

*Most modern compounds, such as the PSE eccentric shown, offer adjustable draw length. This feature will be useful as skill progresses, so keep that in mind when choosing a bow. Normal adjustment range is one to two inches.*

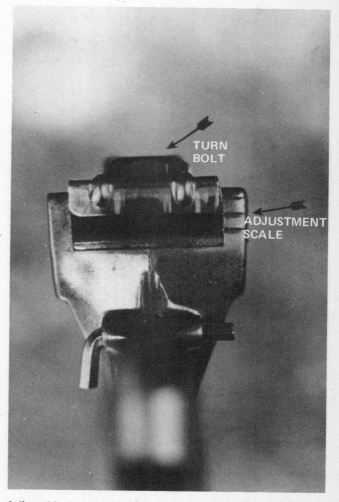

TURN BOLT

ADJUSTMENT SCALE

*Adjustable draw weight is another feature of the modern compound design. Turning the limb bolt in increases draw weight by about five pounds for each full turn.*

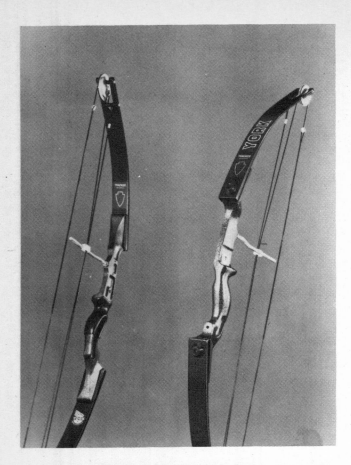

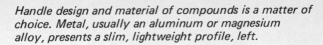

*Handle design and material of compounds is a matter of choice. Metal, usually an aluminum or magnesium alloy, presents a slim, lightweight profile, left.*

away from him, curving backward, or recurving.

There was a time when the recurve bow was *the* bow to shoot. Much faster than the longbow, it is also easier to draw, and its shorter tip-to-tip length makes it easier to handle in the field. Arrow flight offers a much straighter, less arched flight, which means the arrow reaches its mark much quicker — a particularly popular plus if you are after game likely to jump the string.

Among those archers entering the hunting fields with recurve bow and arrow was an individual destined to become a legend in archery lore. It wasn't easy to fill the shoes of a man like Howard Hill, and Fred Bear probably

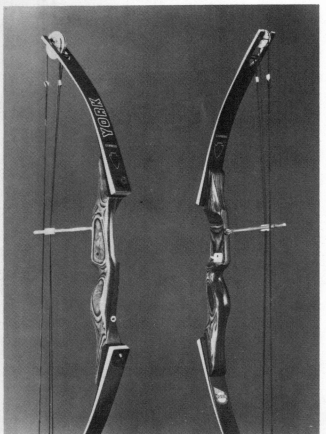

*Two common methods of attaching eccentric wheels to the limbs are the hanger brackets, left, and through a split limb design, at right. The hangers are less expensive to produce, requiring no additional tip strength. Split-limb designs cost more but generally offer higher performance.*

*The other popular choice for handles is natural wood, often laminated and/or impregnated for added strength.*

would be the first to insist that he never has tried. After all, Howard Hill was the lord of the longbow. As for Fred Bear, he didn't seem to cater much to the straight stick, opting for that recurve design Hill had tried and discarded.

With his recurve, handcrafted initially, Fred Bear was able to transfer archery from a spectator sport to one of participation. He gave it nationwide notoriety through his films presented on the popular sports programs of the Sixties, shooting elephant in Africa and polar bear in Alaska. And he made it look easy enough for anyone, male or female, to try.

Like Hill, Bear found quality archery equipment difficult if not impossible to obtain during those early years of the 1930s. But that proved no problem. He simply made the bows himself, in his garage. The quality of his recurve spread quickly and he soon found himself producing more bows than his small garage could handle; thus he began looking toward archery manufacturing as a business. Today Bear Archery is one of the leading names in archery

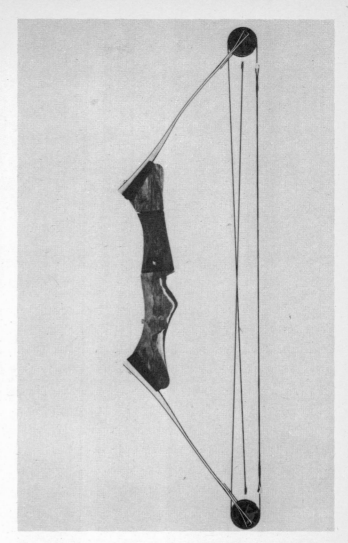

Two-wheel compounds are fast and forgiving, cost less to produce than more complicated four- or six-wheel models.

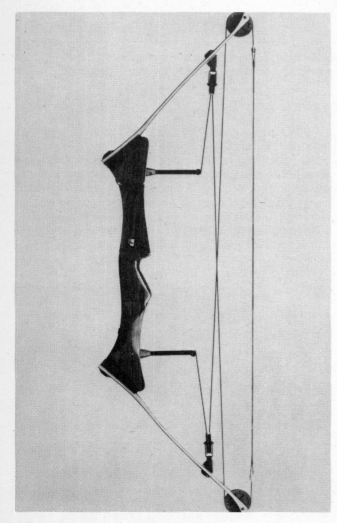

Four- or six-wheel compounds offer greater ranges of adjustability for personalized shooting, but are more complex. The choice is up to the archer.

equipment, manufacturing top-line bows for experts and quality bows for beginners.

One of the major drawbacks to the recurve during its earlier development was the mass needed to provide the necessary draw weight. To shoot such a bow meant a heavy, enforced hold on the bowhandle, often resulting in torquing of the bow and a resulting poor release.

With the introduction of plastic and fiberglass, the problem of mass gave way to gloss and glass, and there was no stopping the recurve's growth. Bowling alleys were transformed into archery lanes, high school and college athletic programs introduced archery to their curriculums and nearly everyone was using the recurve.

The recurve bow was *in*, and you could find it in countless different styles, from heavy to lightweight, long or petite, as durable as denim jeans or as fast as a falling

*An excellent way to learn construction and function of the compound bow is to actually build one from a kit. The Jennings was the first kit compound on the market with its Model K. Instructions are complete and understandable.*

*Alloy handle of the Jennings Model K still has flashing ridges from casting moulds to be filed and sanded off.*

In selecting a recurve bow, you must consider both your draw weight and length. The recurve is extremely simple in design involving, as the National Archery Association describes it, "a handle, two flexible limbs and a string." The modern recurve is both accurate and reasonably inexpensive. It is also highly adaptable, performing with the same ease and accuracy on the tournament field as it offers in the bowhunting field. For many bowhunters who prefer the compound bow for most hunting, the recurve bow is

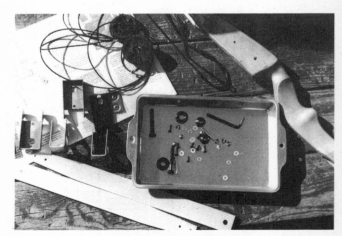

*After reading over the instructions, the first step is to assemble all parts. Keep small washers, bolts and clips in a pan or jar container to prevent loss. The kit builder should learn name and function of each part.*

star. You needed only to determine your needs and find the bow that best suited those needs.

Although the popularity of the recurve is not nearly as dominant today as it was in the Forties and Fifties, it is still a prominent part of archery, especially if you are into tournament archery on a worldwide or collegiate scale. For although the compound bow is by far the more popular style of bow for novice archers, it has yet to gain legal status among collegiate or national archery competition.

*Particular care and attention must be paid to flash around limb cup mounts where pivot plates rock for weight adjustment.*

still a popular choice for bowfishing and small-game hunting, due largely to its lowered cost.

If you are purchasing your recurve bow to be used in bowhunting, you will need little in terms of accessory capabilities. The addition of a simple sight and bowquiver, perhaps a hunting stabilizer or adjustable rest, and you're set to fill your gamebag, provided skill and luck are with you.

For tournament shooting, you'll want to be sure your bow offers the maximum in adjustability, allowing you to "tune" it to your varying archery abilities as practice makes you better. Here an adjustable rest is a must, along with one or more stabilizers.

The recurve bowman who takes to the tournament field today may be shooting a bow patterned after the bows of the ancient Chinese, but you'll be hard pressed to realize it after one quick look at these bows parading along a tournament line with sliding sights and gleaming silver stabilizers sticking out in front and toward the sides of each bow. Here is archery at its gleaming best.

If you are considering tournament shooting, you will be wise to purchase a bow that will accept these modifications, rather than hope to modify your bow later. It's true that you can drill and tap your bowhandle to accept a stabilizer or sight, but it's much more simple to purchase a bow that is already drilled and tapped. Most recurves on the market today, whether tournament or bowhunting model, already are thus machined for all archery accessories.

What should you look for in your first recurve bow? Look first for the draw weight and length. It doesn't make any difference how pretty the bow might be or how many accessories it might have, if it doesn't fit you. Of the two —

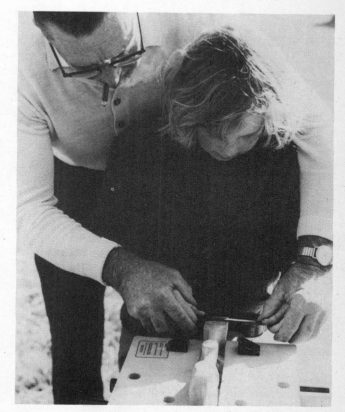

*Compound kit building is an ideal family project. Archer Ed Noyes assists granddaughter Eva with her filing technique.*

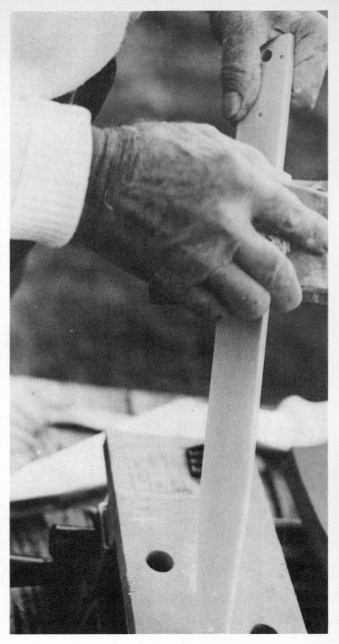

For final finish on the alloy handle, fine grade sandpaper and a lightweight power sander are handy. Degree of finish is option of builder but handle dimensions are not altered.

Use of sanding block is recommended when working on fiberglass limbs of Model K. Fiberglass contains tiny slivers which are painful. Avoid too much sanding.

weight and length — the former will be the most important. You can draw a twenty-eight-inch recurve bow back to twenty-nine or even thirty inches, or shorten the draw to twenty-six or twenty-seven, if that is what your draw length needs to be, and your bow still will shoot well for you. The only difference will be in the draw weight you experience. A general consensus is that for every inch you draw your bow back beyond the indicated draw length, you increase the draw weight by four pounds. The reverse is equally true. Thus a person who has a twenty-nine-inch draw, shooting a twenty-eight-inch bow, will experience a draw weight four pounds heavier than that of the individual with the twenty-eighty-inch draw length.

Draw weight is a characteristic of bows you will need to match to your physical capabilities. To be sure, the novice archer who can only handle a thirty-pound draw weight during the first few months of his archery participation undoubtably will be able to handle heavier weights as he

Handle and other metal parts to be spray painted may be hung on bent coat hangers. First coat on handle is zinc chromate, to which final color will adhere.

Lacquer or enamel paints may be used for final coat, but enamel is usually more durable; both dry rapidly on warm, sunny day. Bow limbs may be same, or complementary color.

progresses, but if the first bow he purchases is too heavy for him — "over-bows" him — he will find archery far too difficult and perhaps even damaging to his physical abilities. So match your bow to your *realistic* draw weight — that weight you can handle without experiencing the shakes before you get to or immediately upon reaching full draw. You should be comfortable in the draw weight, feeling the pull but not fighting it.

In order to determine what the draw weight of a particular bow might be, you will need to read the legend printed on one of the limbs, normally the bottom limb. There it will tell you the draw weight of that bow at twenty-eight inches, unless otherwise noted. For example, the designation 45-lb means that the bow will have a draw weight of forty-five pounds at twenty-eight inches.

As an archer will gain strength and be able to shoot heavier draw weight bows as he practices, it may be wise to delay purchase of your first bow until after you have

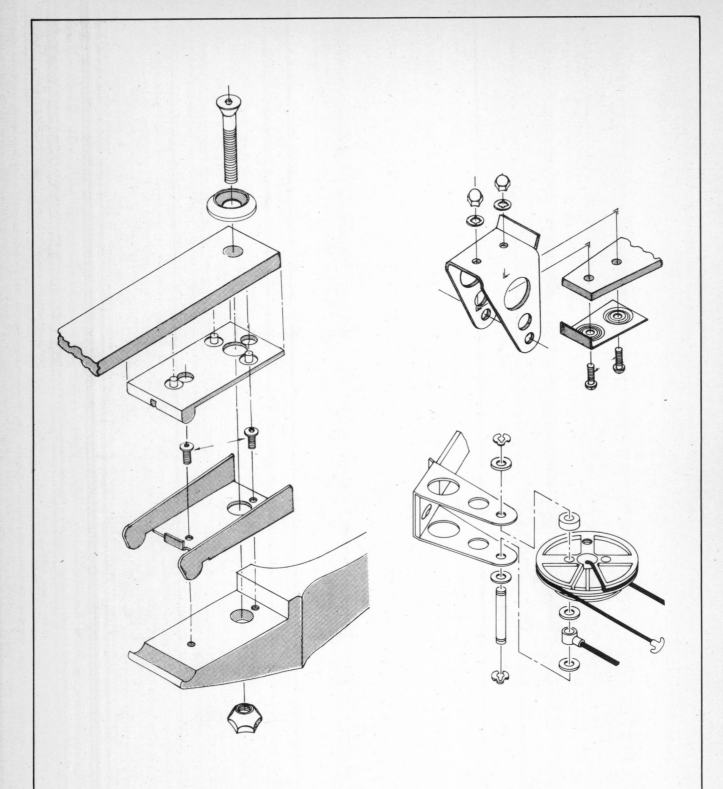

*Exploded drawings showing assembly of handle, limb cups, pivot plate, limb butt, and weight adjustment bolt and nut, left. At right, assembly of important eccentric hanger, end of limb, limb end clip and eccentric wheel.*

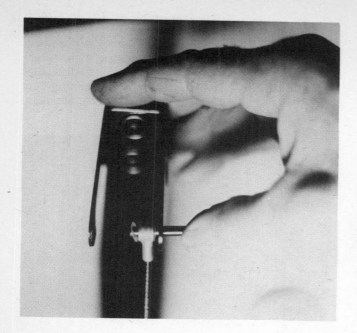

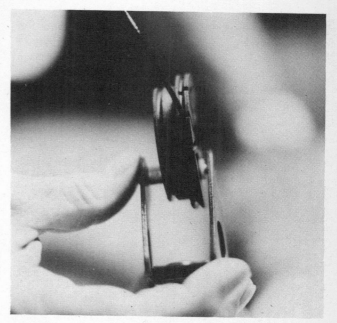

At left, axle is slipped through bracket axle hole, cable end fitting and axle washers. Outside washer and retainer clip are assembled on axle, hidden behind builder's thumb.

practiced with a similar bow for a few weeks, beginning to develop your shooting technique and style. A good place to borrow or rent a bow while you learn the basics is at your local pro shop, provided it has shooting lanes, or at your archery club. Call or write to your state archery club for information on clubs and shops near you.

Once you have determined your draw weight and length, look toward your personal shooting needs. If you intend using your bow primarily for bowhunting, don't buy a bow heavy in silver and gloss-finished paint. The reflection these surfaces offer from sunlight will frighten off even the bravest and dumbest of game. If you will be shooting primarily in tournaments, high gloss and shining beauty are fine.

Eccentric wheel, large inside and outside washers, axle, outside washers and clips are all installed on hanger. With assembly locked in place, bowstring may be attached.

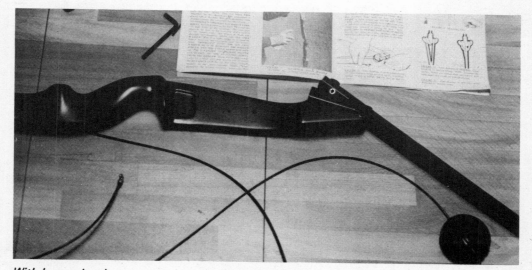

With hanger brackets mounted, eccentrics and cables are ready to be assembled on flat surface.

If you are among the more than seventy-five percent of today's archers who wish to shoot both tournament and bowhunting style, then consider whether your bow can be converted from a tournament bow to a hunting model and how difficult that transition might be. Will the addition of a bowsock do it, or will you need to paint your bow limbs and handle? Could you purchase a bowhunting model, and use it in your tournament shooting? Frequently, you can do just that.

Finally, examine the workmanship of that bow you intend on buying. Even the best name in bows cannot

The completed kit compound bow shoots as well as its factory-assembled mates. Jennings' instruction booklet contains procedures to tune and adjust arrow flight.

many capabilities to the novice archer not necessarily available to the longbow shooter. It offers increased speed, greater stability and compact size. It can be extremely accurate. You can purchase bows that offer a combination of these capabilities. What you cannot have is a recurve bow that offers all of these characteristics: speed, accuracy, stability and compact size.

Large archery manufacturers such as Bear must warehouse thousands of items to satisfy demands of archer-customers. The kit builder, however, may spend as much time as needed.

escape an occasional lemon, so spend the time necessary to determine that your bow is exactly what you believe it to be. Examine the limbs while unstrung. Are the laminations tight? Is the limb straight on line with the handle? Are there visible flaws in the finish? Is the rest the type you desire or can you substitute it for your preferred model with little difficulty? Take your time in making your selection and you will have years of pleasant shooting with it.

It is not unusual for whole families to become involved in archery after the initial introduction by a single member. After all, archery is a sport in which everyone can participate and do well. Shooting a recurve bow offers

Bear Archery's new factory at Gainesville, Florida, is an example of a modern production facility worth millions.

A dependable recurve that could shoot accurately, quickly and consistently, yet offered little overall length to tangle in brush was the dream of many a bowhunter. Such a challenge gave many homemade-equipment archers a run for their money in the Forties. As late as the mid-Fifties, archers still were making their own bows. In garage or basement workshops, they produced quality bows for their own use and, in limited instances, for others as well. Two such individuals were Holless W. Allen and Tom Jennings. It was their quests for a bow design that would offer all of these characteristics that led to the development of the step-child of bows, the compound.

## COMPOUNDS

Just as many of the other sports have given way to modern, mechanical aids, so has the bow — and while only a few of the major manufacturers mass produce the recurve bow on a large volume today, nearly all manufacturers offer

*Bows and arrows have been built for centuries. Today's factory workers combine wood and fiberglass to produce modern laminated limbs for compound bows on a scale unheard of only a few decades ago.*

*Much of the equipment required for the construction of modern archery equipment is of a specialized nature. Many, such as the bow press above, must be designed and built for use by the workers who will operate them in production.*

*Address for new facility on 35 wooded Florida acres was changed to Fred Bear Drive at Archer Road.*

its mechanical brother, the compound bow.

By definition, the term compound refers to the union of several parts into one unit. It's a perfect term for the mechanical bow, whose eccentrics, cables and hangar brackets combine to make a smooth-drawing, fast-shooting bow that has become the most popular choice for the bowhunter.

Looking at a compound bow for the first time, it may be difficult to place it in the same family with the recurve or longbow. Yet its concept and design were born of an overwhelming desire of recurve bow shooters to achieve greater accuracy and speed than their homemade bows were offering them.

Credit for the concept and basic design of the compound bow generally is attributed to Holless W. Allen.

Construction of Bear plant included many windowed public viewing areas from which to see entire process. Bear hopes to introduce archery to some of the 10-million tourists who pass factory each year along Interstate 75.

Even with modern production line facilities, much of the work is by experienced craftsmen. Skills are passed from long-time workers to new employees at Bear. Skill courses are also taught at nearby Santa Fe Community College.

From his son comes this story of how the late Allen came to create his "mechanical bow."

"Dad was an avid bowhunter," explains Doug Allen, "and so it was that on one particular morning he was tramping the woods, seeking venison. He spotted a fine-looking buck, well within his range, and eased back on his homemade recurve."

Allen should have downed that buck easily and it may have taken a few moments for reality to break through the visions of venison steak crossing his thoughts.

"His shot missed," Doug Allen says. "It missed so badly that the buck was not even alarmed and instead went right on feeding.

"My dad nocked another arrow...another release...and another miss. The buck remained. He inched closer and tried again. Another miss.

"By this time he was within eight yards of his quarry and could very well have thrown arrows at him and scored. Instead he eased back on the recurve and released. Again the arrow missed, but by this time the deer had finally taken note of what was happening and, with a leap, disappeared."

Allen was an excellent archer. How then had he missed so badly, so many times? It would have been easy to blame the misses on his equipment, but it was only after agonizing investigation and testing that Allen finally determined that the equipment actually was to blame. Determined not to allow such a thing to happen again, he set about designing a bow that would give him the accuracy he knew he had a right to expect. Combining his knowledge of physics with his love of archery, he designed and patented the first compound bow.

Pro Line Archery, Hastings, Michigan, is another major firm manufacturing quality products in modern facilities.

Construction and selection of limbs are perhaps the most important component of recurves, longbows or compounds. Pro Line limbs are of fiberglass-backed hardrock maple.

Special sanding machines, called profilers, shape the maple into basic form to produce bow limbs at Pro Line.

manufactured are in the compound classification.

While each compound bow offers its own special characteristics to make it unique to that manufacturer, compound bows are basically alike in composition and performance.

What is it about the compound that finally made it attractive to so many people? The term, *attractive* may be a poor choice of words, for in a world where simplicity and smooth lines are the sign of beauty, the compound, with all its cables and metallic additions, is hardly smooth and simple. Yet, it is based on two simple, ancient tools of physics: the lever and the pulley.

A pulley is used to reduce resistance on a given point, by staggering that resistance among several points rather than a

Top-grade epoxy cement is used to bond fiberglass and wood to form laminated limbs. Stacks of limbs are glued and pressed at one time, prior to heat treating.

At about the same time another avid archer/bowhunter, Tom Jennings was experimenting with a mechanical bow. To Jennings is generally credited the advancement of the design of the compound bow to its current high-performance level, and the acceptability of the compound as a legitimate addition to an archer's line of tackle.

This last was by far his greatest challenge, for upon its introduction there were few archers interested in trying the mechanical monsters. These first prototypes were hardly what a novice archer had in mind when he thought of archery. Experienced bowmen certainly weren't likely to shoot one of these ugly, bulky pieces of wizardry. Besides, they wouldn't last very long anyway — or so the sages foretold. Today nearly seventy-five percent of all bows single point. In the case of an individual attempting to lift a heavy weight, as in the case of an automobile engine from its mountings, a pulley is used to stagger that weight from the engine, to a top pulley wheel, down to a lower pulley wheel, then back over the top wheel before it is pulled toward the mechanic. The weight of the engine is shared by each of the pulleys and the mechanic, so that he is able to lift the heavy engine with relative ease. The addition of the pulley allows a change in the direction of the resistance, thus reducing that resistance.

In the case of the compound bow, weight is exchanged for resistance of the bow's limbs against bending. By positioning pulleys at the tip of each limb, then attaching a cable from that pulley to the opposite end of the

Sanding device will sand up to five limbs at a time.

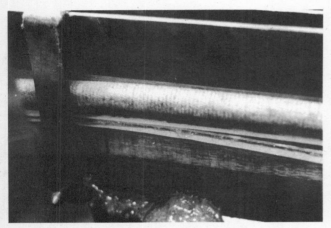

Combination of heat and pressure ensure perfect bond of glass and wood. Procedure is closely controlled.

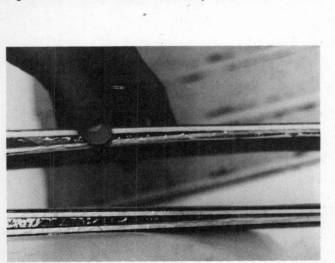

After pressure/heat bonding, each limb is inspected.

bowstring, the resistance of the limbs can be shared between the archer and the pulleys. The lower pulley provides a fulcrum, or pivot point, which essentially lifts the lower limb as the resistance offered by that limb is divided between the archer and the upper limb. The combination of pulleys and cable allows a change in the direction of the resistance from the vertical pull of the cables to the horizontal pull of the bowstring.

The lever action takes place about midpoint in the draw, and is effected by the use of eccentric wheels in the pulley mechanism. The term *eccentric* means "off-center." That description applies to the axle placement on the eccentric wheel, with the axle drilled slightly off-center to give an oval loop rather than a circular loop. The eccentric is

*Photo above shows bonded limbs in clamps before and after profiling to remove excess epoxy from edges.*

positioned so that when at its lowest resistance the bow is at rest and the curvature of the cable around the eccentric wheel is at its greatest arc. About mid-draw, positioning of the axle allows the wheel to swing over to a wide arc, reducing the curvature dramatically and allowing the eccentric to function as a lever, giving a straight pull between the archer and the wheel.

Undoubtably the greatest advantage to this pulley/lever mechanism is that it allows any archer to shoot a much heavier draw-weight bow, for with the mechanism and the bow itself sharing either one third or one half of the load, the archer need only contain the remaining resistance. The petite secretary is able to shoot a fifty-pound-draw-weight compound even though she might never be able to shoot a fifty-pound recurve bow, because at mid-draw she is suddenly only pulling against the compound's twenty-five-pound resistance.

For the bowhunter who prefers heavy hunting bows, the compound means being able to shoot a seventy or eighty-pound draw weight without the risk of muscle strain.

*After profiling, limbs are finished off on abrasive wheel.*

*Photo below shows split limb during final shaping, sanding.*

Phenolic tips are added to Pro Line split limb tips to add strength yet retain thin profile for fast tip speed. Eccentric wheel axles are mounted through holes in tips, rather than through limbs themselves.

And with that heavier weight, he gains increased arrow speed and a straighter cast to the released arrowshaft.

In selecting a compound bow, what does the novice archer look for and how does he decide which bow is best for him? Again, his first consideration will have to be why he wants the bow. What will he be using it for? If he intends it for bowhunting, he must consider where he will be shooting, the type of terrain and weather he will likely experience. Not all bows shoot well for every archer, but with the wide range of styles and models available, there should be several bows that will shoot well for you.

Begin your selection by checking draw length and draw weight; both extremely important. If the bow you select is too long in draw length, for instance, you will not get the full benefits of the bow's let-off. Instead of holding twenty-five pounds at full draw, you'll wind up holding thirty pounds or more, dependent on how short you underdraw. If you must overdraw, your latitude is even less, for you can draw only an extra inch or so before the cables stop your draw and will not let you draw any farther back. In that extra inch of draw, you will experience an increase in holding weight as well.

Most bows on the market today include a provision for adjusting weight and draw length. Changing the draw weight is accomplished generally by turning the pivot bolt (that bolt which holds the inner edge of the limb to the handle or riser section) either in or out. Turn the bolt in and the draw weight increases. Turn it out and you reduce that weight. Most bows offer a ten-pound weight adjustment, while some afford as much as fifteen pounds variance.

Changing the draw length can be a little more complicated, although if your bow offers a length variance, the maker should provide instructions on how to achieve that variance. With bows offering a tri-slotted eccentric, draw length variation is achieved by changing placement of

Variations in wood density and amount of epoxy retained between laminates, determines actual draw weight of limbs. At Pro Line, each limb is measured, above.

Protective mesh surrounds testing area for finished bow. Test bows are dry-fired until they fail; results are recorded.

the cable hook-up to the eccentric. Most bows offering a length variance provide a range of two inches.

The handle of your compound may be made of lightweight aluminum or magnesium. However, wood-handled models are becoming more prominent. An advantage of the wooden handle is the warmth it offers on a cold winter hunt, as opposed to the frigid metal handles. However, a snap-on or wrap-around grip will protect your hand and the metal handle is more economical than the wooden models. You'll also find the wooden handles to be somewhat bulky compared to the thinner metal models.

The limbs of your compound will be either of solid fiberglass or wood with fiberglass lamination. The fiberglass/wood combination offers the fastest shooting bowlimb, but is more expensive. The solid fiberglass, while inexpensive, is noticeably slower. Many of the economy compounds found at discount stores offer solid fiberglass limbs. Another undeniable advantage to the fiberglass laminate/wood version is increased beauty. The lamination gives the limb far greater strength and action, while allowing the beauty of the wood to show.

*Riser end of limb is carefully shaped to fit riser cup.*

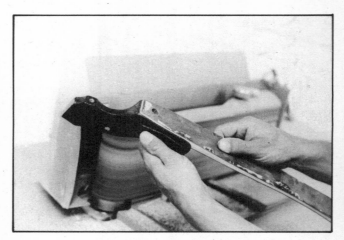

*Rocker cup is fitted and epoxied to bow limb, above.*

*Producing thousands of limbs, even affixing the company logo requires production line methods to accomplish.*

*Pro Line's risers are produced outside of Michigan plant but final preparation — holes drilled and tapped, fitting of rockers, limbs and risers — is part of final assembly.*

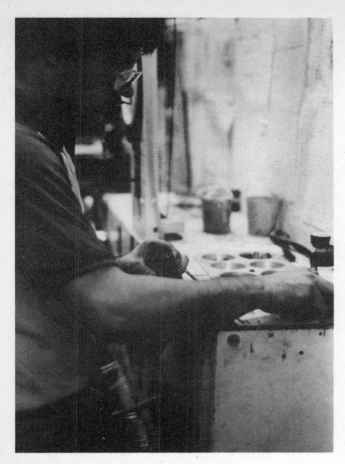

With final assembly, testing, and inspection, new compound bow is ready for shipment, surrounded by protective plastic.

Final assembly of cables, eccentrics and bow strings at factory is basically the same as that of Model K kit.

The eccentrics are attached in one of two basic styles: via hanger brackets or using a split-limb design. The hanger bracket is essentially a metal housing for the eccentrics, suspended from the tips of each limb. While this type of attachment removes the possibility of limb weakness at the tips, it adds mass weight to the bow and, for the bowhunter, can cause hangups amid heavy brush.

The split-limb design refers to the gullying of the limb tips, carving out a "U" which houses the eccentric via an axle running through the limb tip from the side. Bows using a split-limb design have an additional laminate core at the tips to provide the bulk necessary for the axle holes. The axle runs through this fiberglass buildup, rather than through the bowlimb itself. Which style is best is a source

One of the latest developments in archery is Bear's Delta V, billed as the world's fastest bow. Unusual cam design on central frames produce greater arrow speed. Added complexity brings greater cost, however.

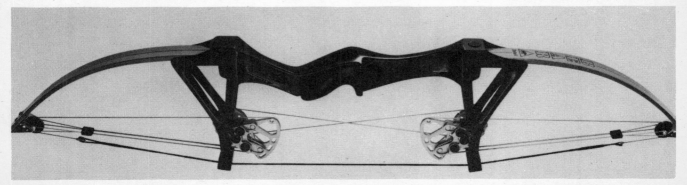

*At right, Browning XLM.*

*Far right, Darton 35 GL.*

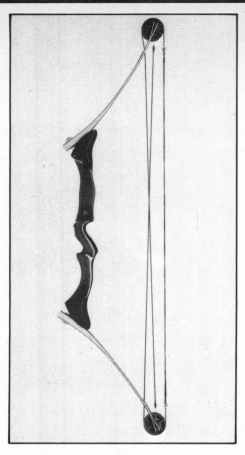

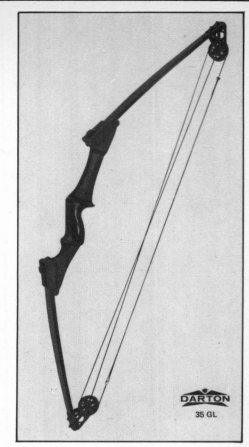

*Right, the Bear Magnum with wood handle.*

*Far right, the PSE Phaser in camouflage coloring.*

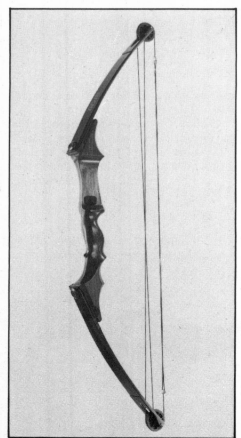

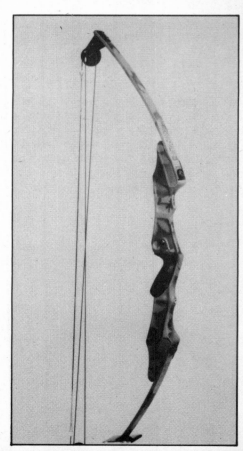

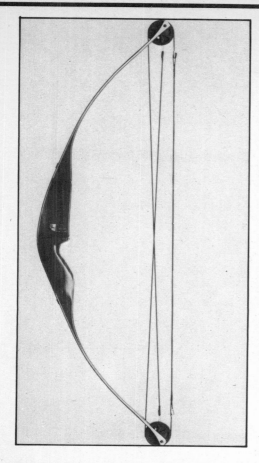

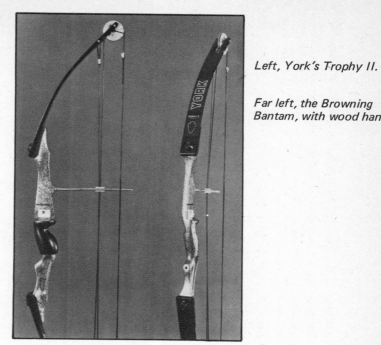

Left, York's Trophy II.

Far left, the Browning Bantam, with wood handle.

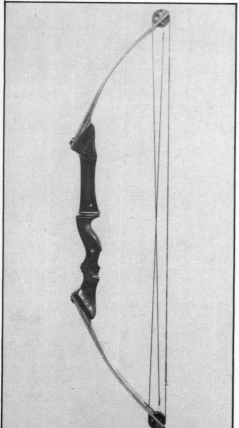

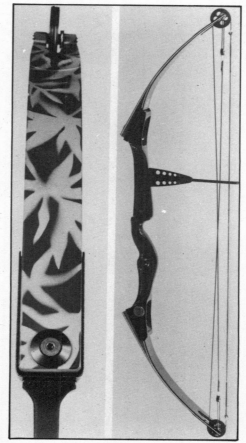

Left, the Jennings T-Star Hunter with Camlimb pattern.

Far left, Martin Archery's popular two-wheeler.

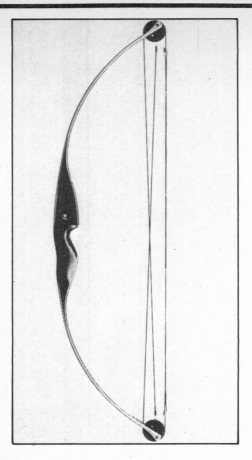

*Right, Browning's Cobra lightweight two-wheeler.*

*Far right, the Bear Hunter.*

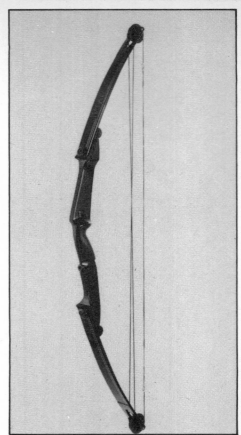

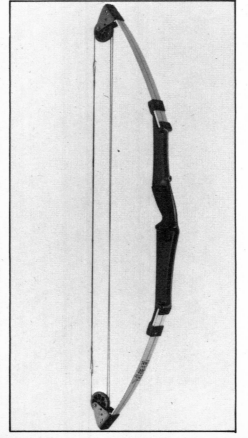

*Right, Bear Archery's Silver Magnum tournament bow.*

*Far right, PSE's Vulcan with alloy riser.*

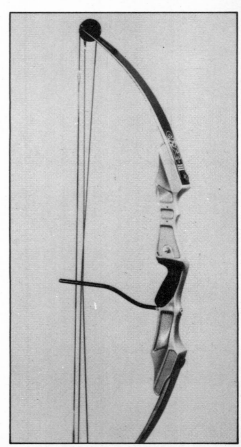

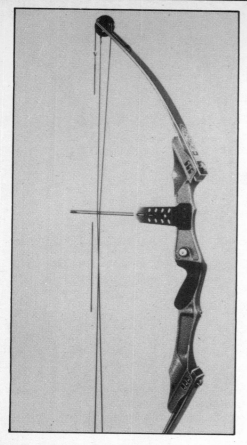 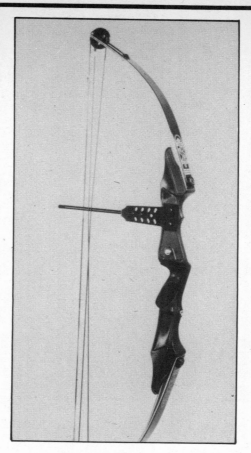

*Left, the PSE Laser Mach I.*

*Far left, PSE's Laser Magnum.*

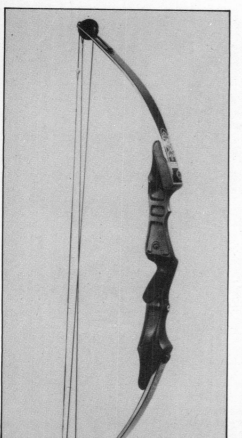 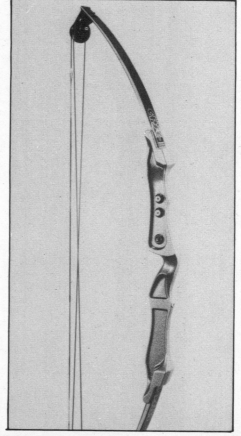

*Left, the PSE Viper.*

*Far left, PSE Laser II.*

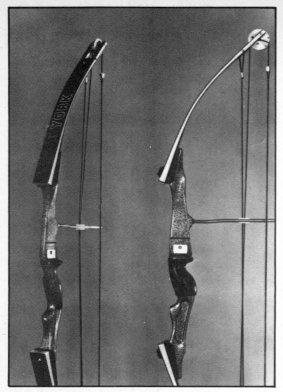

York's Trophy is a popular
tournament compound.

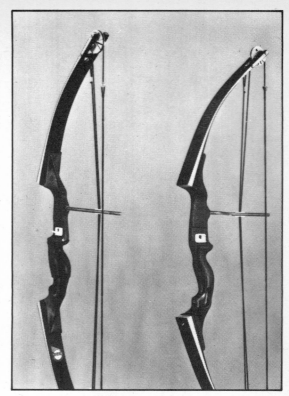

The York Thunderbolt is better
suited to the bowhunter.

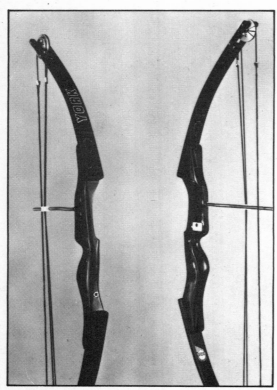

The York Excalibre, introduced in 1982.

DARTON
Archery Equipment

Studying a number of archery catalogs
is a good start on selection. Most
manufacturers offer catalogs free.

of heated debates among seasoned archers. Both are effective.

The bow you choose may be either a two, four or six-wheel model. The four and six-wheel models are said to be faster and smoother shooting, but also are more expensive. The two-wheel model also shoots well and, by virtue of the reduced number of parts, is more economical.

Although your compound is manufactured ready to shoot, there are a few maintenance considerations you must understand and provide in order to keep your compound in shooting shape.

## BASIC MAINTENANCE

Whether a compound, recurve or longbow, always check your bow before you shoot it, especially if it has been a while since you last shot. Look for frayed or cut strings, worn cables, loose attachments.

For recurves and longbows, your primary concern will be the condition of the bow laminations and the condition of your bowstring. Make it a habit to keep a spare

*One of the first maintenance/safety measures to be taken by the archer is a simple visual inspection of all the bow's bow's components. Cables must be seated in wheel grooves.*

bowstring on hand at all times. Never shoot a string that is frayed or cut. Replacing that worn string takes but a few minutes and is worth the time.

If you must replace the string on your compound — and at some time you will need to do so — you will need a bowstring changer. This is nothing more than an excessively

long bowstring with metal claws attached to each end. These claws grasp the cable ends above the anchor fitting. Placing the center of the string changer beneath your foot, you then can lift the bow toward you until the shorter, shooting bowstring is relaxed enough that you can slip it off and slide a new one in its place.

You'll also want to lubricate your compound's eccentric housing. A number of excellent, inexpensive lubricants work well, including some manufactured especially for compound bows, like the spray-on silicone lubricant packaged by Bohning Adhesives.

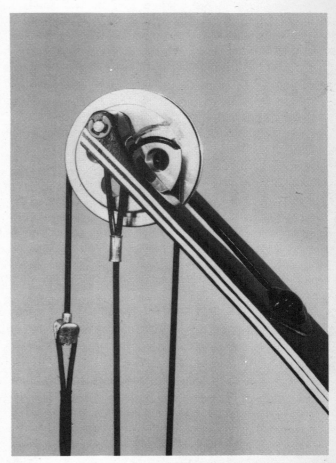

*Eccentric wheels or cams of compounds should periodically be lubricated with a non-corrosive spray-on silicone.*

Do not store your recurve or longbow in a strung position, as it will weaken the action of the limbs. Compound bows are intended to be left strung.

If you desire to alter the draw weight of your compound, remember to turn both the upper and lower limb bolts the same number of turns. If you do not, your bow will become out of balance. We refer to this as "out of tiller." The distance between the riser and the bowstring, tiller is measured at both the upper and lower end of the riser. To be correctly set, the upper limb measurement should be approximately one-eighth-inch more than that of the bottom limb measurement. A clip-on bow scale will give you a readily available reading of tiller.

Never shoot the bow without an arrow. The energy normally transferred to the arrow shaft will instead remain with the bow, causing a sudden surge in force and could possibly break or crack the limbs or handle. Even the friendliest of pro shop dealers will lose his enthusiasm for helping you select a bow if he catches you dry snapping his bows.

Should you become confused as to exactly what weight your bow is set and need to know, you can do one of two things. Either weigh the draw with a bow scale, if you have access to one, or tighten the bow limbs all the way down to their maximum weight. Then release the weight on each limb alternately, turning one full turn on the top limb, then a full turn on the lower limb. Each turn will reduce your draw approximately one pound.

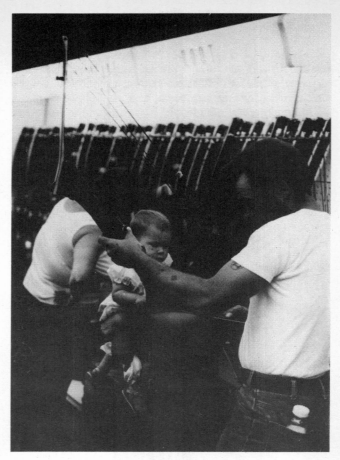

*A well-stocked retail archery dealer is one of the best places to start making a selection for a new compound bow. The knowledgeable dealer will provide valuable advice to the novice as well as the expert.*

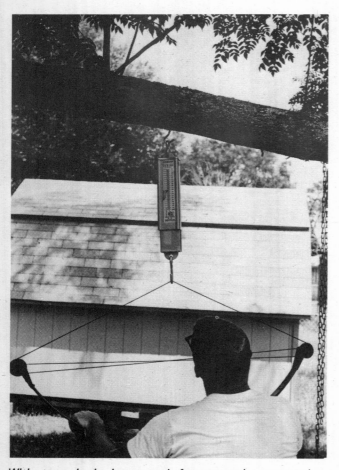

*With atmospheric changes and after use, each compound bow should be checked by the shooter for draw weight. A simple and inexpensive spring scale will do it.*

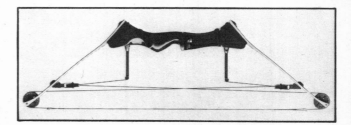

*While the industry seems to be moving away from the four-wheel-design compound, Browning still catalogs the Explorer line in various weights and draw lengths.*

When you reach the desired weight, you again will need to check the tiller, remembering that you want the upper limb to measure one-eighth-inch greater than the lower limb.

Try to learn the names of each of the parts of your bow, whatever style of bow you may be shooting. (Refer to the drawings in this chapter.) And read the literature packed with your bow. Not only will it offer helpful information about your bow, but there usually is a scaled drawing of the

With hundreds of designs and models to choose, picking the right bow isn't easy.

American Archery's Cheetah Mag bow features laminated, impregnated wood handle requiring little maintenance.

parts and their assembly, plus maintenance and shooting tips.

An excellent aid to learning how and why a compound bow performs as it does is to purchase one of several bow kits now on the market. These kits allow you to finish your own bow from basic parts already shaped and drilled. The kits are so simple that a child really can put them together — provided he is supervised by an understanding, patient adult. A bow kit is an excellent family project and the finished product can be a source of great pride.

Glean as much information as you can from your pro shop dealer and from veteran archers. Keeping in mind that they often are prejudiced to their particular bow or inventory stock, there is still a host of information to be gathered from friendly target-side chats.

Whatever type of bow you select, do not be afraid to ask questions about it. Shoot it several times, if the opportunity presents itself. Ask around to see who else might have a similar bow and how theirs performs. Finally, be realistic in your selection.

The finest of bows will do you no good, if all you do is take it home and hang it from your wall on a bow rack. To enjoy a bow, you must shoot it, so purchase a bow that you *can* shoot. Then keep on shooting and let the spirit and achievement of the sport grab ahold of you.

Arrow shafts, often pre-fletched with feathers or vanes, are available at archery shops in a variety of draw lengths.

# Chapter 5

# ARROWS

## The Choice, Care And Maintenance Of Your Arrows Is A Personal And Somewhat Complicated Matter

Anderson Archery, in Michigan, stocks arrow shafts in bulk, pre-wrapped for shipment to buyers across nation.

Left: When the question comes up as to what arrow shaft one should use, this is best determined by finding the one that best matches the draw weight of a specific bow.

WHICH ARROW material is best? Depending on who you ask, the answer will be: wood, aluminum, fiberglass, graphlex, perhaps even steel, although they are hard to come by these days. You'll find that nearly every archer is positive that his arrows are of the best type shaft material on the market, and he'll probably be more than happy to tell you why.

"They're fast" "They shoot straight as a bullet" "They last" "I score well with them." All are frequent and

*A good archery pro shop, usually has a wide variety of shaft materials on the shelves for a customer's wants.*

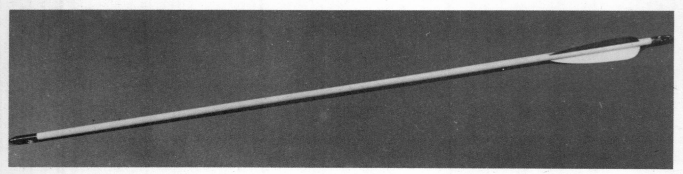

*The oldest known arrow material, wood is the least expensive, but it also is the most susceptible to weather changes.*

accurate reasons for choosing a particular type of arrow. The problem in determining which shaft material is best for you is that these same statements can be made about all arrow shafts, provided the shaft matches the bow from which it is being shot.

In determining which shaft you should use your first and primary concern should be for matching your arrows to your bow. But don't be alarmed; matching arrows to bows is not difficult.

## MATCHING ARROWS TO BOWS

Matching your arrows to your bow means that you must select an arrow shaft with weight and stiffness compatible to your bow's performance capabilities. All arrow shafts will not fly well from a given bow. In fact, unless the match of shaft to bow is within limited bounds, your arrows will probably fly poorly.

If the arrow you choose is too light in stiffness for your

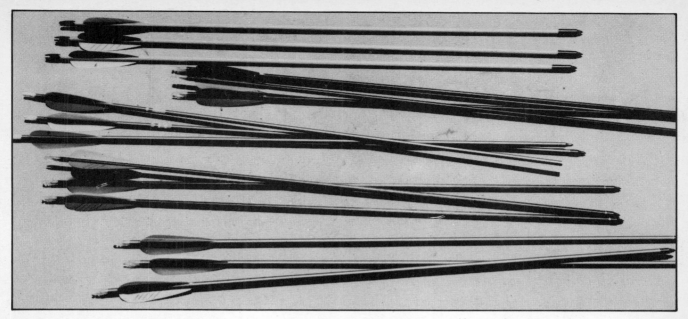

Arrows today are available in three types of materials. Top three arrows are of wood; beneath and at bottom are aluminum shafts, while the other two groups are of fiberglass marketed as Graphlex and Lamiglass.

From top: These arrow shafts are made of cedar, Graphlex, Lamiglass, followed by a pair of Easton XX76 aluminum shafts, same maker's GameGetters.

bow the arrows are likely to soar off to the right of your target. If the stiffness is too great the arrows will sail to the left. There's a reason for this. The straight-as-an-arrow flight you think you see is not truly a straight line. The arrow actually must bend around the riser of the bow. It begins its flight by bearing slightly to the left, then curves toward the right to straighten itself out. If the shaft is too stiff it will bend to the left and stay to the left. If too light it may bend far to the left, then far to the right, leaving it bent too far to straighten itself out before impact.

In purchasing your arrow shafts you will be asked the draw weight of your bow. Even if you plan on making your own arrows you must purchase the shafts on the basis of draw weight. You also should tell the salesman whether your bow is a longbow, recurve or compound. The shaft needed will be different for longbows and recurves than it is for compounds, the compounds requiring a much lighter shaft.

For recurves and longbows the salesman will attempt to match the maximum draw weight of the bow at your full draw. Keep in mind that this does not necessarily mean the maximum weight posted on the bowlimbs. That bow weight is accurate only if your draw matches the draw length given on the legend. In other words, if the legend states "45 pounds at 28 inches," then you must draw the bow back to twenty-eight inches to record a draw weight of forty-five pounds. For every inch less that you draw that bow back you can expect the draw weight to decrease by approximately two pounds. For every inch over twenty-eight inches it will increase by two pounds. Thus, if your draw length is twenty-six inches, the draw weight of your bow at full draw will only be about forty-one pounds, and your forty-five-pound-test arrow shafts may be too stiff.

*Both sets of arrows (above and below) are of Port Orford cedar, which is the best wood available in this country for the manufacture of arrows. The grain is straight, which means that the material is less likely to warp.*

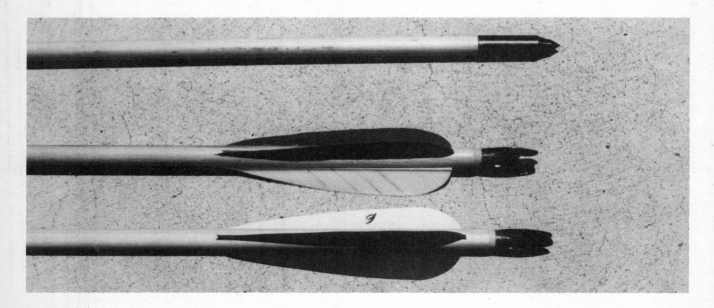

Due to the let-off factors of compound bows and the acceleration effect of the arrow, there is less stress on the shaft at the onset of the release and, when shooting fiberglass or aluminum shafts, a lighter-spined arrow may be used. A recommended formula for determining the bow weight figure needed to match your arrows suggests that you add the peak or maximum weight of your bow to the holding weight, then divide that answer by two to get the actual weight you must match for arrow shafts. Thus, a compound bow with a peak weight of forty-five pounds, and a let-off of fifty percent that reduces its holding weight to 22½ pounds, will shoot an arrow whose stiffness matches a draw weight of about thirty-four pounds. In ordering or purchasing your arrow shafts you would want to give the salesman a draw weight figure of thirty-four pounds.

Whether you intend to purchase your arrows premade and precut or are simply going to purchase bare shafts that you will convert to arrows at home, you also must know

*In this age, aluminum is the most popular shaft material and often is anodized, then crested for identification. However, a drawback is that the aluminum bends easily.*

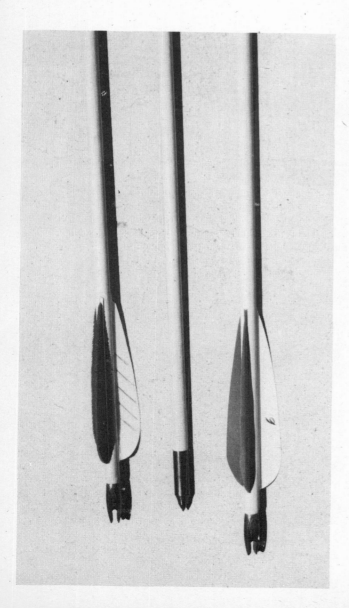

*Left: Plastic vanes often are installed on arrows as they are uniform in size, thickness, which aids in the archer's continued quest for uniformity in accuracy.*

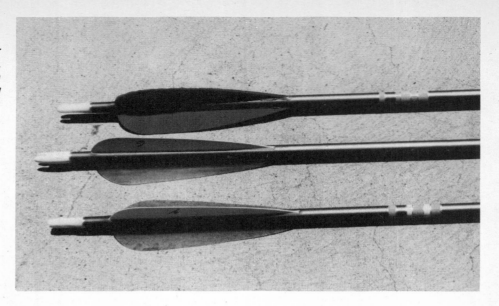

*In attaching vanes or feather fletching to an aluminum shaft, it is important to remove polish from the metal so that bonding material used adheres properly.*

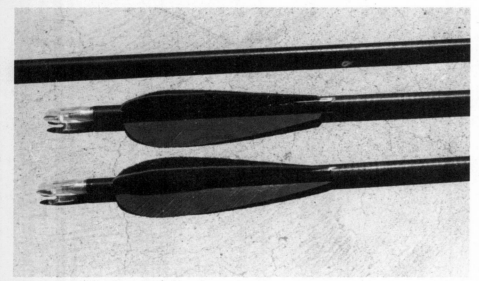

*Gordon's Graphlex arrows are a combination of fiberglass and carbon. When the material is bent, it springs back straight.*

*Feathers can be used to fletch fiberglass arrows with no difficulty, but if feathers become wet, as is the case with the fletching shown above, it sometimes is difficult to return them to their original shape.*

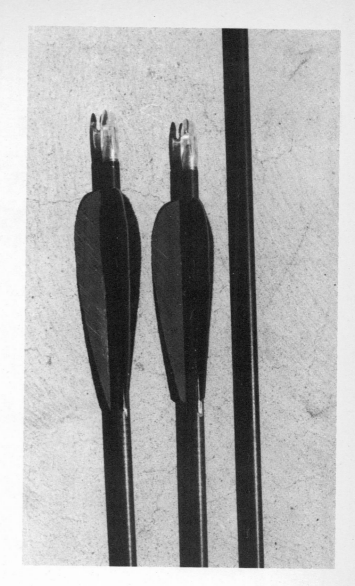

*It is a simple matter to attach nocks to fiberglass shafts, as they can be cemented directly to shaft.*

your draw length. This is *not* the draw length of your bow, but rather the length of your arrows; there may be a big difference, perhaps as much as two inches.

The draw length of your bow refers to the length from either your nocking point to the back, far side, of the bow, called traditional measurement, or from your anchor point to the cushion plunger or rest, called true draw measurement. In either case, cutting your arrow shafts to this measurement will mean your shafts are too short for you to shoot and you may find yourself looking for a fellow archer with shorter arms to whom to give these arrows. If your draw length is, for instance, twenty-eight inches and your arrow shafts are cut to twenty-eight inches, you will have little or nothing extending beyond the arrow rest when at full draw. On occasion, you may overdraw the rest, and have your arrows drop off entirely.

In determining proper arrow length, add a minimum of one-half inch, and preferably a full inch, to the length of your draw to allow the shaft to extend slightly past the bow. If you intend to use broadhead hunting tips, this will be especially important, as you must give clearance between your hand and the razor-sharp inserts of the broadheads. Some archers will add as much as 1½ inches to their arrow lengths when shooting broadheads, even though the added length means added weight, preferring the extra safety to the greater speed of a shorter arrow.

Once you have determined the arrow match of your bow you are then ready to look in to the types of shafts available to you.

*Unique to Lamiglas is its aerodynamic design, with the nock end of the shaft smaller in diameter than the front end.*

*Gilmore's all-fiberglass arrow shaft is much heavier than some, making it slower in arrow speed. However, it offers greater penetration capabilities because of that weight, outdoing lighter weight arrow shafts.*

## TYPES OF SHAFTS

Three basic materials currently are used in the production of arrow shafts: wood, aluminum and fiberglass (either as all fiberglass or in a combination carbon/fiberglass mixture). Each style has its advantages and disadvantages.

Wood, particularly Port Orford cedar, has long been a favorite for archery, especially for the novice archer or small-game bowhunter. Wood is undoubtably the oldest material known to archery. It is also the least expensive shaft material currently on the market, with a dozen shafts costing less than five dollars.

In explaining how you went about determining the proper draw weight to use in ordering aluminum and fiberglass shafts for compound bows, we omitted wood shafts. This was deliberate, for when shooting wood shafts

## AVERAGE WEIGHT IN GRAINS
*(includes all arrows, feathers and vanes)*

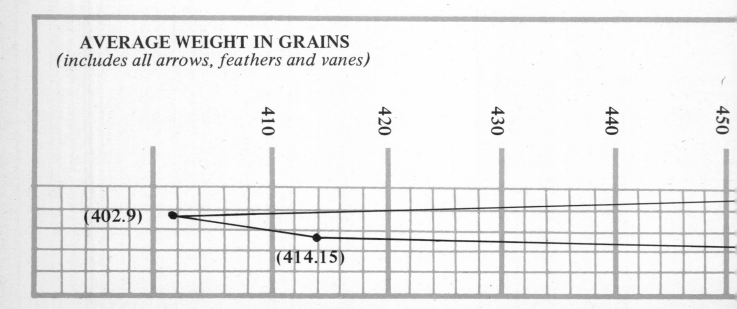

410  420  430  440  450

(402.9)

(414.15)

*Differences in shaft diameter and wall thickness result in a specific arrow shaft that matches a particular bow.*

from a compound it is recommended that you use shafts of spine *equal* to that of the *maximum* weight of the bow. This is due to the lack of elasticity in the cedar shafts. Some pro shop owners will recommend that you actually increase the weight requirements of your cedar shafts as much as five pounds over the peak weight of the bow. Whether you choose to exceed the peak weight of the bow by five pounds or stay at the peak weight is a matter of choice, but you would be unwise to go below that weight.

Another advantage to the cedar shafts is that they can be found in much more abundance than can the other arrow

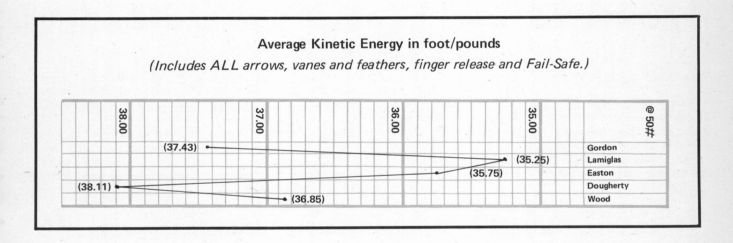

### Average Kinetic Energy in foot/pounds
*(Includes ALL arrows, vanes and feathers, finger release and Fail-Safe.)*

| | @ 50# |
|---|---|
| (37.43) | Gordon |
| (35.25) | Lamiglas |
| (35.75) | Easton |
| (38.11) | Dougherty |
| (36.85) | Wood |

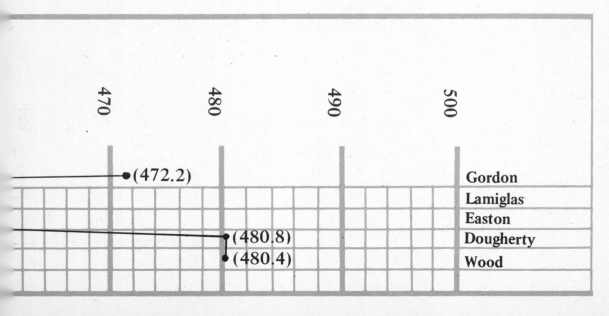

| | | | | |
|---|---|---|---|---|
| (472.2) | | | | Gordon |
| | | | | Lamiglas |
| | | | | Easton |
| (480.8) | | | | Dougherty |
| (480.4) | | | | Wood |

# Average Speed in Feet Per Second (fps)
*(Includes ALL arrows, vanes and feathers,
finger release and Fail-Safe release.)*

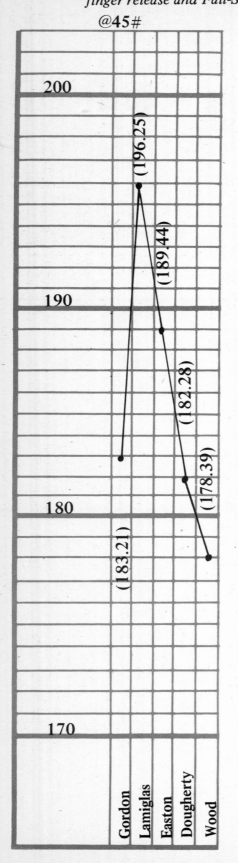

@45#

@50#

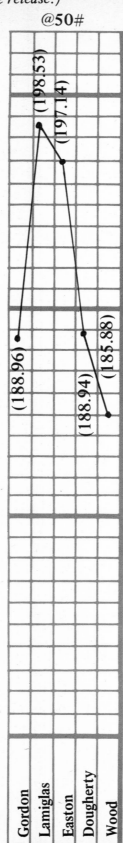

**Average Kinetic Energy
in foot/pounds.**
*(Includes ALL arrows,
vanes and feathers,
finger release
and Fail-Safe release.)*

materials. You'll find cedar shafts being sold in department stores and discount shops that carry only a limited amount of archery items.

For plinking and small-game hunting the cedar shaft can be an excellent choice, especially if you are shooting in terrain that is likely to result in lost arrows. For more serious shooting, as in bowhunting of big-game or tournament shooting, however, you rarely find archers shooting cedar shafts. This is especially true in damp, rainy weather. Cedar shafts do not fare well in wet conditions; they tend to warp.

Should you purchase cedar shafts and find that after a period of time they have warped, it is possible to return them to a degree of straightness by holding them over steam for a few minutes, then easing the shaft back into alignment. You might also want to dip your cedar shafts in a clear or lacquer-based paint to waterproof them.

The most popular arrow shaft material on the market is aluminum, produced in large part by Easton Aluminum. The California-based company has seen its arrows used in winning in every major state, national, international and Olympic archery competition for some thirty-five years.

Easton's aluminum shafts can be purchased in three basic grades of aluminum: Swifts, GameGetters and SRTs of 2024 alloy; XX75s of a 7075 alloy; and the X7 series of 7178 alloy. Easton also manufactures a softer, more ductile and thus easier to manufacture and less expensive series of shafts for the economy-minded archer.

When you order arrows of aluminum you order both a series and a size. The size is given in an identification number of four digits, e.g., 2014. From this number, you can determine the exact size of both the outside diameter of the shaft, and the thickness of the wall of the tube. The

*Penetration is not the same for all arrows, although they have been shot from the same bow. Differences in weight, speed, texture of the shaft's surface tend to increase or to reduce the penetration capabilities.*

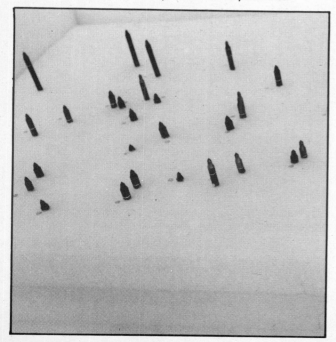

*Speed of an arrow is measured by an Arrometer made by Micro Motion. The speed is given in feet per second, with adjustments allowing for varying arrow lengths in tenths of an inch. Not the seemingly bent arrow, shaft is straightening itself after release around the bow.*

*Although the same type of points have been used in the penetration test performed by the author, differences in the degree of penetration become quite obvious.*

outside diameter is given in sixty-fourths of an inch. Thus a shaft with an indication of 2014 will have an outside diameter of 20/64 inch. Stiffness of the shaft is determined largely by this outside diameter measurement.

Overall weight of the shaft is credited to the amount of thickness of the wall that makes up the shaft tubing. The thicker the wall, the heavier the shaft will weight. Wall thickness is measured in thousandths of an inch, thus our same 2014 shaft will have a wall thickness of .014 inch. It is this combination of wall thickness and outside diameter size that combine to give each arrow its spine and weight and determine whether a particular arrow should be used in a particular bow. Easton put a good deal of time and effort into determining the best arrow shaft for a given draw weight and draw length. You are able to make the same determinations in a matter of seconds with the aid of their readily available chart for arrow selection.

Although the aluminum shaft is more expensive than the cedar shaft, it is still reasonable in price. A dozen bare shafts of the GameGetter series, a popular choice for new and veteran archers alike, costs less than $30.

Unlike cedar shafts, aluminum is nearly impervious to weather conditions, and is extremely uniform in weight, spine and straightness.

*A log of the various arrow materials and weights was maintained during tests so proper comparisons could be made.*

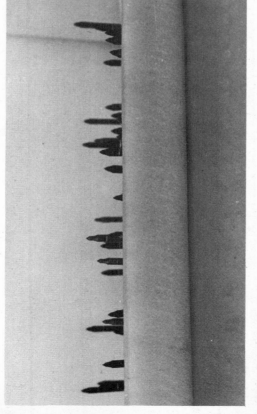

Quality control is checked constantly at the Gordon plant in southern California to maintain uniformity of shafts — an advantage of man-made materials. Uniformity can vary with wooden shafts where density of grain differs.

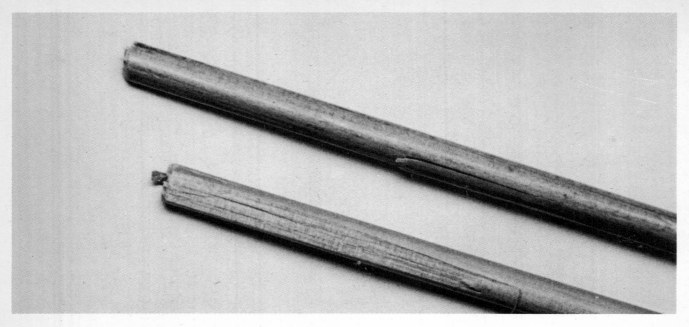

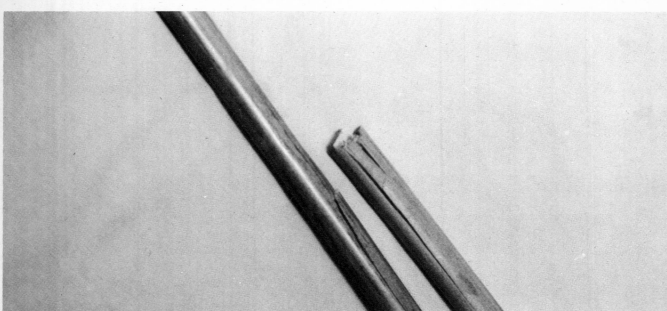

*Port Orford cedar or other wood shafts can be damaged beyond repair if a hard surface such as a rock is hit by the arrow. Such splintering can happen anywhere on shaft at its weakest point; some are nearly invisible.*

The most common maintenance problem seen in the use of aluminum shafts is bending. Frequently you will notice the bend before you shoot the arrow. If not, it will become immediately apparent upon release.

Straightening aluminum shafts is not difficult, but takes some practicing. Although arrow straighteners come in varying stages of complexity and price, all work on the same basic principal requiring a support at either side of the bend to provide an upward push as a central wheel is drawn down on the bend at its highest point. The bend is "walked" out by providing a series of moderate thrusts to the bend. If the bend is slight, a few minutes' time will straighten it out.

If your aluminum shaft has a long bend in it remove the largest percentage of the bend by hand, using your palm as the push of the wheel.

In checking aluminum shafts for straightness you may see archers spin the shaft as it rests between the thumb nail

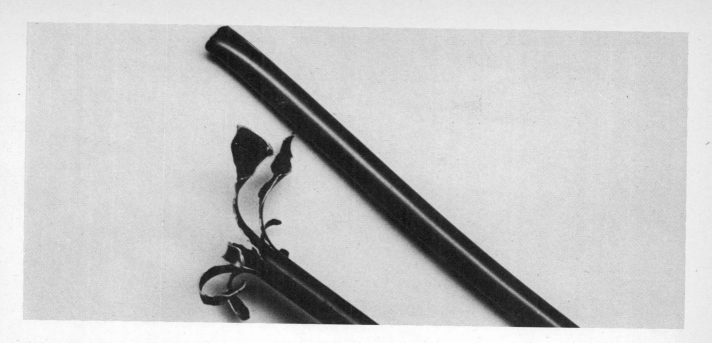

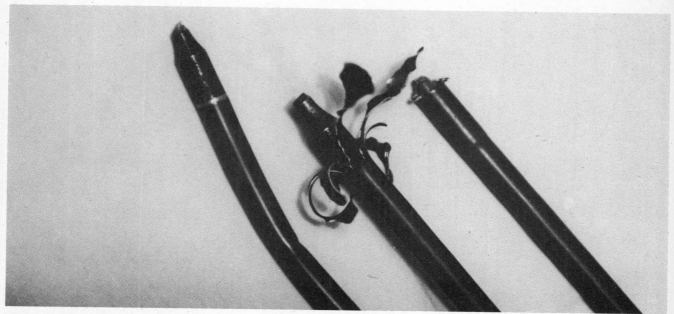

*Aluminum shafts do not splinter. They tend to bend or, if suffering impact from an extremely hard obstacle such as a rock, they may peel back from the arrowhead, resulting in what archers term the tulip effect.*

and middle nail of their hand. The union of the two nails gives a smooth surface for the arrow to spin on. If the shaft is straight it will glide smoothly; if not, it will bounce against the nails and is easily seen.

You might also test for straightness by rolling the arrow across a flat surface, such as a table top, looking for wobbles. Or, using your same thumb and middle finger nails as a pivot point, blow on the fletching and note whether the arrow turns uniformly or wobbles.

Aside from occasional bending, aluminum shafts will hold up extremely well for normal shooting. Tree trunks, walls and rocks are something else, however, and you can expect your aluminum shaft to come out on the short end of the battle, sporting flower-petal ends as the impact peels the aluminum tubing in ornate sections.

There are three major manufacturers of fiberglass arrows currently on the market: Gilmore, Lamiglas and Gordon.

*Fiberglass shafts can be mistreated, too, as is evidenced by the split ends of these Gilmore shafts after an arrow outfitted with a field point was deliberately shot at rock.*

Each has its own special makeup, characteristics and advantages.

A stiff competitor with the aluminum shaft is Don Gordon's Graphlex arrow. Graphlex is not the traditional fiberglass shaft, but rather a fiberglass/carbon combination, designed to provide a fast, yet sturdy shaft. The unique combination gives the Graphlex arrow what Gordon terms "memory," which means that the arrow will spring back to its original straighness if bent.

When Graphlex arrows were first manufactured they proved to be extremely expensive; however, improvements in manufacturing ease have reduced their price to where they are now a match for that of the aluminum shafts. Like aluminum they are unaffected by changes in weather.

*When shot against a hard surface deliberately, the ends on these Lamiglas shafts splintered and even shattered.*

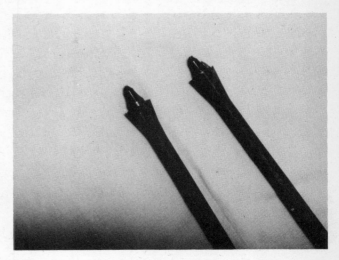

*Gordon Graphlex shafts suffered damage, too, displacing the points rearward, when they were shot into hard rock.*

*Left: All arrow makers, regardless of the type of material used to make shafts, place great store on quality control. Arrows are tested for their spine, degree of flexibility.*

Available in four basic sizes, Gordon uses color coding to differentiate between sizes: Green for bows giving a peak weight of forty pounds; Black for fifty-pound ranges; Yellow for sixty-pound ranges; and Red for seventy-pounders.

Although the Graphlex arrows snap back when bent, repeated impact can lead to shattering of the shaft; this requires that the archer examine the shafts periodically for wear marks.

When Lamiglas arrows were first introduced to the market they were said to be "the fastest arrow" being made. That boast may still be true. They are extremely fast, due in large part to their limited mass weight and the aerodynamic design of the shaft. Lamiglas features a tapered shaft design, with the shaft narrowing as it proceeds to the nock end of the shaft. This design yields a faster, flatter-flying shaft.

Were it not for the high cost of purchasing the Lamiglas arrow it might well be a preferred choice of shaft for many archers. However, a dozen bare shafts are priced at around $60, making them an unlikely choice for the novice archer who is apt to lose a good number of arrows before he is able to hit his targets with regularity.

Composed entirely of fiberglass, the Gilmore shaft is a heavy-duty shaft, much heavier than its counterparts. Because of that weight it is a fairly slow flying shaft, but is also an excellent choice for bowhunters who require good penetration in their hunting arrows. The added weight

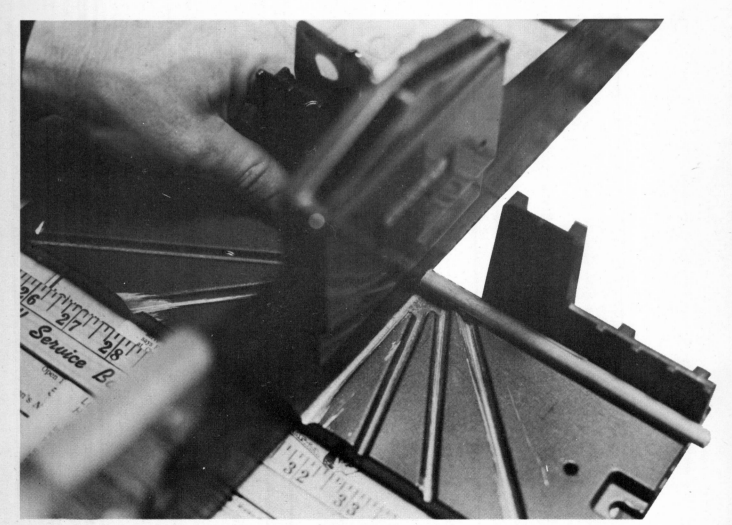

When cutting cedar shafts to your proper length, the job can be done with a hacksaw; miter box makes straight cut.

*Easton's cut-off tool makes cutting aluminum and fiberglass to proper size easy and accurate for novice.*

*A friction disk does the cutting of the shaft, while sizing is maintained by means of a sliding measuring gauge.*

results in a harder punch, and a deeper penetration.

Offering a cross-fiber makeup, which gives it its bulk and strength, the Gilmore shaft ranges in sizes from 2 through 9X, the numbers indicating the pound weight recommendations.

## SPEED AND PENETRATION

In determining which arrows you will use, you must now concern yourself with two characteristics of those arrows: their flight speed and their penetration capabilities. Penetration is especially important to the bowhunter, whereas speed is important to both tournament and bowhunting archers, and is a vital portion of penetration ability. In determining the penetration or "punch power" of an arrow archers use a simple physics formula: $V \times V \times W \div 64.32 = E$. The figure 64.32 represents twice the acceleration of gravity, V represents velocity in feet per second and W represents the weight in pounds of the arrow.

*Wooden shafts must be tapered with a tapering tool to accommodate the nock and point. The tapering tool works much like a child's pencil sharpener, with one end tapering for the nock, other for the point.*

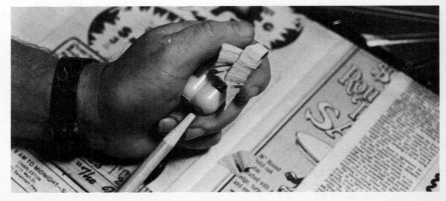

*Although not necessary, dipping aluminum or fiberglass shafts into a lacquer-based paint adds color and allows for a better bonding between the shaft and fletching.*

*A plastic dip tube, such as this one marketed by such firms as Bohning Adhesives, makes coloring the shafts simple, consistent, allowing for excess to drip off.*

Folks wise in the ways of mathematics will probably recognize this formula as the formula for determining kinetic energy, what we refer to as punch power.

This same formula that marksmen use to determine the energy of their ammunition can be used by archers if we remember to convert the normal weight in pounds to weight in grains, which is the measurement used for arrows, there being 7000 grains in one pound.

To determine the weight of your arrows you can use a grain scale, found in gunsmith and sporting goods stores who cater to the home bullet loaders. To determine the velocity of your arrows you will need a chronograph. Your pro shop may have one you can use, or perhaps you can find one among your archery club members.

A chronograph particularly popular for archery is the Arrometer by Micro Motion, Incorporated. The Arrometer

*A simple line rigged between a pair of chairs allows freshly painted shafts to dry untouched. They are held in place with clothespins. The lacquer-based paint should dry to the touch within thirty minutes.*

allows us to adjust the meter for each individual length to 0.1 inch, and gives a digital readout as the arrow sails through it.

Shooting through an Arrometer has become a featured attraction at outdoor archery tournaments, allowing archers to determine the actual speed of their bow when *they* are shooting it, with releases and shooting styles all playing their part in the resultant speed readings.

*As an afterthought, before dipping or fletching, arrow shafts should be cleaned of body oils and all chemical residues. Household cleanser, running water are used.*

*Once the point has dried, you can add the nock. Remove paint from the area beneath the nock with lacquer thinner or acetone. Remove only the paint that would otherwise be under nock.*

## YOUR GUIDANCE SYSTEM

Once you have determined the type of arrow shaft you will use and the size of those shafts, you must then consider the type of fletching you will use. Fletching — the guidance system of your arrows — is available in two basic materials, either feathers or vanes. Each comes in assorted colors and sizes.

The oldest form of fletching, the turkey feather, is a popular choice for the young archer as well as many bowhunters. Due to their high degree of flexibility, they are more forgiving to poor releases, are lighter and thus faster than their plastic counterparts. When shooting off the shelf of a bow; feathers are nearly a necessity as they lay down well. Plastic vanes, far less flexible, tend to kick off the shelf, causing erratic flight. The greatest drawback to the feather is its poor performance in foul weather. Feathers do not fare well in damp air, absorbing the moisture and thus becoming soggy and waterlogged. They may also separate themselves from the shaft, leaving behind only the bead of glue that once held them in place.

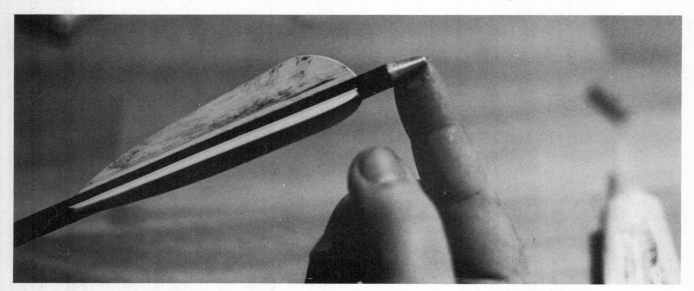

*When gluing the nock in place, apply your glue to the shaft rather than to interior of the nock. Spread the glue evenly with your finger, then quickly position the nock. Make certain it is straight, in line with shaft.*

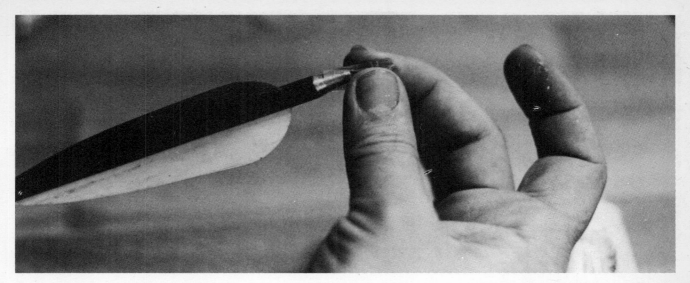

*An excellent cement for arrowmaking, Fletch-Tite dries rapidly, requires having the nock handy before gluing.*

*If you wish to add cresting to your arrow, a cresting tool allows you to apply the lacquer to the shaft as it is spinning. Using the tool in this manner it is possible to provide an even, smooth line of bright color.*

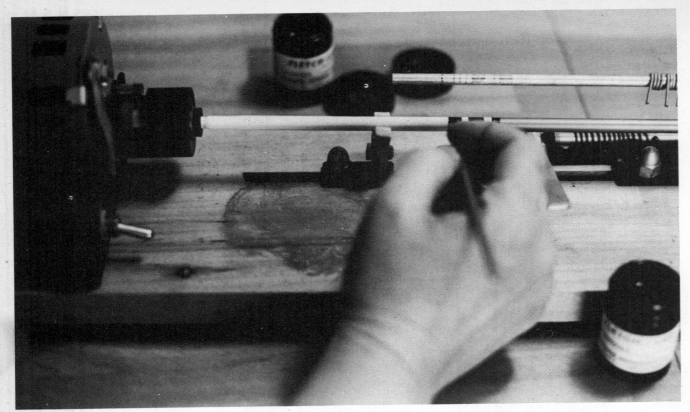

*Cresting is done after the nock is installed and even after you have completed fletching the arrow.*

*To add fletching to the shaft, one needs to use a fletching jig such as the highly-favored Bitzenburger. This particular type of jig allows for variations in the number of fletching and the angle at which set.*

For the archer apt to shoot during inclement weather, the introduction of the plastic vane came as the answer to a prayer. Plastic vanes are unaffected by moisture. Because the composition and design of each vane is identical to any other vane of that manufacturer, they also are consistent in weight and should group better than do feathers with their varying weights. Most competitive archers shoot with vanes because of their consistency.

Both feathers and vanes may be purchased precut in varying sizes. The size of the fletching should be determined by the weight of the bow, with light weight recurves of the twenty to twenty-five-pound range requiring only small, one-inch fletching, whereas larger fletching is the choice of heavier draw-weight bows.

Although color choices are seemingly endless, you may find some colors more appropriate to your use than others. If bowhunting you may prefer shades of green, black and brown for camouflage. But if you are apt to lose your arrows in the brush or wish to see where the arrows have struck you may do well to use brighter shades, such as the reds, yellows and fluorescent colors. A single round of shooting will tell you exactly how difficult it is to find your arrows in the grass. For tournament shooting any color of fletching will do and many archers choose their colors for purposes of personal identification. A guaranteed method of identifying your arrows is to make your own.

## MAKING YOUR OWN ARROWS

Were you to poll any group of archers you would find an

extremely small percentage who had actually made their own bow, even though bow kits make home workshop projects relatively easy. However, were you to poll the same group of archers regarding making their own arrows that percentage would jump dramatically. Why? Because making your own arrows is easy, it's enjoyable, and the end result is one in which you can take great pride. Then, too, homemade arrows are less expensive than premade arrows. The adage "so easy even a child can do it" is appropriate here with arrow making becoming a popular parent/child project.

The first step in arrow making is to cut the shafts to proper length. Most arrow shafts come in lengths of thirty-two inches, far too long for most of us. Remember the time you spent in determining your correct draw length? You will now use that measurement to cut your arrows to length, one-half to one inch longer than your actual draw length.

For best results you will find a high-speed abrasive-wheel cut-off tool or metal friction wheel mounted to a circular saw works best. Both produce a smooth, even cut with little or no rough spots. Folks have been known to use a rotary tube cutter or hacksaw to cut their arrow shafts to size. However, the frequency of rough spots is high and splitting of fiberglass shafts may occur. Take care that your cut is clean, smooth and even. There are a number of arrow cutters currently on the market, including the arrow cut-off tool manufactured by Easton Aluminum. If you prefer you

*A scale alongside the blades allows you to position each fletch identically to all others. The spring-loaded blades hold fletching firmly in place.*

*It is important to clean fletching prior to addition of glue. Chemical residue on the fletch as well as oil from the hands will resist bonding and allow fletching to separate from the shaft during use. A cloth dipped in lacquer thinner and wiped across the surface of the fletching will remove any dirt, oils or residue remaining.*

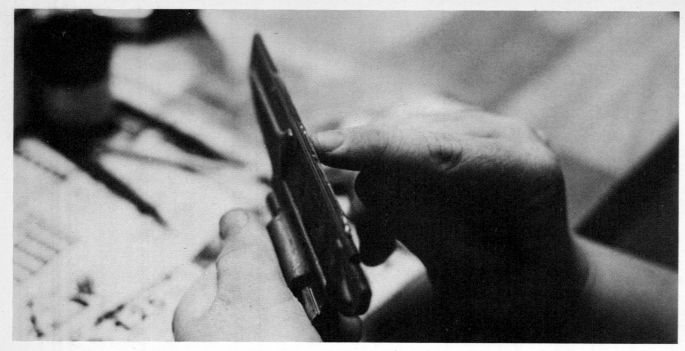

*Spread a thin, even line of Fletch-Tite along the length of the fletch, avoiding the temptation to apply more glue than is necessary, as it will only squeeze along the sides of the fletch when positioned on the shaft.*

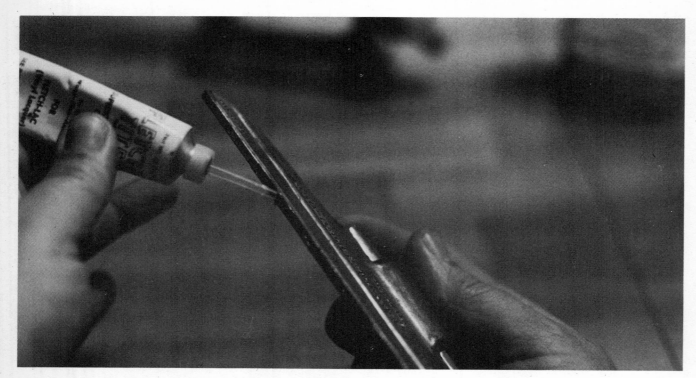

*To remove excess glue from the fletch, run a finger along each side as it is held in the fletching jig. The finger will pick up the excess, not affecting the line of glue needed to hold the fletch in place.*

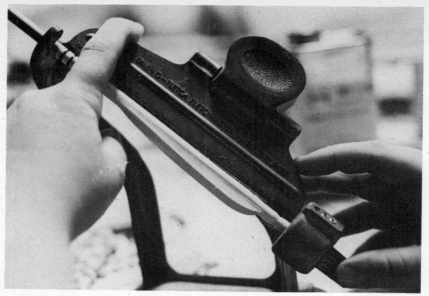

*The clamp is held in a perpendicular position to the shaft by a large magnet, requiring only that you slide the clamp down onto the shaft for correct placement. Leave the clamp in position until the fletching has dried completely. This usually takes fifteen minutes.*

can purchase your bare shafts precut, although for a slightly greater cost. Many pro shops also will cut them for you, often at no cost.

If wooden shafts are used, you will need to taper each end. The shafts come blunt cut and must be tapered to accept the nock and point. Archery tapering tools available for little cost offer two separate cuts to match the taper of nocks and points, and work much like a simple pencil sharpener.

Once tapered and cut, it is time to consider color. Although it is not necessary to coat aluminum or fiberglass shafts, you may find it advantageous to at least partially dip

these shafts to provide both color and a better bond for your fletching. If using cedar shafts, you will want to dip each shaft fully, not only for color and bonding, but to provide a degree of protection against the weather.

Cedar shafts normally are dipped in a clear lacquer. Before dipping wipe the shaft down with lacquer thinner on a paper towel to remove any body oils deposited by your hands. Fiberglass shafts also must be wiped free of dirt and oils using the same thinner. For aluminum shafts you must use additional care.

There are two methods currently recommended for the cleaning of aluminum shafts. One method involves the use

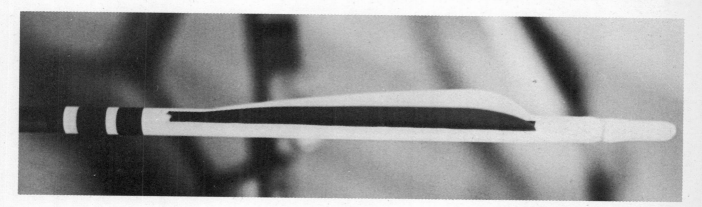

*When the feather is in place, a good glue line should show no seepage of glue beyond the finished fletch.*

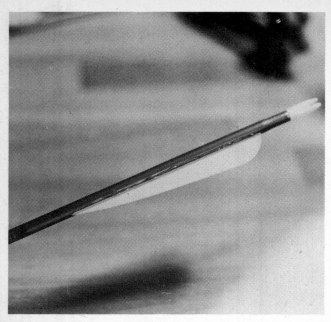

*If too much glue is used in setting the fletching, the excess squeezes along fletches, causing a buildup.*

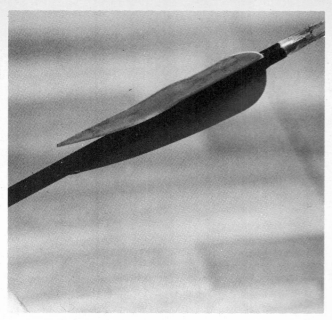

*A common arrow maintenance problem is loose or missing fletching. Pull off the old fletch and replace it with new.*

of a cleanser scrub, wiping the shafts down with a damp cloth coated with cleanser or a similar abrasive cleaner, then rinsing under running water before drying. Another method involves the use of a metal conditioner offered by Bohning Adhesives, a Michigan-based company that manufactures a number of quality products for arrow making. Shafts are dipped in the conditioner for a minute or two, then rinsed off under running water and allowed to dry.

After cleaning the shafts, take great care that you do not touch the area that you will be coloring. You will want to dip these shafts as quickly as possible after drying. If delay

extends beyond eight hours, reclean the shafts with a cloth dampened in lacquer thinner before dipping.

The use of dipping tubes makes coating your shafts extremely easy and efficient. Use only plastic or aluminum tubes, as other metals may not be compatible with the lacquer-based paints. Fill the tube with your base coat, allowing the paint to settle until all air bubbles have come to the surface. You'll need to skim these bubbles off the surface before dipping your shafts. Should you find air pockets in the finish of your dipped shafts, you probably have air pockets trapped within the lacquer in the dip

*Do not attempt to shave the remaining glue from shaft. Unless one is extremely careful, this can leave nicks and cuts in the shaft, making it difficult for the new fletching to adhere properly to the shaft.*

*Right: Method for making fiberglass arrows is complex, with intricate machinery being required to combine the strands of glass with the resin that, when properly dried and formed, presents a straight hollow tube.*

*A rag dipped in lacquer thinner or acetone will remove the old glue, leaving the area of shaft clean, smooth.*

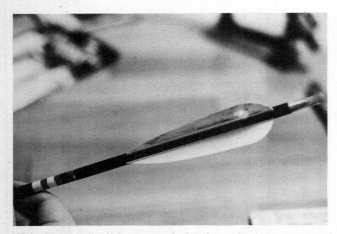

*With the new fletching properly in place, the new arrow is almost ready for use with little additional work.*

earlier provides the same degree of taper to wooden shafts. If you have dipped your shafts in lacquer paints you will need to remove this paint from the nock area before adding your nock. Simply dip a rag or paper towel into lacquer thinner or acetone, then rotate the shaft against the towel as you wipe the lacquer off. Removal should be easy and quick. You want to remove only that paint that would be beneath the nock.

A common cause of improper nock alignment is the trapping of air bubbles inside the nock. These bubbles lift the nock up and possibly tilt it slightly. You may not even notice the tilt until you try shooting your arrows. To avoid air bubbles make it a habit to apply your glue to the shaft itself, rather than dropping it inside the nock. Apply to the shaft a large drop or two of glue such as Bohning's Ferr-L-Tite developed especially for archery needs. After applying the glue rotate the shaft against your finger, allowing your finger to spread the glue evenly around the shaft. Quickly position the nock into place before the glue dries. Fletch-Tite dries rapidly and you will need to have your nock handy before you begin.

If you wish to crest your arrows, you will want to do so at this point. During the Middle Ages, knights would label their shields and clothing with their names, using crests. Each crest was special, used only by that royal family, and readily identified the individual. Cresting your arrow shafts can produce the same results for you, immediately identifying your arrows as your own.

Cresting is the addition of lines of color just below the fletching, intended to give the arrow a personalized look. To give your arrows a smooth, professional appearance, you

tubes, and will need to dilute the paint slightly to allow the trapped bubbles to rise to the surface. Do not thin the paint any more than necessary, or you are apt to get runs in the finish.

Mark the shaft at the level you wish dipped, then dip the shaft to that mark. Remove the shaft and allow it to run freely until it reduces to an occasional drop. Now redip the shaft to give the shaft a full, complete coating. Hang the shafts in a vertical position until they are completely dry, about thirty minutes.

You are now ready to add your nock. It is extremely important that the nock be correctly aligned if you hope to have good arrow flight. A nock that tilts even slightly will cause erratic arrow flight.

Aluminum and fiberglass shafts are pre-tapered at the nock end of each shaft to give you a perfect match to the inside taper of the nock. The tapering tool mentioned

*To finish off the fletching, add a drop of Fletch-Tite to each end of the fletching. The glue thus can prevent lift-off should arrow pass completely through target.*

will want to invest in a cresting machine. The crestor spins the shaft at a constant speed while you add your color. Select the color and pattern you wish, marking them with a piece of paper taped below the crestor or mark with tape on the guide wand above the crestor.

Among the types of cresting being used is the incorporation of the International Morse Code to your rest. Dots and dashes are represented by varying widths of

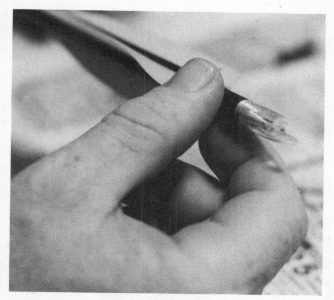

*Nock damage generally results from breaking off one of the lips of the nock. As one cannot accurately predict the flight, never shoot an arrow with a damaged nock.*

bands around the shaft. Slim lines represent dots, wide bands the dashes. To give the shaft that finished look hairlines are added; the fine, extremely thin lines are used to frame the crest or perhaps to separate the different letters in a coded crest. Once the cresting has dried a coating of clear lacquer is applied to protect the finish against scuffing. A popular overcoat is Fletch-Lac; a clear lacquer that not only protects the cresting but seems to brighten the colors.

### INTERNATIONAL MORSE CODE

| | | | | | |
|---|---|---|---|---|---|
| A | .– | J | .– – – | S | . . . |
| B | – . . . | K | – . – | T | – |
| C | – . – . | L | . – . . | U | . . – |
| D | – . . | M | – – | V | . . . – |
| E | . | N | – . | W | . – – |
| F | . . – . | O | – – – | X | – . . – |
| G | – – . | P | . – – . | Y | – . – – |
| H | . . . . | Q | – – . – | Z | – – . . |
| I | . . | R | . – . | | |

Once your cresting has dried you are ready to apply the fletching, either feathers or plastic vanes. An important step in fletching comes before the first fletch is ever applied. In order to have a good, secure bond between shaft and fletching there must be no interference, either from the body oils in your hands or the chemical residue in the makeup of the plastic vanes. To avoid interference from body oils, simply resist the temptation to grab your shafts at the nock end. To be sure they are clean; unpainted shafts may be wiped down with a rag dampened in metal cleaner, lacquer thinner or isopropyl alcohol.

You will need a fletching jig. This jig is used to hold the fletching in place against the shaft while the glue dries. A

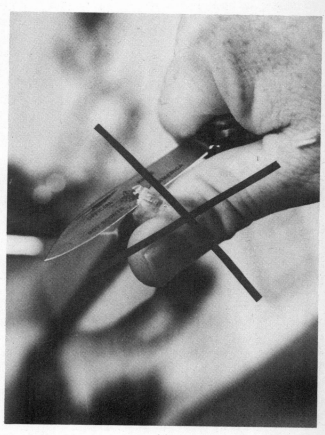

*Do not remove a broken nock by cutting it from shaft. You are apt to cut into the nock taper. This, in turn, can mean that replacement nock will not seat properly.*

popular model is the Bitzenburger which provides optional setting for exact placement of three, four or five-feather fletching, with either left or right-hand helical twists. The fletching is held in place between two spring-locked blades.

Once the fletching is in place between the jig blades wipe the fletching down with a rag dipped in lacquer thinner or isopropyl alcohol to remove chemical residue or oils from the fletching that might interfere with the bond. Next,

*Another indication that an aluminum shaft is less than straight is to place it on a table and roll it. If you can see light between shaft and surface, it is crooked.*

*Left: There are several types of shooting machines that can be used to test your bow and arrow combination. (Above) To test aluminum arrow straightness, sight down it with one eye or roll it on a flat surface. If the shaft wobbles in the roll, it will need straightening.*

apply a thin line of Fletch-Tite along the length of the fletching. Use your glue sparingly to avoid messy oozing of excess glue alongside the fletching. A good glue line will leave little or no glue lying visible along the vane or feather, and yet will completely line the fletching to avoid air holes.

Once all fletching is added you will want to finish off your fletching job with the addition of a small drop of glue at both ends of each fletch. The glue keeps the vane or feather from lifting off at either end upon impact with the target.

The final step in making your own arrows is the addition of a point. Aluminum and fiberglass shafts require the addition of inserts inside each tube to accommodate the points. Inserts may be of either tapered or screw-in style. Most popular is the screw-in style which allows you to change points whenever you desire.

In applying the inserts most manufacturers recommend using a blow-torch and hot melt, such as Ferr-L-Tite, available in stick or tube form from Bohning Adhesives.

With the addition of the inserts your arrowmaking is complete. Simply screw-in the point of your choice and take to the range to show off your handiwork. Your arrows should give you years of pleasure with very little maintenance required.

## ARROW MAINTENANCE

Although arrows require little in the way of maintenance there are some periodic inspections that should be made. It's a good idea to check your arrows after each round of shooting. Look for loose or missing fletching, damaged nocks, splits in fiberglass or wooden shafts, bends in aluminum shafts.

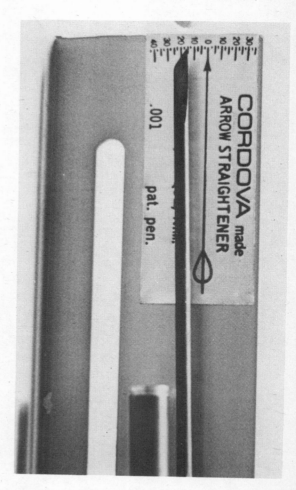

*Commercially made instruments can be used to straighten aluminum arrows. Although there are numerous styles and prices, all straighteners use the same principle.*

*A straightener uses a force applied above the high point of the bend, support offering upward thrust at the ends. Most straighteners have a gauge that registers results.*

The grouping on this target would tend to indicate that some of the arrows are not too well matched or shooter is not paying attention or not using the same anchor.

If your arrows are closely balanced for weight and length, you may even shoot an occasional Robin Hood, if lucky, but certainly grouping should be excellent.

Testing your arrows on a target face such as this will help to sort out those that perform less well than one would expect. Discard these for any serious competition.

Performance of various arrow materials in relationship to each other also can be tested on a backyard range. It helps determine match-up of arrows to your own bow.

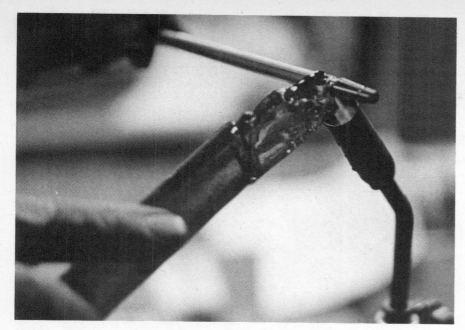

*Nocks and points are applied to the plastic or aluminum shafts by hand, using Ferr-L-Tite and a blowtorch.*

If fletching is loose or missing you will probably notice it immediately. Loose fletching causes fluttering of the arrow in flight. If the fletching is missing, the arrow balance will be distorted, again resulting in erratic arrow flight. While shooting arrows with no fletching whatsoever is not only possible, but in many cases deliberate, shooting arrows with damaged or missing fletching is not recommended.

Replace damaged fletching by peeling it from the shaft. Do not cut it with a knife or you may nick the shaft itself. Residual glue may be removed with lacquer thinner. Do not attempt to replace the original fletching, as removing the residual glue is extremely difficult. New fletching is extremely inexpensive, a hundred four-inch feathers costing less than $7, a hundred similarly sized vanes about $8. Many pro shops will sell you feathers and vanes in assorted colors and sizes, in packs of twelve for about a dollar a pack.

Never shoot arrows with damaged nocks. The nock functions as the control system of the arrow. It holds the arrow in a constant, secure, straight position, providing a smooth release from the bow. With a damaged nock there is no telling where your arrow might go.

To remove a damaged nock heat it slightly near an open flame, then pull it off with a pair of pliers. *Do not* cut or shave the nock from the shaft. You may alter the angle of the nock taper, causing the new nock to seat slightly off center, resulting in erratic flight.

For arrow shafts that are split or appear to have weakened areas along the shaft walls, there is nothing that can be done in terms of maintenance other than to retire the arrow as a tomato stake or, perhaps, if the damage is located only at the end of the shaft you might cut off the damaged area and donate the shaft to one of your shorter-draw friends. Never shoot an arrow if you suspect shaft damage. The thrust from the bow upon release may be just the stress that is needed to shatter the damaged shaft, causing it to splinter in several directions, and possibly cause injury.

Also get into the habit of checking your arrows periodically during shooting, especially if you have reason to feel that the arrow may have suffered damage, as from impact with trees, stones, etc.

With a small amount of effort on your part, you can guarantee yourself years of enjoyable shooting, and with archery you'll not need to worry about the frequent need to resupply your stock of ammunition. You can shoot your same dozen arrows day after day, target after target, at a cost that is hard to beat, even at today's prices.

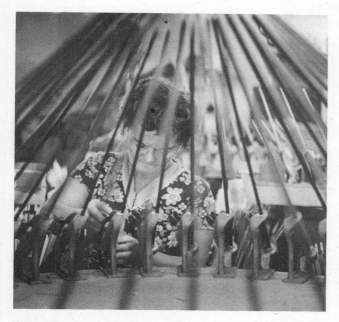

*With the aid of Bitzenburger jig, which is mounted on a rotating table, worker at Arrow Manufacturing is able to fletch as many as forty-eight arrow shafts at a time.*

To make your own bowstring, you first need the makings. That includes a string jig, a ball of Dacron thread, a serving thread and a server, along with a tape measure for determining proper length or the bow so that you can use the string that already is installed to determine the proper length. Don't let technicalities frighten you.

# Chapter 6
# THE BOWSTRING
## Construction Of Your Own
## Custom Bowstring Is Challenging
## — And Rewarding

THE BOWSTRING is an important part of your arrow-casting equipment. After all, there must be something between the two limbs of a recurve or longbow, or the cable ends of the eccentrics or computed cams on modern-style compound bows.

For every rule there is an exception, of course. Indian Archery made several models of a compound bow that used a full-length cable, no string; the cable acting as the string. One thing for certain, you won't likely break or cut that cable guidance system.

Bob Learn is a bowhunter who has constructed several of his own bowstrings of a variety of materials. In so doing he has developed a number of procedures and little tricks to make the task easier. The following is his advice on how to avoid pitfalls and be a successful bowstring builder.

Making a bowstring is easy after you assemble the right gear. It doesn't take long and you can buy a large spool of

Dacron that will produce many strings. If you prefer the Kevlar material, you can buy a quantity of that, too.

Bowstrings were made of many available materials in the past — fibers woven from plants, sinew from animals, anything that would work and could be found. Silk was used by archers in the Orient since they had quite a bit of it. Today, most archers have settled on Dacron. Several types are on the market and all work well for bowstrings. The newer Kevlar is good, used mainly by those who shoot in FITA tournaments and Olympic competition.

To construct a bowstring you need a convenient method of winding the string material. You can make a string jig from two pieces of two-by-two lumber and a two-by-four split down the middle. Or you can make one of old bed rails and machined aluminum as Bob Learn did. If you prefer, you can buy a jig from an archery mail-order company. Martin Archery, Bohning, and Bingham Outdoor

*The material for making your own bowstring can be either the Dacron B-50 at right on a one-pound spool, or you may choose to use the newer Kevlar also shown. Many of today's top competitors have come to favor this newer material.*

Projects are a few of those who list a string jig in their catalogs. Cost was about twenty dollars in 1982.

Also required is a string server. This is a device to hold a serving thread, usually nylon, on a metal or plastic keeper that will allow you to set tension for serving the ends, loops, and the midsection on the string. These are also listed in several catalogs.

Buy the jig, the server, some Dacron string material, a spool of serving thread and you are in business to make strings, says Learn. You could buy a ready-made string, but with the right equipment you can save dollars and fine-tune your gear to your specifications.

When you buy or build a string jig, make it to fit the equipment you use. Perhaps the longest strings needed would be for longbows. Learn says he has one that measures sixty-nine inches, and his string jig is long enough to make that length string. Compound bows require shorter strings; as short as thirty-four inches. If you build your jig make it adjustable for the longest and shortest strings you may ever need.

The first thing to consider is how many strands you want for the bow on which you plan to put the string. Bow-company and string-manufacturer charts will indicate how many strands are required for different bow weights.

*One also has a choice of serving materials. Available are the nylon installed on the Bjorn server at right or the orange-colored monofilament which is shown left.*

Learn's hunting strings are all made sixteen strands. This, believes Bob Learn, is strong enough for a bow up to and including eighty pounds draw. Even if you don't shoot that heavy a bow, making an extra strand or two in the string builds in safety in case you should nick a strand of the Dacron with the sharp edge of a broadhead. It has been known to happen. That extra one or two strands allows the hunt to continue.

For this project Bob Learn made a Dacron bowstring of

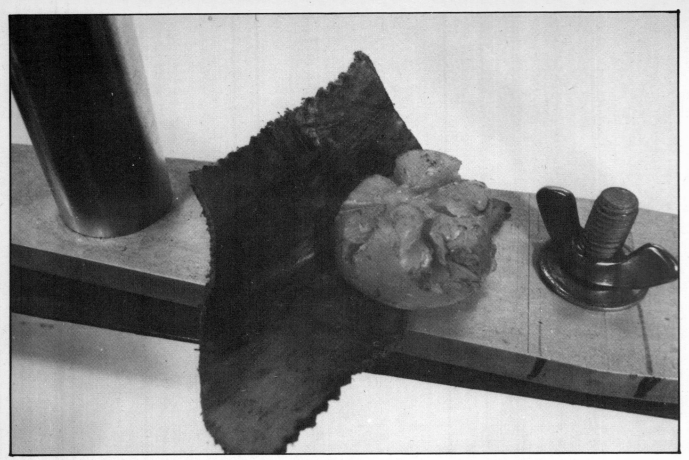

*An important part of Bob Learn's string-making effort is a hunk of beeswax with a section of light leather. The latter is used to burnish the string for smoothness before the serving is completed in the string's center.*

*To start the string-making operation, start with the arms of the jig positioned parallel to the base. This is necessary for proper measurement of the bowstring.*

sixteen strands to fit a modern compound bow, the Martin/Howatt Cougar II. According to the chart the bow requires a string length of thirty-eight inches. The string on Learn's bow was thirty-nine inches. Dacron stretches under pressure of shooting and the tension of the compound system. The experienced builder will allow about seven-eighths-inch for stretch, making the new string almost an inch shorter than the existing one. If not sure, measure the string on the bow and shorten that measurement by one inch or three-quarters-inch for the new string. A shorter string decreases the draw length and draw weight of the compound; a longer string lengthens the draw and increases the poundage. You can adjust bow and draw weight by experimenting on your own bow.

*In this instance the length of the string is to be 38 inches, so Learn measured to the outside of the opposite post, adding two inches to the three-foot tape length. It is at this distance that the string is wound to post.*

The string jig has two arms: One is fixed at one end but pivots in place. The other arm is movable down the length of the jig and also pivots in place. To set the jig arms for proper string length, consult the charts or measure your bowstring as it is on the bow. Deduct seven-eighths-inch and set the movable arm at this distance. Learn uses a cloth measuring tape with a loop on one end. This loop goes over the post of the jig arm, measuring from the tip base where the string will be made. Measure to the outside edge of the opposite arm post with the two arms swung parallel to the base section of the jig. This is the length your string will be when finished. For this project, Learn set his arms thirty-eight inches apart.

Next, pivot the two arms into position at right angles to

*The cloth tape has a looped end that fits over the post of the server. This helps determine proper string length.*

**B-50 DACRON\* AT 50 LBS. PER STRAND IS OVER 35% STRONGER THAN TYPE B. YOU MAY FIND THAT YOU WILL WANT TO USE FEWER STRANDS THAN INDICATED BELOW.**

### SUGGESTED STRAND PER BOW WEIGHT

| BOW WT. | STRANDS |
|---------|---------|
| 20-30 # | 8 |
| 25-35 # | 10 |
| 35-45 # | 12 |
| 45-55 # | 14 |
| 55-80 # | 16 |

**FOR BEST RESULTS BOWSTRING SHOULD BE TWISTED ⅓ TURN PER INCH AND WELL WAXED. DO NOT SERVE TOO TIGHTLY.**

\*DUPONT POLYESTER

If one chooses to use Dacron B-50 for his bowstring, the manufacturer, DuPont, includes with the material a chart that indicates the number of strands that should be used in relationship to the draw weight of the intended bow.

In surveying the efforts of a young field archer during competition, Fred Bear appears to ponder. He is one who knows the importance of an extra bowstring in the field.

With the arms swung out at right angles to the jig base, wrap the strands of Dacron around the arms. When this much has been accomplished, set-up should look like this.

the base and set the wing nut hard on the arm base so it can't move during the string layout. Tie the loose end of your Dacron string material to either end post of the fixed arm or make a separate pin to tie the loose end onto. Removing the excess string later is easier if you use the extended pin tie. Take one turn around one of the arm posts on the end arm. Maintain constant tension on the string as you go around each post of the string jig. Learn suggests wearing a leather glove to get more tension and not cut fingers as pressure is applied. Count each turn as you place the Dacron on the posts. A sixteen-strand string means eight loops on the entire jig system. When you have sixteen make a turn on the opposite post you started from and tie off the tail to a post or tie screw.

This is the basic layout for any string. Measure the

length with the arms lengthwise, pivot and lay on the strands you need around the post ends. The only differences in this procedure is the number of turns — less for a lighter bow, more for a heavy bow — and the length as determined by the individual bow.

Learn built a plastic guide for marking the serving area for the loop ends of his bowstring. Alternately, the maker may measure to the middle, mark off two inches on each side of the midpoint for a string loop of four inches. This is

No serious competitive shooter goes into a tournament without an extra bowstring easily accessible should he break a string during an important part of the shoot.

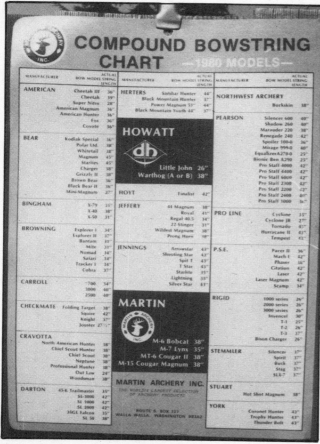

Martin Archery offers a handy chart that suggests string lengths for the most popular compound bows. This length is what should be made, as it will stretch when installed.

One must be certain the string threads go to the bottom of the machined post. Sizes of posts should be matched.

fine for the upper loop of a recurve says Learn as that loop usually slides down the upper limb when stringing the bow.

The larger upper loop is also applied to the longbow, but for the compound you don't need a big loop, only one big enough to go over the cable-end teardrop; too big a loop and it might come off, too small and it won't fit over the end unit.

A yellow wax pencil will clearly mark the black Dacron for reference. After marking the area to be served, turn your attention to the string server loaded with nylon serving thread. Most makers use a heavy thread, but Learn has used a No. 16 sewing thread, which works well but takes longer to serve. The server facilitates laying the thread tightly around the multi-strand string to help hold the

*Learn contends that a few simple, homemade gadgets can help in string-making. This plastic serving marker he made from clear plastic. It hangs on the serving area so black material can be marked with pencil of yellow wax.*

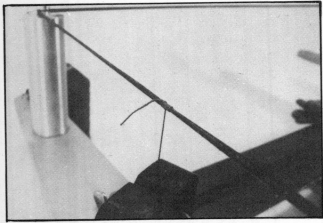

*To begin the serving, one has only to lay a section of the serving thread on the start mark made with the wax pencil, then turn a few wraps around the bowstring.*

strands together and prevent any from being severed by arrow nock ends or compound teardrops.

Check the server to determine how much tension is on the thread. You should be able to pull it out with some force. If too tight, the serving thread will break or strands of the layered string material might cut through. Learn uses the Bjorn server which permits tension adjustment through the number of holes the serving thread passes through prior to the outlet hole. You can also apply tension to a wing nut that holds the crossbolt on the spool in the server.

Pull out an inch or two of thread and lay this at the end mark for the loop serving. Wrap the string around the Dacron by hand, holding the server until you have it started. When the serving thread is about one-half inch down the Dacron, increase the tension on the server by back spinning the spool. This places the grooved center section of the server against the Dacron. Now all you need do is turn the server around and around the string as the serving thread lays along the Dacron in a tight pattern. This makes a good serving and once you have determined the proper tension on the server you need not change it till you run out of serving thread. If the serving thread is too loose the serving on the string will separate, causing problems.

When you have spun the server down the length of the loop section to your second mark you are ready to tie off the thread. This is easier to do than to describe, says Learn. You may use the same finish knot as used when serving line guides on a fishing pole.

Never served line guides? Neither has Bob Learn, but this is how to do it: When you reach the end mark pull out about a foot or thread from the server and cut it off. You will not have a loose end beyond the served area. Keep one

finger on the served thread to prevent it from unraveling. Back off on the served section about one-quarter inch, or until you are just a bit back of the end or finish mark.

With the one finger of the hand on the serving end, check to see which way the serving is wrapped on the Dacron. Move up the loop end area about two inches, take the loose end in the opposite hand, and place it over the strands in the opposite direction from the serving.

Now move down the inside of the loop you have formed and lay loose serves around the Dacron moving back toward the served area. Learn makes his looped ends with about ten turns for the tie-off. With ten turns lay the loose end of the serving thread along the served section of the Dacron.

Hold this loose end close to the served section and with one hand continue the serving by laying the wraps over the loose end and continuing from the served ending. As you wrap by hand from the end, the loops formed around the

*One should bring the server to the hand wrap and turn the server down the strands until the end is reached.*

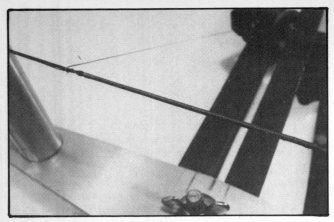

*When you reach the end mark on the Dacron string, pull out about a foot of excess thread to use in tying off.*

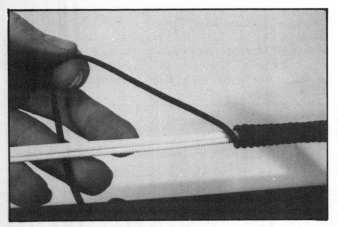

*As the standard thread is too small to be seen clearly, Learn used parachute cord to illustrate points. Take one end of the serving thread, place it over Dacron strands.*

Learn's illustrations on this tie-off procedure show large strands of nylon cord for better visibility of the procedure.

After marking, serving and tying off one end of the string, move to the other jig arm and repeat the process. When you have both loop ends served you can place a drop or two of Fletch-Tite on the tied-off end. Run it in for a better finish.

Cut the Dacron close to the serving where you tied the Dacron to start laying the strands for the string.

To form the loops on the string ends you now pivot both arms of the string jig simultaneously until they are again parallel with the jig base. This will bring the strands of the Dacron closer together. If you make your strings as tight as Bob Learn, you will probably have to loosen the movable arm to rotate it. While you have the tension off the arm, pull the string until the two served ends are around the posts of the arms. The midsection of the post where you wrapped the Dacron on the jig will form the loop ends for the string. Pull the string around the posts until the ends of the serving on the loop ends line up. The servings should evenly meet on both ends and on both arms.

Learn changed this procedure slightly for the following reason. If you serve the loop ends evenly and they match nicely, when the arms are pivoted back to align with the jig you will have a big hump where the served ends meet. These ends are then served down to form the end loop. Learn marks his end loops so the served ends don't meet

Dacron will unwrap as you lay new wraps down. When you finish, if you have done it right, you will end up with one large loop and about one-half inch or less of slightly looser serving. Get a good grip on the loose end of the serving thread which lays along the served section and pull it tight. As you pull, the end of the loop will decrease until it also is tight against the Dacron string. Pull this loose end tight and snip off the loose serving thread where it emerges from the serving.

It may sound complicated, but when you do it you will be able to see it happen. If you form the end loop the wrong way the thread will wrap on the Dacron rather than unwrap as it is supposed to. If that happens, undo it and wrap the loose end from the other side of the Dacron.

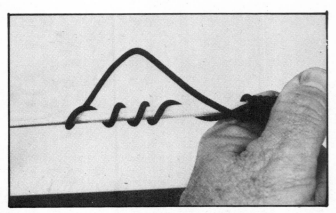

*Holding the loose end of the thread — in illustration, parachute cord — wrap back toward the end of the served area. Make about ten turns, keeping the loops loose.*

exactly. This leaves about one-quarter to one-half inch difference when the arms are swung. When the next procedure is begun, these two served ends won't meet in one big hump but will be slightly separated and the finished string is smoother and neater.

Learn first took measurements of the Martin/Cougar string to make his new one. The loop of the string end started 1½ inches from the end of the loop. He then measured down from the looped string on the post the same distance. This provides a starting place for making the new loop end. Martin made their serving come down four inches from the start so Learn marked that distance on his string with the yellow marker.

Lay a short section of serving along the marked upper end by the jig post. Hold the two sections of the string together — they want to separate as the diameter of the jig post is holding them apart — and start serving down the

doubled Dacron the same as when forming the loop ends. Learn says that after he has wrapped about one-quarter inch by hand he pulls the loose end of the serving thread between the two string sections and runs it down the middle between the served loop areas.

After enough wraps to get the serving started pull the tension on the server as before until the slot is on the string. Now rotate the server and it will move down the Dacron toward the middle. When you reach the end mark, pull out a foot of serving and tie off as you did on the string loops.

Repeat the process on the other end. When you make that second tie-off the string is almost completed. At this point you can remove the string from the jig and check it against the string on the bow. If it is shorter than the original not to worry, claims Learn. That is the way it should be. Each bow has its personality, and after you

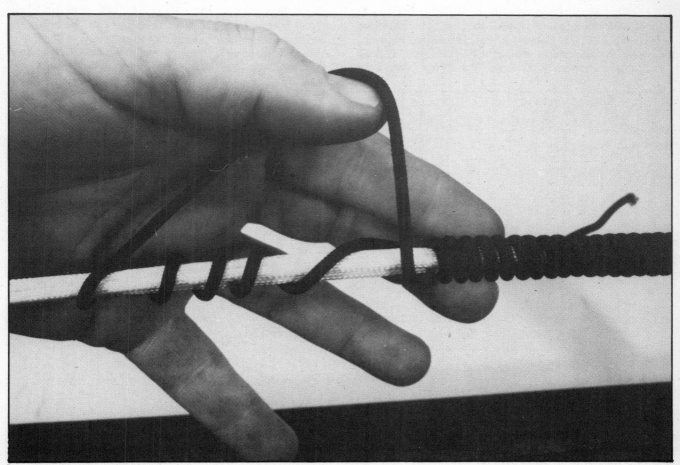

*Serve at the end of the served area by pulling the thread tight. Then wrap the strands from the serving end. As one wraps by and onto the Dacron, the other end will unwrap. Learn says it is more simple than the explanation sounds.*

Turn the arms of the jig so they once again are parallel with the base of the jig. Pull the served ends until they are around the posts and almost meet in the middle.

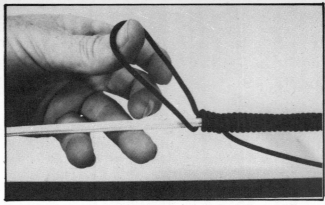

When you have a single loop, merely pull on the straight length you laid along the string. This should shorten the loop and pull the excess into hand-wrapped serving.

know its kinks you will know exactly how long to make a new string so the bow will perform at its best.

Before placing the new string on the bow Learn suggests serving the midsection. Return the string to the jig with the loops over the posts and pull it as tight as you can.

If you shoot nothing but target you can place your midsection serving dead center, balanced above and below the nocking point. If you are a bowhunter or field archer you need to make this center section off-balanced. Martin's original midsection serving was about seven inches long. Learn lengthened his to eight inches. He wanted his string longer on the bottom to protect the Dacron strands from abrasion when carrying the bow. The string often rides against the arm when carrying a bow. This added serving length will take wear far better than the multi-strands of Dacron.

Learn is a right-handed archer. For a three-fingered release he puts tension on the string to the right. For this reason, he serves all his center sections from the bottom to the top. When he draws and releases, the center serving will tend to pull together and not unwrap.

Beeswax rubbed into the string will impregnate the string with extra wax. After waxing, Learn burnishes the wax into the string by pushing and pulling with a piece of soft leather until it feels hot to the hand. This sets the string and helps stretch it before remounting on the bow.

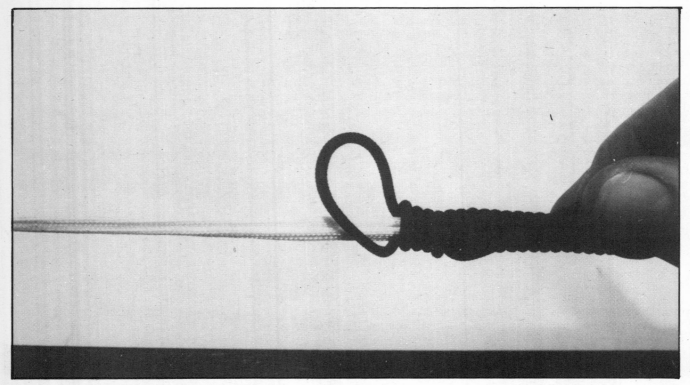

As the loose end is drawn up, the loop gets smaller until it disappears into the serving. There should be no lump.

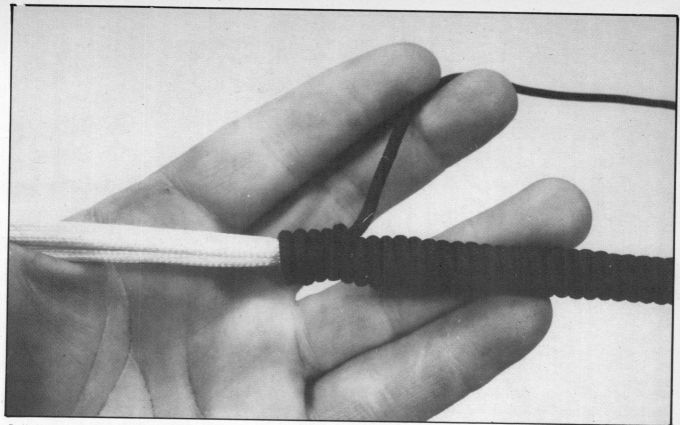

*Pull the loop tight into the hand-wrapped area, then snip off the loose material as close to the serving as possible without cutting into adjacent material. The resulting wraps should be smooth to touch of finger.*

After burnishing pull the jig arms as tight as possible. Start your serving at the bottom mark. Lay it on by hand, pulling on the server and moving up the string until the end mark is reached. On the center serving, fifteen extra turns for tie-off will protect the work from the added whipping action as the arrow is released.

Your new string is now ready to remove from the jig. Learn's Cougar II compound has the double teardrop cable fitting and changing strings is a breeze. Place the riser on a soft rug or other surface and pull up with one hand on the string. Place one loop of the new string on the empty teardrop, move the new string over to the other teardrop and loop the string end on that empty end. Now remove the old slack string. The new string will have taken the pressure. The new string will stretch with time until it becomes the same length as the original.

There are a few variations to consider for other bows. For the longbow and the recurve the upper loop should be big enough to slide down the limb when you unbrace the bow. The lower loop will be smaller so it will stay on the bow end nocks and not fall off when bracing. Learn always serves his center serving on a recurve rather than on a jig for simplicity.

How long should a recurve bowstring be? Measure the full length from bow nock to bow nock. Subtract three inches for the proper string length. Learn says it comes

*The need for a well made and adequate string becomes obvious in big money shoots such as in Las Vegas.*

Notice that the completed serving is offset. This is to allow the loop serving to vary in thickness. If one had both ends even it would create a larger hump in the area where the two ends will meet and be secured.

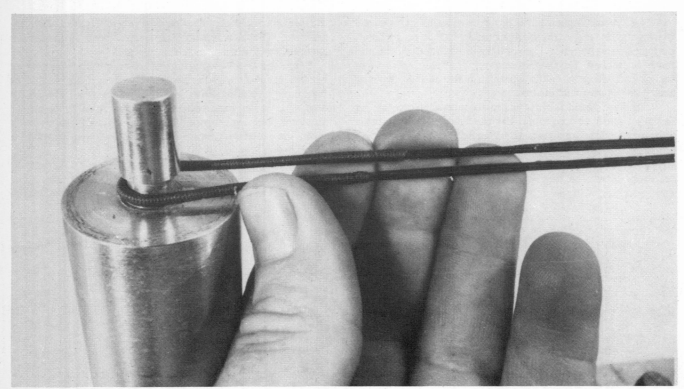

One must turn the arms of the jig so that they once again are parallel with the base of the jig. Then pull the served ends of the string until they are around the posts and almost meet in the middle of this practical setup.

easier after making a few. If you lay up the strands without enough tension the string will stretch and eventually sag. Terry Martin of Martin Archery said they use about sixty pounds tension on their string-making machine.

There is some disagreement as to the proper brace height for a recurve. Most old timers measure the brace height from the back of the arrow shelf, where the broadhead will be, to the point on the string at brace position. The AMO specifications state brace height is measured from the pivot point on the handle to a point at right angles to the string. On Learn's Howatt Hunter brace height measures ten inches from the arrow rest and eight inches from the pivot point of the handle.

The proper brace height for a recurve should be low enough so the tips start to curl over. There are often string grooves on the belly of a bow and the string should lay in that groove when at proper brace height. If it's too low you will get a sore arm from the string slapping it on release. Some argue that the lower brace height, longer string position gives the bow greater speed since it can follow through on the arrow longer.

If you brace the bow too high, the string too short, you won't get the speed built into the bow. Some will use that slight curve on the tip as a judgment for proper brace height and string length.

A recurve bowstring that comes out about a quarter to one-half inch too long can be removed from the upper end and twisted to correct length. Turn it clockwise so the string draws into the twist, not away from it. When you brace the bow again you will find the twisting has shortened the string a bit, making it a stronger and better string.

This technique works on a recurve or longbow string as the string is held solid on both ends. But don't try this on your compound; it will merely untwist and might impart some weird problems in the cable system.

One other string variation should be considered. The Dynabow systems use two strings, one for shooting and another called a tiller string. They are both Dacron but

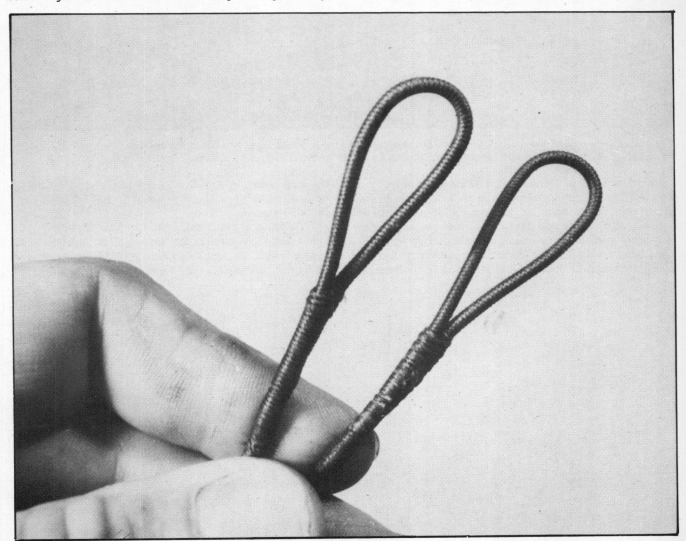

*After serving the loops together on both ends of the bowstring, one has the loops completed and it is time to remove the string from the jig and install it on the bow to learn how well the work was done for a fit.*

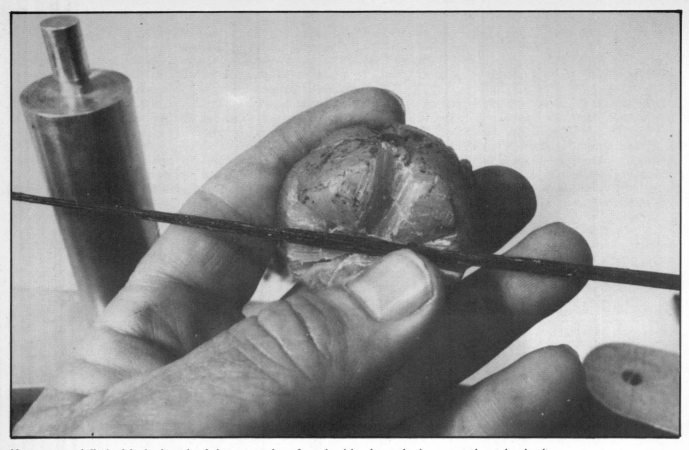

*If you are satisfied with the length of the new string after checking it on the bow, put the string back on the jig and pull it tight. Next, rub beeswax into the entire length of the string, using the wax liberally.*

loops are smaller on the tiller string. These loops go over the small tips on the upper limb and are held on the lower section by screws used for adjustment. If you own a Dynabow system you will have to drill and tap on a metal jig or merely screw a small hook in a wooden jig arm. The string ends can be held in these hooks, tension pulled on the jig arms, and by some careful attention to the start of the loop ends you may construct your strings. Both strings have center servings; the tiller string to prevent wear when shooting across it.

Making a string for your longbow is basically the same procedure except for brace height. Use the older system called fistmele measurement. Most longbows have little or no window cut out. Learn has an old York longbow

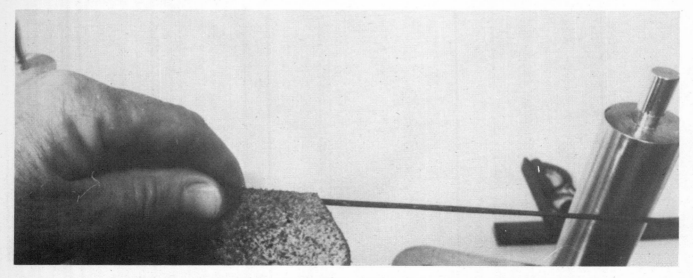

*Next, burnish the waxed string with piece of light leather. This melts wax into string. Burnishing stretches string.*

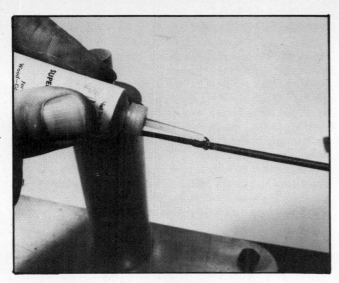

As an added precaution, one can place a drop or two of Fletch-Tite cement on the ends of all sections and rub it into the end sections. It will help prevent raveling.

with no arrow rest; the arrow rests over the hand of the bow arm. To adjust the string for this bow you make a fist on the handle, extend the thumb to a vertical position and that is the proper fistmele. You may raise or lower the hand to fit your shooting style but you still use the doubled fist for a measuring system.

All bow strings should have a nocking point. Most bowhunters have the nocking point at the top of the nock so the arrow nock slides up to it and stops at the proper point. You can nock an arrow properly without even looking at the bow. The nocking point may be above or below the arrow nock or you may use two points with the arrow nock between them. If you are a release shooter you can tailor the nocking point to your particular style.

For his hunting bows Learn starts with the nocking point above the arrow nock, placed one-half inch above the ninety-degree angle of a bowsquare to the arrow rest. If you don't have a bowsquare you can use a piece of paper, make

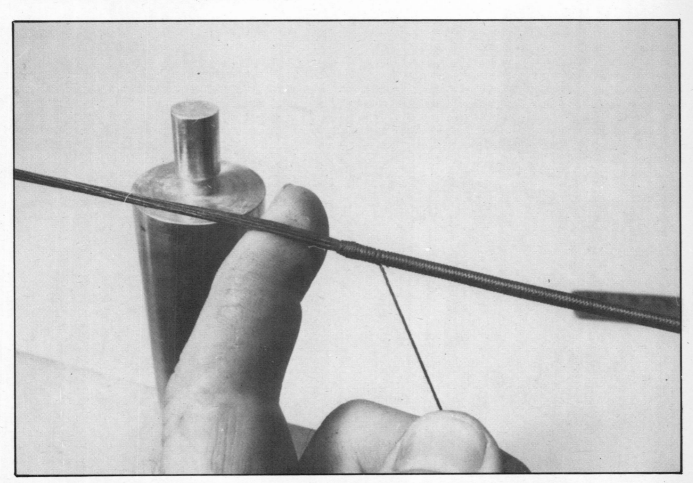

Serve the center section, but when you tie off, allow enough extra serving thread to make at least a dozen, even fifteen backwraps. The center serving, of course, undergoes a great deal of added stress during shooting.

the marks, and lay it on the arrow rest and place your nock. Some bows require the nocking point to be moved from this basic position, but it always gives a point to start from. The Graham DynaBo required raising the nocking point to get proper arrow flight for Learn.

The arrow shaft you are using and the type of nock on the arrow can be factors in determining where you place the final nocking point. A short piece of nylon serving thread wrapped on the center serving of the string may be used as a nocking point or you can use one of the many types of clamping metallic units. Bob Learn says he uses the Saunders NokSet. This is a small metal ring, open on one side and backed with rubber. Placed on the serving at the

proper point as determined with a bowsquare and clamped by a pair of pliers, the nocking point won't slide during shooting.

All archers whether on the tournament trail or hunting grizzly bear in Alaska need a backup bowstring. When you have the right length and settings for a string you have made, make note of it. Some archers write the measurements right on the string jig, always having them where they need them.

Make your backup bowstring, place it on the bow and shoot it until you are certain it has stretch-stabilized. Check the nocking point on your old string and on your new string to be sure they are the same. Learn will make a new

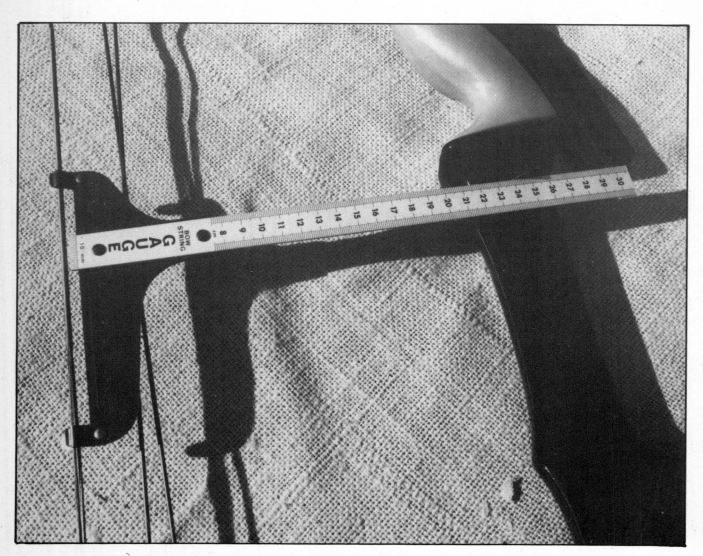

*It is time to install the new string on the bow so that a bow-square can be used for determining the nocking point.*

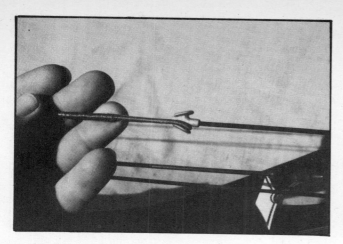

The newly completed string has been installed on the Cougar II bow with a double cable teardrop ending. The loop, of course, can be shorter than one illustrated.

Specifications of Archery Manufacturers Organization state brace height of a recurve bow is measured from the pivot point of the handle. This measures 8 inches.

string, relegate the older shot-in string for his backup unit as he knows it is correct, then shoots the new string for his field system. He often carries three strings with him.

A backup string is no good unless you have it handy. The target archer should carry it in the quiver for the field ranges, the FITA shooter should have it in the tackle box, making certain he complies with the rules for the shoot concerned. Some matches do not permit the shooter to go behind the shooting lines after the tournament has started.

Most bowhunters carry their spare string in the bow quiver or in their pack. A good idea is to tape it directly to the bow. If you cut your bowstring with a broadhead all you need do is take out the other unit, ready with a nock point. If you are in an area where game is moving it would

be horrible to have to return to camp to get another string.

Regardless of the type bow you shoot, you should have a field method of bracing it to remove and/or replace that old string when needed. The longbow can be push/pulled without much trouble. The best way to work the recurve is with bracing cord that has pockets of leather on the tips so you can safely replace a bad string. The old step-through method works but is frowned on in today's safety-conscious world. If you use the push/pull improperly, the bow can slip the string, the bowtip comes back and usually will pop you right in the eye. Carry a cord bow-stringer with your recurve and learn how to use it, says Learn.

The compound presents little problem if it has the

The Saunders NokSet is placed about half an inch above the right angle of the string to the arrow rest. This is a starting point and can be adjusted as necessary.

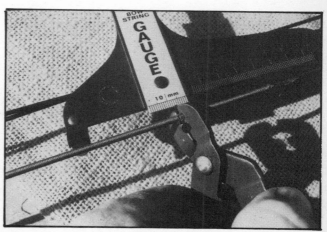

With the NokSet pliers, crimp the small metal rubber-backed unit to the bowstring. It does not move on the nylon serving, but it may on a monofilament bowstring.

*Old-timers prefer to measure from the back of the bow to the point where the broadhead will be drawn. This makes a decided difference in measurement of the bow's brace height, as evidenced by the new 10½-inch measurement.*

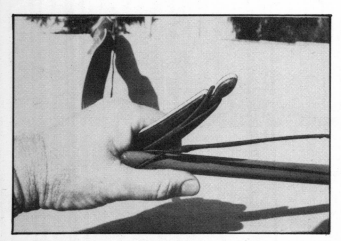

*End loops are compared to those on a recurve (upper bow) and an old longbow. The longbow is braced with a twist in the end loop. The twist disappears as bow is drawn.*

double-teardrop cable end design. Unless you totally sever the entire string you can pull up on the old string, place the string loops of the new string in the empty cable ends and replace the old with a new. If your bow has the older-style single string attachment system you will need to buy a compound string-changing device. There are several of these on the market for a reasonable price. They usually work by having hooks or slots on the ends of metal units with a nylon cord between them. Place the metal hooks over the inside of the cable ends, pull up on the nylon cord and use this to help change the old string for a new one.

A unit Learn carries with his compound has a center rod that works similar to the stays on a tent guyline. This works by placing the metal ends on the cable ends, pulling up on the cable by lifting the nylon cord, and when the cables are high enough, merely set the rod in position and it holds the bow in a partially drawn position permitting a change of strings.

There are all types of string attachments to aid in aiming: Kisser buttons, constant nocking positioners, peeps that fit between the strands of the string for a rear sight system, string silencers that go between strands to quiet the noise when the bow is shot, and the list goes on.

Something that isn't really new but used by many archers is the monofilament material used for center serving. It is slick and aids in getting a cleaner release. Learn

has made strings using it and it is so slick that he had to tie an old-style nocking point because the NokSet kept slipping on the monofilament.

If you want to try the monofilament material, be extra careful when serving with the string server. You can set tension too tight and cut the Dacron bowstring material. When the serving is tied off at the end you must retain tension or it will unravel all the way back.

There is a newer string material on the market. It has been around for several years but was seen primarily on target and tournament shooting lines; Kevlar.

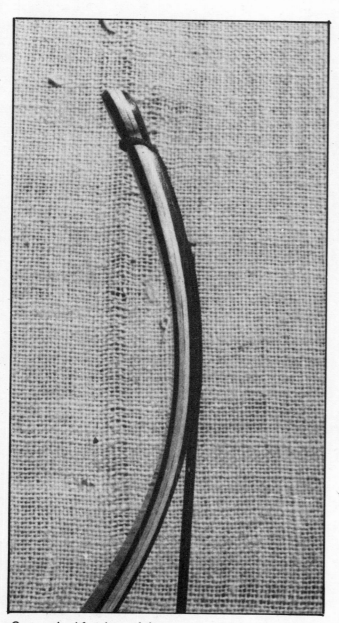

One method for determining proper string length for the recurve is to get a small tip curve as illustrated with string lying along the tip of the bow when it's braced.

Checking your string from time to time during tournament can prevent trouble, allow you to change during a lull.

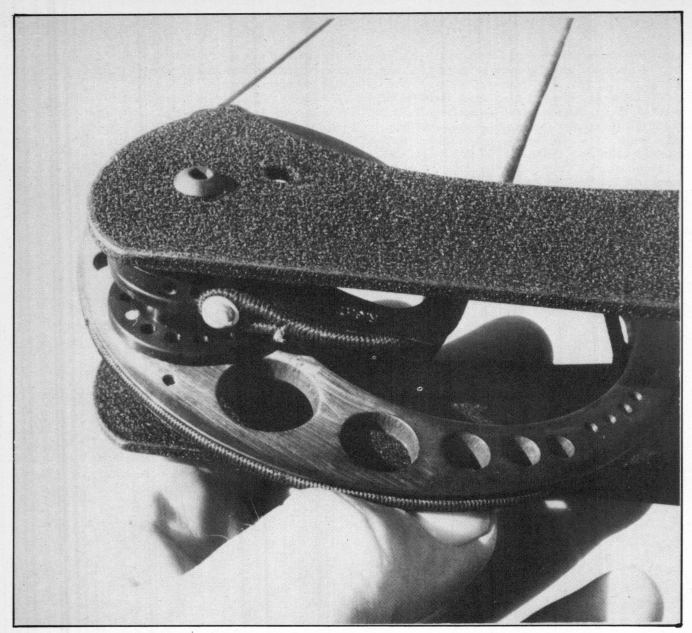

*The Graham DynaBo, a compound model, utilizes a set screw for proper adjustment of the string and draw. In making a string for this model, it will be required that a small end loop be incorporated in this section.*

Kevlar is lighter and stronger per strand. Learn tried a bowstring of Kevlar to speed his arrows. The lighter the bowstring the less mass the bow has to move, goes the theory. When he made his Kevlar string, he made it with fewer strands. However, Learn found all his arrow nocks were too big and would fall off. Kevlar recommends using a specified number of strands to get the same thickness you would have with Dacron.

Kevlar does give a faster arrow, it stretches less, but it is also noisier than Dacron. Most target shooters who use it

have several in their tackle box and replace the old string after each tournament. Here again, you should try it to see if you like it.

Bowstrings now cost several dollars over most shop counters. A Dacron string will got for about $3.50 and a Kevlar for about $5. For a small initial outlay you can set up to make your own strings. Your jig is a one-time investment. Better yet, make your own jig from materials on hand. Buy a quarter-pound of Dacron, a good string server along with the nylon serving thread, and you can

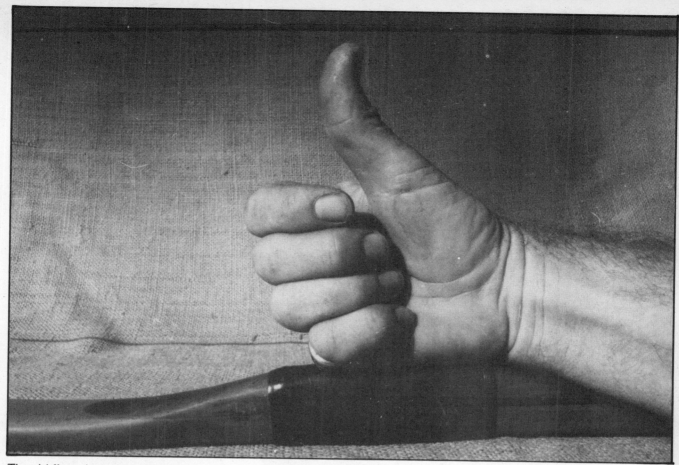

*The old fistmele system of checking proper brace height is used when dealing with the traditional longbow. You can twist the bowstring and raise the fistmele a bit, but this particular bow should shoot well as it is set.*

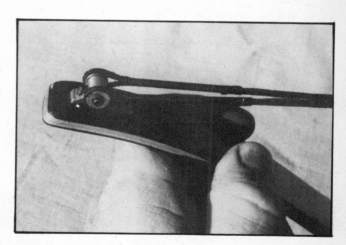

*When you make your own strings, it is possible to adapt your system for these small end loops on the upper limb of the Graham DynaBo. Versatility is the watchword!*

make many strings. You can try the Kevlar and the monofilament; you might like them for your style shooting.

There are some preacutions. The monofilament for fishing line is not the same material used for bowstrings. All strings require some maintenance. When you use a bow that hasn't been shot for some time it doesn't hurt to apply bowstring wax, such as that made and marketed by Bohning, rubbed into the string and burnished with a piece of leather. Naturally, you check your arrows before shooting, but if the string goes, your hunting or target shoot is over.

*The target arrow point is designed to be extremely light in weight and also is streamlined against wind resistance.*

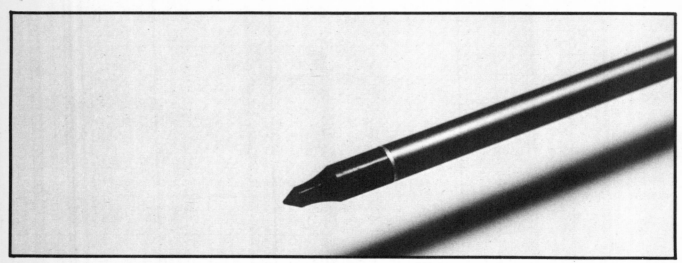

*With the most common type of field point the major difference from the target point is the bulk weight of the former. The field point is deliberately weighted to match the 125-grain weight that is found in most hunting points.*

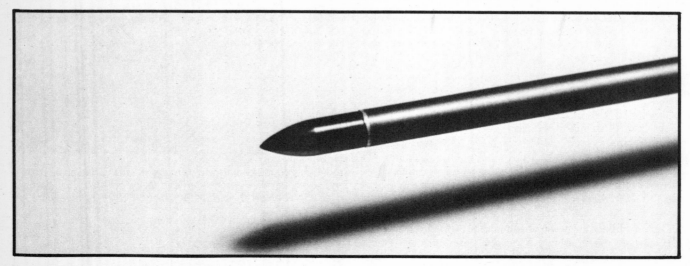

*Eastman's bullet point is another style of field point that has been designed for maximum aerodynamic flight.*

# Chapter 7

# THE WHY OF ARROWHEADS

## With Numerous Styles Available, An Archer Need Not Limit Himself To One Type Of Shooting

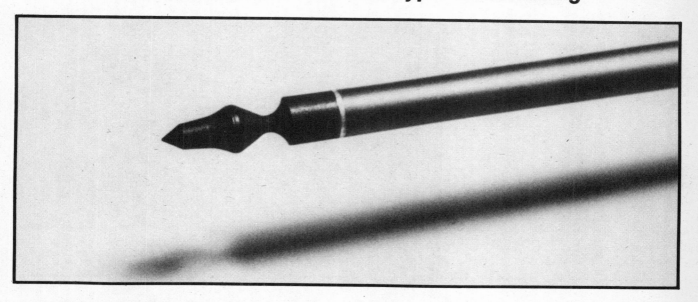

The slim neck on this breakaway field point allows the tip to break clear of the shaft upon impact with a rock, tree or other immovable object. The theory is that such breakage should shield the shaft from most possible harm.

THE BUSINESS end of the arrow is called the point. It may be of three basic styles: target point, field point, or broadhead. Each has its own special characteristics making it ideal for its particular use.

Back when archery was confined to the American Indians or other primitive peoples, arrowheads were made from rock or flint. Asked to describe an arrowhead, even the most uneducated of individuals probably can describe the shape of these early points, a triangle or wedge with rough, sharp edges. But that same individual would be hard pressed, perhaps, to recognize the points of today as arrowheads. Like nearly everything else, archery has given way to metals and physics. Metal has replaced rock. In some cases, even wire and plastic are prominent. The design of the arrowhead has certainly changed as well, with points resembling balls and sugar cones. But the task of today's arrowhead, to hit the mark and to remain in that target until removed, is still the basic requirement of a good arrowhead.

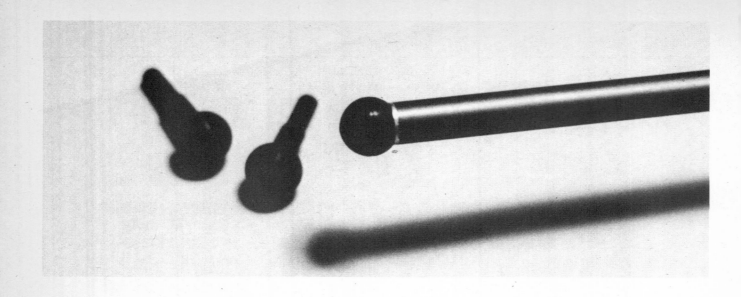

*The small-game heads (above and at right) are designed to kill through shock rather than penetration. The Bludgeon II (right) features a wide head for maximum hitting capability. Both points are by Saunders Archery.*

## TARGET POINTS

Target points are, by design, extremely light in weight, intended to guide the arrow with the least resistance and drawback to speed. The pyramid-shaped end cuts through the air with as little wind resistance as possible, allowing the arrow to fly straight and true. If you purchase wood arrows already fitted with target points, you probably will find that those points cannot be removed, but are intended to remain on the shaft, a band of the metal point being crimped into the shaft.

Aluminum and fiberglass shafts normally are equipped with screw-in adapters that allow you to use screw-in target points. The advantage of this type of point is that it allows you to change from one style of point to another quickly and efficiently.

The Frontier Star is a plastic small-game head. Light in weight, it is available in two- and four-blade styles. Also, do not let the plastic construction fool you as the head is extremely sharp along the cutting edges.

## FIELD POINTS

Most common among novices and field archers is the field point. Similar in shape to the target point, the field point has its greatest difference in its mass weight. It is designed to match the weight of most hunting points — about 125 grains — to allow one to practice in the field with arrows that will fly similarly to hunting broadheads.

Ideal for hunting practice, field points will penetrate pine boards or small game easily. They also will score well on traditional tournament targets, causing no more damage to the target than does the regular target point.

The biggest drawback to the field point, as well as to the target point, is seen readily when shooting at outdoor

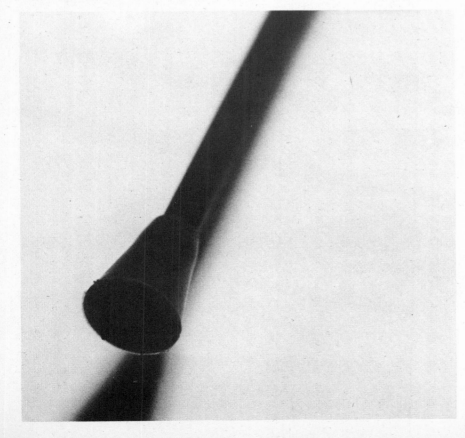

Saunder's Bludgeon, designed as a small-game blunt, is of rubberized plastic. The wide face is meant to maximize arrow's shocking power.

targets. Miss the target, or have your arrow pass through the target, and you may have a devil of a time finding your arrow. That same design that reduces the resistance of the point to wind in flight also reduces the resistance of the arrow to grass and weeds. The arrows are apt to embed themselves in the grass so deeply that you may not find them for weeks to come. For this reason, many field archers fletch their arrows with bright fletching in the hope that the coloring will show even if the shaft does not.

A unique style of field point is the break-away point, which features a narrow neck midway down the length of the point. This neck allows the lead end of the point to break away upon impact with immovable objects such as trees and rocks, and is intended to limit the damage to aluminum and fiberglass shafts normally seen in such situations.

*Although a number of two-bladed broadheads are available with or without razor-blade inserts, Zwickey's Black Diamond is one of those styles that relies totally upon the cutting power of the two blades to take down game.*

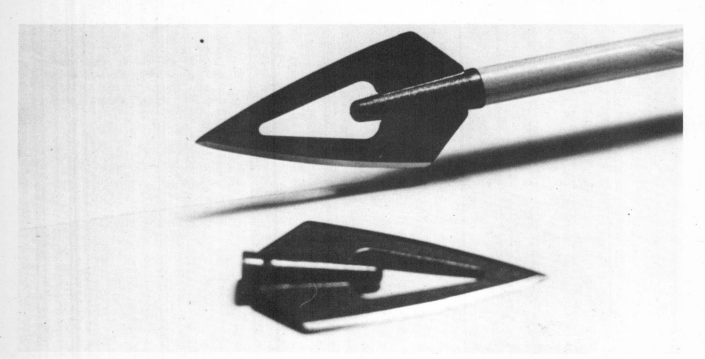

*The Pearson Switch Blade is another style, popular after years of use by hunters, that relies on its own sharpness.*

# BOWHUNTING POINTS

Although this book is not intended to provide insight on techniques of bowhunting, you cannot help but wonder why there is such a variety of bowhunting points available on the market and what the purpose of these points might be; hence, this brief explanation.

You may never desire to give bowhunting a try. Or, that may well be the reason you are entering archery in the first place. You may wish to hunt only small game or perhaps even trophy animals. If you're a fisherman who would like to add a new dimension to your sport, you may want to try bowfishing. A golfer may become interested in archery golf. You may wish to try shooting at moving targets, such as milk cartons tossed into the air or perhaps would like to fill your quota of ducks in a more unique manner. You can do all of these things with a bow, arrows and the right type of point.

*PSE's Brute 3 also is manufactured in a vented style. Choice is pretty much up to the individual hunter.*

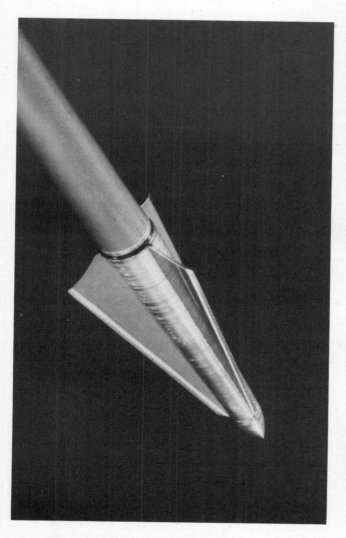

*Among today's three-bladed broadheads is the Brute 3 Low Profile from PSE, unique in design, hunting capabilities.*

In hunting small game the intention of the arrow-point design is to kill the animal by shock much as a bullet does. Consequently, all small-game points have the same basic design — they are wide at the head, or front. This wide head provides a greater impact capacity, and produces the greatest shocking effect.

As an especially popular style of small-game point, the Judo point features four spring-loaded arms that fan out to catch the target. The Judo point is seen frequently during outdoor field shooting in heavy foliage because of its unique design which makes it very difficult for the point to dig into the ground. Loosing an arrow outfitted with a Judo point may actually be an impossibility.

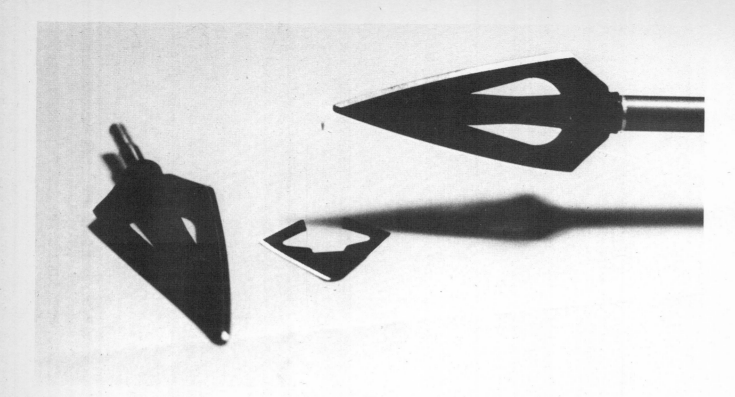

The Bear Razor Head, perhaps today's most popular big-game hunting head, is a two-blade broadhead featuring accommodations for razor inserts. Purpose of inserts is to increase the cutting power of the head as needed.

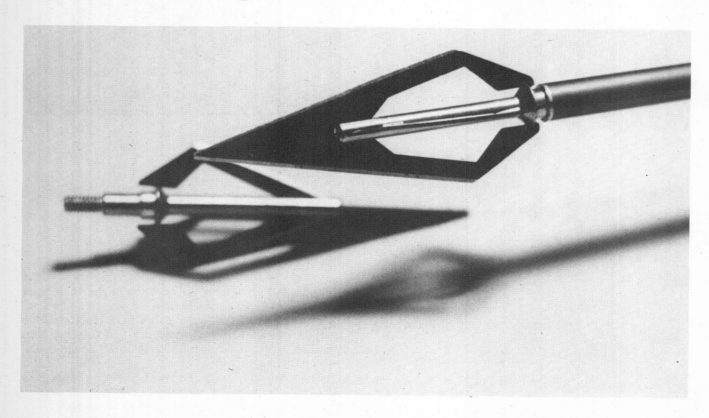

For large game, today's four-bladed broadhead is especially popular with bowhunters. The added blades double the cutting power and effectiveness.

Points called "blunts" are seen in varying styles for use against small game. Although there are several styles of blunts available, all have that same, flat-faced front that gives them their name. Discarded firearms cartridge casings make excellent blunts for cedar shafts. Although naturally lightweight, the weight can be increased easily by pouring melted copper into the casing before mounting it to the shaft.

For the more sophisticated small-game hunter, the Bludgeon features an inverted cone shape of rubbery plastic which gives just enough to prevent broken arrow shafts. Or, for use with your field point or a screw-in round nosed blunt, the Bludgeon II quickly converts a field point to a small-game head. The Bludgeon II is simply a section of round rubberized plastic, like that used in the Bludgeon, which acts as a collar around the field point, widening the area of impact for maximum shocking power.

Another popular style of small-game head is the HTM Blunt, considered one of the most effective of heads. Ideal for tree shooting the Blunt may also be used for indoor shooting, as can the Bludgeon.

Typical game for small-game points include rabbits, snakes, raccoon, ducks, prairie dogs, squirrels, rock chucks, birds, groundhogs and fish.

If you really hope to be successful in bird hunting, however, you will probably want to consider the Snaro Head style of point rather than a blunt or Judo point. The Snaro Head is composed of four circular wire rings attached to a central ferrule. The rings allow a shotgun-type spread to aid hitting the game.

If bowfishing is your sport, none of the above-mentioned points will do you much good, although you can certainly hit a fish with most of them. The problem would be in retrieving your fish, for as with

Brute 4, manufactured by PSE, is available in vented model. It is fixed blade, requiring sharpening.

traditional style fishing, you have to hook a fish to bring it to land. For this reason you will need a point that includes a barb, or perhaps two or more barbs — the fish point. Specially designed to allow for the accommodation of fishing line, the fish point comes in various styles, but generally in two basic categories: the barbed and the bladed. Used with solid arrow shafts, the point usually screws into the shaft, allowing easier removal from the fish. The fish line is normally attached to a traditional-style reel taped or mounted to the front of your bow. When you score on your fish, you simply reel it in, just as you would if you were using a pole.

## BOWHUNTING BIG GAME

Because of the limited force with which a bow can propel an arrow, the technique of filling your gamebag by using points that score by shock will not work well against big game. There simply isn't enough force behind the arrow to shock a deer, bear or elk. Consequently you will find that big-game points, termed broadheads, kill by hemorrhage. The animal bleeds to death, often with no apparent knowledge that he has even been hurt, unless the hunter tries to chase him down after the shot.

Because the primary task of the broadhead is to cut, you will find that all broadheads have two or more razor-sharp

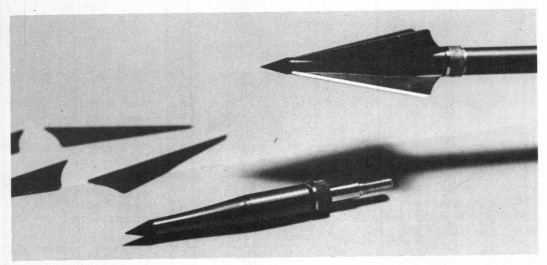

*Satellite broadhead by Sherwin features a central ferrule, with razor-blade inserts for a fast, continuous razor-sharp head. These heads are replaced, not sharpened.*

*For the maximum in cutting power, five-bladed heads are the answer. Care must be given in sharpening these heads due to closeness of the blades. The Razorbak 5 is one of those that has gained popularity with bowhunting clan.*

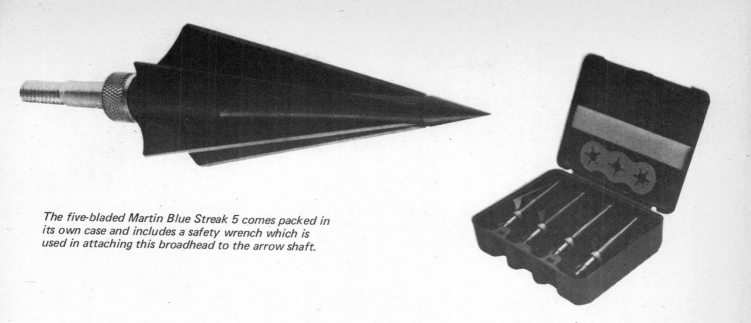

The five-bladed Martin Blue Streak 5 comes packed in its own case and includes a safety wrench which is used in attaching this broadhead to the arrow shaft.

cutting edges to them. In fact, most will have at least four cutting edges, often using razor-blade inserts to provide the additional cutting power.

## ARROWHEAD MAINTENANCE

In terms of maintenance there is little that needs be done to field points and target points. Even a stubbed point will fly and score well, unless it is badly deformed. In this case, simply replace it, as opposed to trying to repair it.

If you desire you can remove a bend in a tip by filing.

For broadheads there is the need for continuous care. Because of the nature of the design of the broadhead and its intended capabilities it is imperative that all broadheads be maintained in a razor-sharp condition. Taking to the field with dull, rusted or dirty field points may not even be noticed, but to take to the field with broadheads in the same condition is to invite the ridicule of any bowhunter in your vicinity. You might well be asked to leave the hunt.

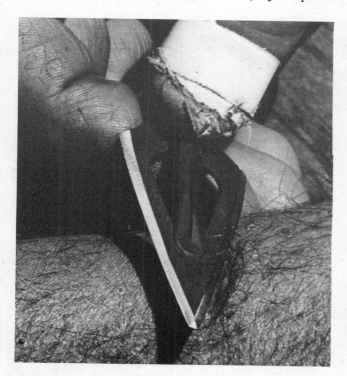

When a hunting broadhead is properly sharpened it can be used to shave the hair from your arm. In fact, this is a popular in-the-field test favored by bowhunters.

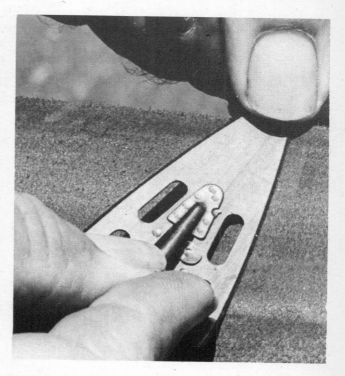

This same rouge-impregnated leather strop has been in use since 1957 and still works great for the finishing touches. Heads must be handled carefully against cuts.

An unpretentious-looking but useful item, this is a piece of soft scrap leather fastened to a piece of wood with a pair of C-clamps. Jeweler's rouge is rubbed on the rough side; it's held in a vise and used to strop final edge.

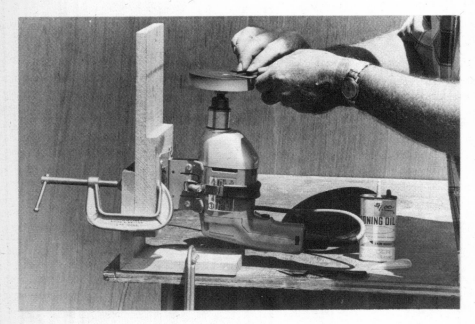

A more convenient means of putting an edge on broadheads is to hold an electric drill upright with a clamp, then install a disc with 600-grit paper for initial honing. Always wear eye protection.

For the final cutting edge, one can substitute a leather-faced disc and use this to hone edges of broadhead.

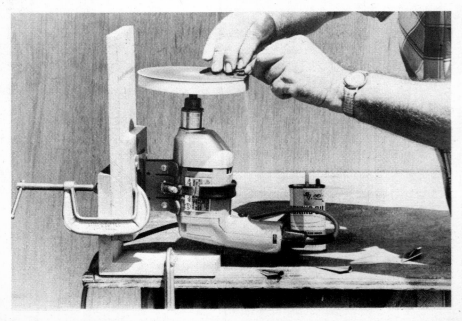

A practiced method for sharpening broadheads requires that you place the broadhead in a vise to hold it secure while you work on one blade at a time. The blades then may be filed with a fine-toothed file, then honed with a stone and some jeweler's rouge to produce that original razor-sharp condition. Do not attempt to sharpen the razor-blade inserts used in your two-bladed broadheads. Replace them.

To protect your broadheads from rust coat them with a rust retardant or oil such as is used on the barrels of rifles. Once you have sharpened your broadheads you will want to be certain that you store them in an area where they will be safe from young hands. A well-sharpened broadhead is just as dangerous as a razor blade and must be kept from prying hands.

In terms of economics, you will find that target and field points are extremely economical, costing approximately a quarter for each tapered field point or blunt, approximately the same for the Converta-point systems.

In comparison, broadheads will cost you as much as $5 per head, depending on the style you select. You should realize that you are not apt to shoot these heads very often. More than one bowhunter has taken to the fields for several seasons without ever having released an arrow at an animal. When your chance does come, though, you'll want the best arrowhead you can have working for you.

If the broadhead you have chosen downs your animal and fills your freezer with several weeks worth of good eating, then the price should be worth the results.

The leather-faced wooden disc is given a coating of jeweler's rouge while spinning in the clamped drill.

The Loray Sharpener also can be used to sharpen broadheads. It comes with three hones in various grit grades and also has a guide to set angle.

134

# Chapter 8
# ARROW RESTS & NOCKING POINTS

## *While A Few Die-Hards Scoff At Such Niceties, These Items Make Shooting Simpler, More Effective*

WHEN PURCHASING a new bow few archers allow the type and style of arrow rest to enter into their decision. Yet it is this small, seemingly insignificant part that they may seek to change first when they begin to shoot the bow. In terms of importance the arrow rests comes second only to the nock locator.

It was not so very long ago that arrow rests were non-existent. Archers provided their own rest, the top of their bowhand doing the honors. But allowing an arrow to soar across your hand could occasionally prove painful, especially if you happen to be using plastic vanes. So it was that introduction of the sight window offered a particularly appealing possibility. The sight window provided not only the ability to shoot from a near center position of the bow, it also provided a natural shelf from which to shoot.

There was a problem with shooting off the shelf. It was hard and inflexible, causing erratic flight for an occasional

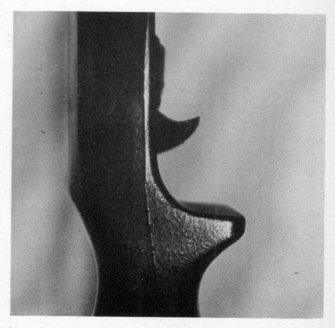

This simple rest used on the Little Bear bow is nothing more than a section of leather curved around riser and shelf to protect the bow from scuffing. (Left) Archer uses his bow hand as a rest for his arrow on a longbow.

Introduction of the sight window in bow design offered a natural shelf from which to shoot, but the shelf was hard and inflexible and in need of some device that could be utilized to cushion the arrow: the arrow rest.

arrow when fletching deflected against the shelf. It was not long before archers began looking for ways to soften that shelf; to make it flexible. The result was the arrow rest.

An arrow rest is more than simply a cushioned ledge from which to launch the arrow, although that certainly is the basic function of the rest. It also provides the arrow shaft a stable base from which to begin its flight, thus controlling to some degree the course of that flight. To understand why this is true, one must first understand what happens to the arrow as it passes across the rest.

At full draw, the shaft lies in the corner created by the rest and the side plate of the bow or the plunger, if one is used. Upon release the shaft sails forward, across the rest

and to its target, gliding smoothly past the rest until the fletched end of the shaft meets the rest. Having needed only sufficient space to accommodate the width of the shaft, it suddenly is faced with the sudden increase in width of the fletching. This requires some adjustment. The bow can't move, so the shaft must; it does so by kicking out from the riser, righting itself after it passes. If the kick-out is too great the shaft will have great difficulty in righting itself and may sail wide to the left of the target. The purpose of the rest is to insure that the shaft passes the bow riser with minimum deflection.

The amount of deflection is dependent upon the amount of fletching that contacts the bow. All fletching — both plastic vanes and feathers — will accept a certain degree of interference from the riser and still guide the shaft efficiently. It is when this interference is great that deflection and erratic flight occur.

You can readily determine whether your arrows are slapping the riser simply by examining the bow. After

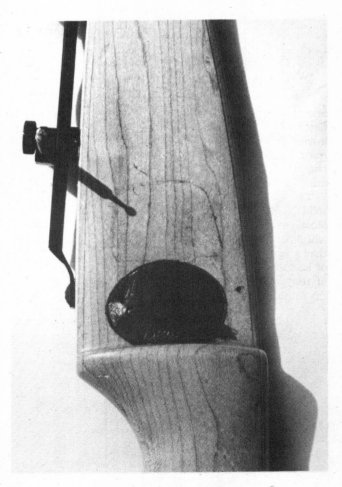

*The rug-style rest provides lift to the arrow shaft, allowing it to clear the shelf. The leather plate beside the riser protects Bear Grizzly's finish from fletching.*

*Brush plate rest on this Bear Bearcat affords clearance, while the depth of the riser plate will move the arrow shaft slightly from riser, increasing fletch clearance.*

*A commonly sold style rest, this particular type features a solid plastic riser plate. It is cushioned by felt and has a flexible plastic finger that yields to the shaft as the arrow is launched in flight toward the target.*

several shots, you will see the marks left behind as the fletching slices away the paint and finish of the bow, leaving scuff marks. To counteract this, one must move the rest out, away from the riser. This is accomplished in one of two ways: with the aid of a wider-sitting solid rest or by using a combination of rest and plunger.

There are many styles of so-called solid rests, the term solid referring to the one-piece construction of the rest. Most recurves and longbows, if they feature a rest at all, will have a solid type. A favored rest for longbows, and one that is both simple and economical, is no more than a piece of leather above the shelf and alongside the riser. This type of rest normally is thin and does little more than protect the finish of the bow.

More accommodating to arrow fletching is the brush or rug style rest. Due to the consistency of their materials, both tend to lift the shaft up and away from the riser, the greatest lift given from the shelf. Again a section of leather may be used to protect the side of the riser or the design of the brush may include a plastic or rubberized side to protect the riser.

Rapidly gaining in popularity among solid rests is the type that combines a plastic wall to protect the riser with a rubberized protruding plastic finger that extends out from the wall to form a shelf of its own from which the shaft may be launched.

The advantage to the plastic finger is that it is flexible; it yields upon meeting resistance from the arrow fletching rather than providing resistance of its own. Consequently the flight of the shaft can progress without interference, and because the strength of the plastic is high, such a rest is likely to last the lifetime of the bow under normal use.

*This is the same rest as in top photo but for a left-hand model and includes an extra felt pad to cushion the shaft from beneath. For the left-handed archer the string moves counterclockwise. As a result the rest must be mirrored if one is to prevent arrow fall-off.*

Circular ring above finger of rest on Indian Tracker
allows for the addition of cushion plunger on soft rest.
Of flexible rubber, rest moves easily with arrow flight.

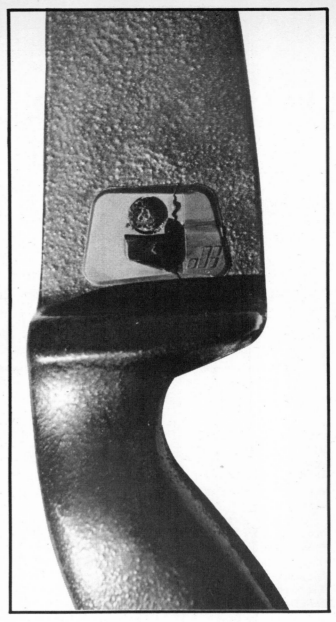

This Jennings arrow rest is manufactured of soft rubber
and includes a cushion plunger that allows for flight
adjustability of arrow for the optimum in performance.

For those who desire even greater flexibility to their rest, the mechanical rest is a top choice. Manufacturers refer to this style as the flipper rest, gleaning its name from the metal finger that flips forward during release, allowing the arrow to pass unhindered.

Similar in function is the springy rest, again deriving its name from its design. A springy rest is no more than a wire coiled into a spring, the last coil extending to form a lip upon which the shaft can rest. Like the flipper rest the springy rest is extremely flexible and offers a minimal amount of resistance to the arrow. If there were a drawback

to this mechanical rest, it would be the increased cost and reduced useful life it demonstrates.

An integral part of both the flipper and the springy rest, as well as an accessory to the solid style rests, is the cushion plunger which passes through the width of the bow, extending out from the riser to push the shaft away from the riser. The plunger serves to adjust the position of the shaft to reach the optimum match between rest and bowstring, the arrow passing directly through the imaginary mid-line of the bow.

It is important to take a moment to adjust this plunger

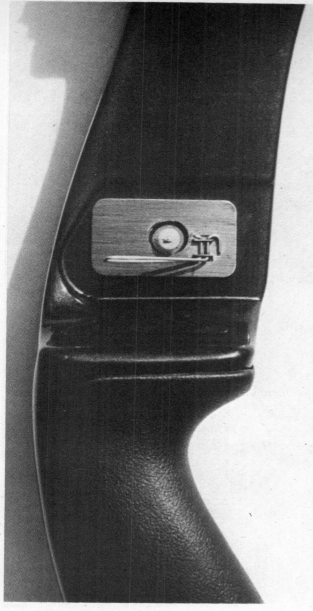

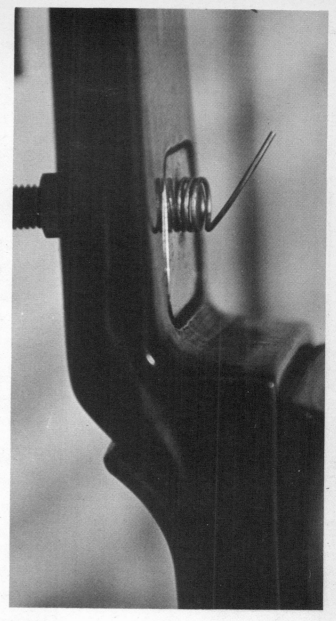

*Flipper rest on Pearson compound offers adjustability at its best. Wire flipper responds to movement of the shaft; cushion plunger makes tuning arrow simple matter.*

*Springy rest on this Jennings Tournament compound has a screw adjustment inside the coil to adjust the rest in or away from riser, functioning like a cushion plunger.*

for the best flight. If the plunger is seated too far inside or outside of the center, the arrow will fishtail, swishing from left to right in flight. The same fishtailing will be evident whether the plunger is set too far in or too far out. To determine which is your problem a simple test can be performed requiring the use of six arrows, three of which are fletched, the others without fletching.

Begin by shooting the three fletched arrows into a target, giving special attention to your shooting form to avoid invalid results. Although the group size of these

arrows will vary with your archery skill, you should be able to see a grouping of some sort.

Using the three bare shafts perform the same test, shooting at the same target and again using your best shooting form. You should again see a grouping, but the position of each group should differ. If the three bare shafts impact to the left of your fletched arrows, the cushion plunger of your rest is sitting too far away from the bow, and needs to be turned in. If the impact of the three bare shafts lies to the right of the fletched arrows, the cushion

If the arrow fishtails, swishing from left to right, the shaft is sitting too far to the left or right of the centerline of the bow. Move the cushion plunger in or out, dependent upon which side of centerline the arrow rests. A simple test involves the use of three fletched arrows and three bare shafts, as described fully in the text.

If the bare shafts impact to the right of the fletched arrows (for a right-handed shooter), the cushion plunger is too far inside riser and needs to be turned outward. For a left-hander, the opposite situation is evident.

pressure around the entire locator as it is tightened, rather than pressure on two sides which causes a flattening of the locator.

Most bows do not come with nocking locators installed, requiring that you do so on your own before you shoot the bow. You may find a set of locators included in the shipping box that held your bow. If not, you can get a few for around fifty cents each at most archery shops and many sporting goods stores.

Whether you choose to use two locators — one above, the other below your nocking position — is a matter of personal preference. Most archers use only one, positioned above the nock, to prevent the arrow from sliding upward during the draw. Others like to sandwich the nock between two locators to prevent movement up or down.

To determine where to place your nocking locator, determine an imaginary line running perpendicular to the bowstring. This line should cross directly over the arrow rest. Mark the point at which it also crosses the bowstring. You will want to position your locator so that the bottom portion of the arrow nock will sit approximately one-eighth-inch above that reference point.

*To correct porpoising — up and down flutter of the arrow in flight — change the position of the nocking point. To determine which way to move the nock locator, use the same bare shaft test. If the bare shafts impact above the fletched arrows you know nocking point is too low.*

plunger is resting too far inside the riser, and needs to be adjusted outward. If shooting left-handed, the opposite is true.

Continue to adjust the plunger, or the spring adjustment screw, until both sets of arrows — fletched and bare shafts — impact within the same grouping. At this point your rest is adjusted properly. Archers call this "tuning" the bow.

Although nocking locators come in various styles, the most common is the metal clamp-on type, which is positioned using a bow-square and a pair of nocking pliers. The pliers differ from the household tool in that they have two circular cuts in their jaws to allow for equalized

*In the test, if the bare shafts tend to impact beneath the fletched arrows, it means that the nocking point is too high; it must be moved up until arrows coincide.*

*Installing a nocking point requires a pair of nocking pliers and a set of nock locators such as the pair of half-circle clamp-on locators to the right of pliers. The larger locators are applied by heating, but be careful not to burn the bowstring during the process.*

A T-square or bow-square makes determining the correct placement of the nock locator rapid and easy. If you do not have a bow-square, use a piece of paper, a newspaper or the edge of a large book to gain your reference point. Once you have determined where you should place your nocking point, attach the nock locator. Do not tighten the locator too firmly just yet. Although the one-eighth-inch measurement is a close approximation of your best nocking position, exact placement will be determined only after you have shot the bow.

Once again you will need your three bare shafts and three fletched arrows. First shoot your fletched arrows. If the nocking point is either too high or too low, you will see what we refer to as porpoising; the tail or nock end of the arrow fluttering up and down during flight, as if it is nodding to you.

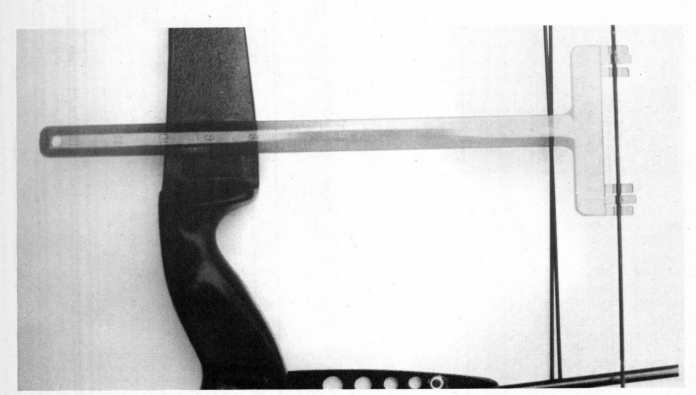

*Application of nocking locators requires the use of a T-square or a bow square such as this type made currently by Bohning Adhesives. A scale is imprinted on the plastic bow square to aid in positioning the locator correctly.*

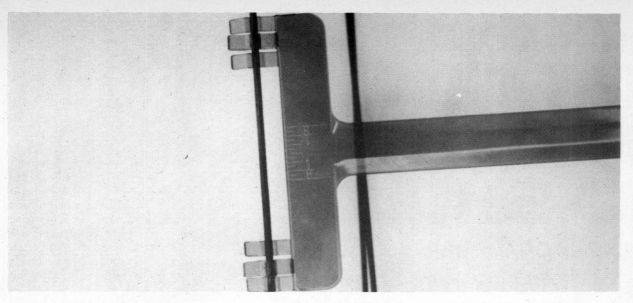

*In order to locate proper position for nocks, the bow square clamps to the string of the bow, then is slid down to rest on the arrow rest. Be certain that the square is at right angle to the string to do the job properly.*

As with the position of the cushion plunger, determine whether the position of the locator is too high or too low. You will use the same three fletched and three bare-shaft arrows in your test. If the bare shafts impact above the fletched arrows, the nocking point is too low and must be raised. Should the shafts impact below the fletched arrows, the point is too high and must be lowered.

To adjust the locator, simply move it up or down around the string. Once you have all six arrows consistently impacting at the same level, your nocking point should be correct and you can tighten the nock locator into position. The procedure for adjusting your nocking point is another part of bow tuning.

NOTE: When tuning your bow it is important that you adjust your nocking point *before* you adjust your cushion plunger, to avoid unnecessary repetition.

*The Posi Pressure Button, offered by Martin Archery, includes a spring inside the plunger channel allowing maximum adjustability to the arrow shaft during flight.*

*Circular design of the nocking pliers allows one to crimp clamp-on locator in position without flattening it. Crimp lightly until you have tested your arrows for correct flight. Once satisfied, crimp it down tightly.*

Periodically you will want to repeat the bare shaft tests, especially if you begin to notice unusual arrow flight or change. This will be especially true if you are headed for tournament competition or are about to take to the woods in search of game. Repeated use of your bow may result in a locator working itself loose or a plunger can change position. There may be nothing wrong with your bow's tuning, but it's nice to be sure. It makes concentration on your target just that much easier.

# Chapter 9
# GETTING READY TO SHOOT

## A Number Of Available Accessories Can Make Archery More Enjoyable

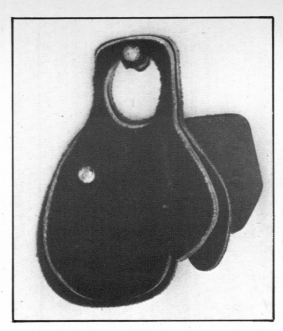

*For the more advanced archer, the divider tab offers added benefit of a wide plastic tab to hold the index finger separate from middle finger, reducing nock pinch.*

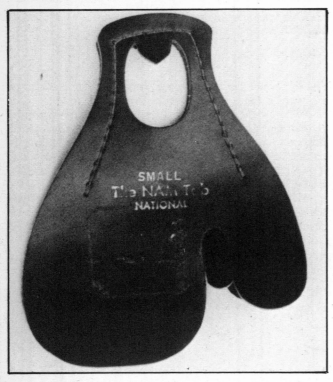

*Among the most economical finger tabs, this model offers ample protection at a cost well within budget of archers.*

ONCE YOU have purchased your bow and arrows, you may never need nor want to purchase another item of equipment. With just the basic equipment you are guaranteed years of shooting enjoyment. However, there are a number of accessory items that not only can make the pursuit of archery trophies easier for you, but can add to the enjoyment.

In considering accessory items, probably the first you will want to purchase would be an arm guard. It takes only one slap of a bowstring on your forearm to teach the value of this simple leather pad. Even the stoutest bowhunter is likely to wear an arm guard while in the field to protect

him from the sting of the string, an experience known to bring a tear to many a hard hunter's eyes.

The design of the arm guard is extremely simple. Normally, it is no more than a section of leather with one or more metal braces running its length. The braces absorb the slap of the string otherwise intended for the forearm, while the leather offers additional protection and a means of holding the metal braces in position.

Arm guards come in a variety of styles and sizes, ranging from economical petite guards that cover only the front forearm, to large, full-length covers that span the distance from the wrist to halfway up the upper arm. Costing

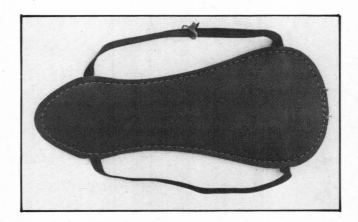

*This economy arm guard provides only limited protection, but is extremely effective if positioned properly on arm.*

anywhere from $3 to $15, the arm guard offers excellent quality for the price.

Regardless of which style arm guard you select, there are some basic requirements to consider. Look first to the material in the guard. Arm guards may be made of leather, vinyl-coated cowhide or even plastic. In terms of durability, the heavy-duty plastic may be the most durable, but is probably the hottest to wear. Especially during summer shooting, heat retention can become extremely uncomfortable for the archer who spends an hour or so in the field. Look for breathability in your guard, either through the materials lining the guard, or through the inclusion of breathing holes or lanes.

Consider the fit and adjustability of your arm guard next. During summer, you are apt to wear the arm guard directly over your bare arm. For cooler months, you'll probably want to wear the protector over a shirt sleeve or jacket. The guard not only protects the arm, but serves to hold the sleeve material out of the way of the bowstring.

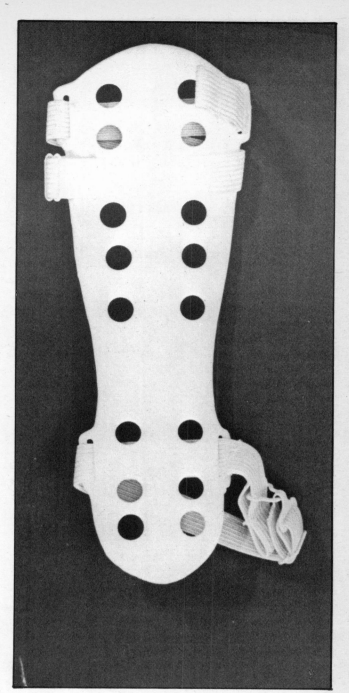

*This plastic arm guard is favored by tournament archers, because it is lightweight, holes allowing ventilation. Even the color of the guard appeals to competitors, since white is the dominant shade used by tournament archers.*

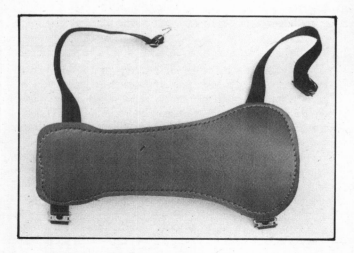

*Another arm guard in the lower priced bracket, this one is of leather and is held in place by elastic strapping.*

Most arm guards currently on the market offer adjustable elastic straps for fitting the guard to your arm. The length of these straps varies considerably and you will want to be sure that your guard will fit. If you've an extremely small arm, a large, hunting-style guard probably will not adjust down far enough to hold the guard in place. If you've a large arm, you will not want to purchase one of the small, economical guards that could wind up cutting off blood circulation to your hands.

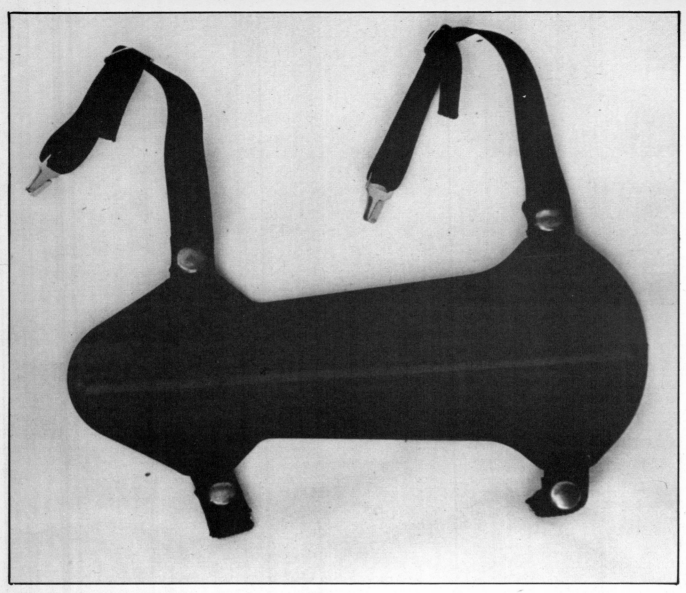

*The clips on this plastic arm guard are more difficult to hook than are Velcro closures, but the adjustability factor of the arm straps tends to make the guard appealing to many who tend to favor a more tight elastic fit.*

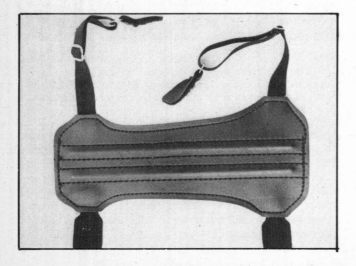

Look also to the type of closing on the arm guard. Remember that, in strapping the guard in place, you will have only the benefit of the use of one hand, so the closing should be easy for you to use. The two common styles of arm-guard closures are the clip and Velcro fastener. Of the two, the Velcro pads are far easier to use.

You may purchase arm guards in a variety of colors, including black, brown, white, and even several camouflaged models. Whatever color and style you choose, remember to use the guard. It only takes one string slap to remind you of the value of this simple protective accessory.

There was a time when only children and women wore fingertabs or gloves for shooting the bow. Men didn't need

*This particular style features Velcro closures as well as adjustable straps. Two steel braces run the length of the guard as a means of affording added arm protection.*

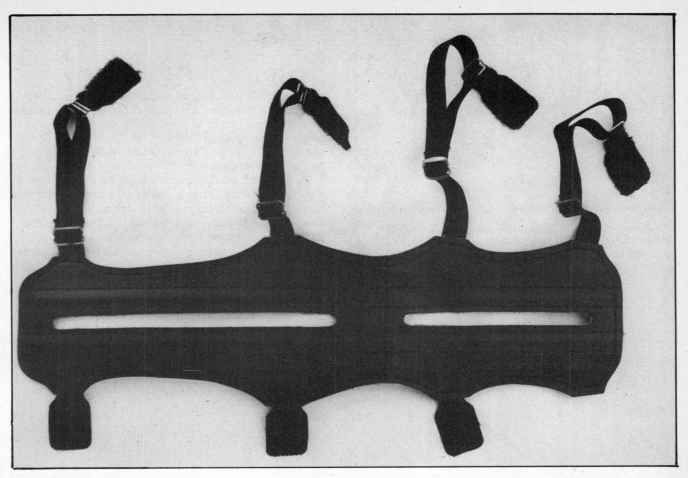

This extra-length arm guard features added coverage for the upper arm and inner elbow, with air channels adding cooling capabilities in hot weather. Velcro closing straps can accommodate the bulkiest of hunting jackets.

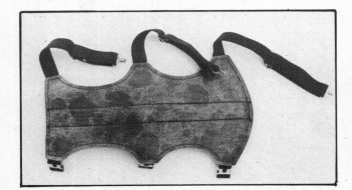

Arm guards come in a variety of colors and designs that include camouflaged models such as this one. Seams at either side of the metal support keep support in place.

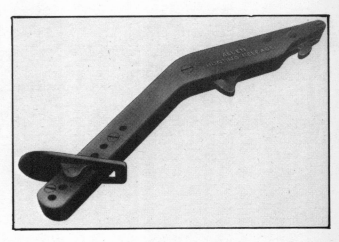

Among the most popular bowhunting releases is one made by Allen. It features a trigger release mechanism that allows for unexpected release of the string and arrow.

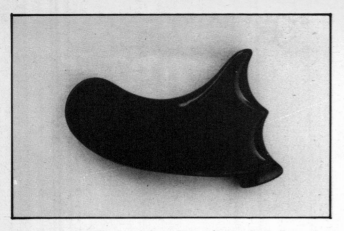

*An extremely simple release, this model by Bulls Eye Manufacturing features a simple lip which is meant to hold the string until released by a twist of the hand.*

this sissy stuff, or so you might hear someone proclaim.

Thankfully that era is behind us and today it is unusual to see anyone, male or female, shooting a bow without some sort of finger protection. A tab or glove is not a necessity, but after fifteen minutes or so of shooting, it certainly becomes a nicety.

As with arm guards, there are several styles of gloves and tabs from which to choose. Finger tabs come in two basic styles; those with a finger divider, and those without. The finger divider is not necessary, but it helps to avoid nock pinch by separating the index and middle finger. Tabs come in both left and right-hand styles and are intended to cover only the string side of the fingers. A hole cut at the top allows the tab to be hooked to the hand by sliding the middle finger through that hole.

In purchasing a tab, look for one that offers the best finger protection, with several layers offering the greatest finger protection as well as protection for the tab itself. A felt pad between the inner and outer layer of leather or calfskin buffers the tab against string chafing and creasing. In terms of price, you can purchase a tab for anywhere from $3 to $8.

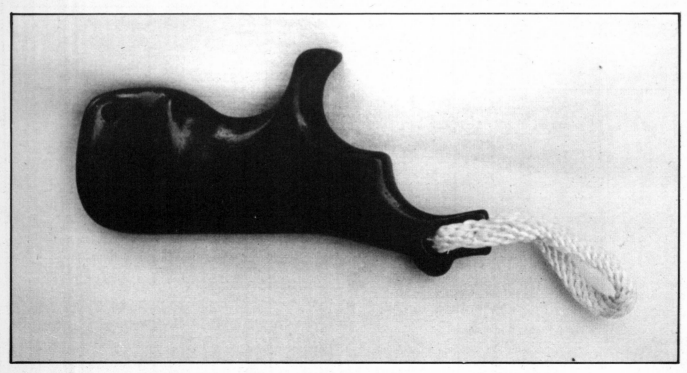

*The rope retainer on this particular release holds the string in place until you remove your finger. It then flips back to release the string. Simple, it's effective, too, and requires little practice to use to perfection.*

For those who want to travel the tournament trail or go afield for serious bowhunting forays, a bow case is a necessity. Cases made today come in both hard and soft styles. They may furnish thin protection or be lined.

An accessory that has become especially popular among the bowhunting fraternity is the Kwiklock manufactured by Saunders Archery. The device holds the arrow in place in the nocked position, releasing shaft as the draw begins.

Cats Whiskers can be added to a bowstring for bowhunts. They serve to quiet the sound of the string as released. The so-called whiskers are attached by tying in place.

Most pro archery shops offer a full line of accessories including such items as these finger slings by Martin.

There are two other methods of protecting the fingers from string sting. One is the use of No-Glov nock locators. These are nothing more than a set of two or more rubber nocks, oversized around the string to provide a cushion of rubber over the string. The use of No-Glov nock locators effectively removes the need for a tab or shooting glove.

A second substitute for the tab or glove is the release. This is a mechanical shooting aid that allows you to grip it while it, in turn, grips the bowstring.

While the release removes the need for a tab or glove, that is hardly the designed intent of the release. A release aid is meant to effect a smoother release by incorporating a surprise element into the release. The archer is unsure of exactly when the release will let go of the string, thus is unlikely to resist the release at the last moment. The problems of a poor release due to improper hand placement or finger release are removed, the archer simply holding his anchor point while the release does all the work.

The major drawback to the use of the release has been the question of its acceptance as a legal archery aid. To date the question of whether or not a release aid can or cannot be used in tournament competition is still up for grabs, with proponents of both sides in heated debate. Whether or not it can be used in tournament play, the addition of a release to your practice or hunting is worth considering.

The list of miscellaneous accessories for archery may seem endless, new additions being introduced each year. Such items as string changers, bow slings, finger slings, and riser grips of all styles and materials are available. Whether you will need or want any or all of these will be a matter of personal preferences and the influence of your fellow archers.

It is the addition of these accessories that makes archery a personal sport. You can be as complete or as basic as you desire and still achieve full enjoyment of the sport. The choices are yours, the equipment is there, just waiting for you to make up your mind.

Shooting gloves are somewhat higher in cost, averaging from $5 to $10. The shooting glove is a series of three leather pockets which slip over the three shooting fingers, connected to a top hand piece with an adjustable strap which encircles the wrist and attaches to one side of the top piece.

The advantages to the use of a glove or tab are two-fold. It protects the fingers from chafing and provides a smoother release, due in part to the fact that the archer is not hesitant in releasing the bowstring, as he knows the string is not apt to sting his fingers.

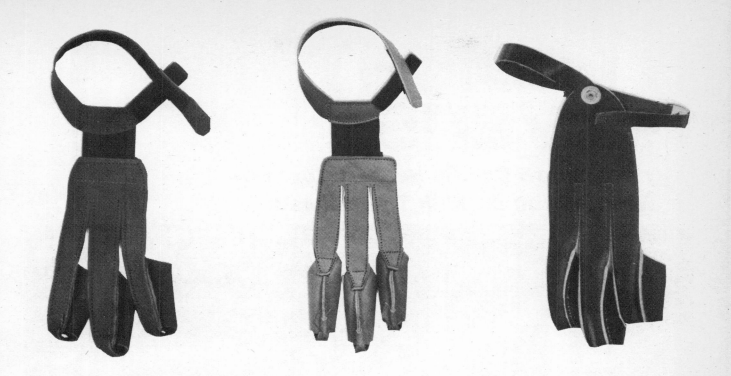

*Martin Archery offers a variety of shooting gloves to protect the archer's fingers. From left are a style of top grain leather, the maker's single-seam premium glove and an economy leather glove that many beginners favor.*

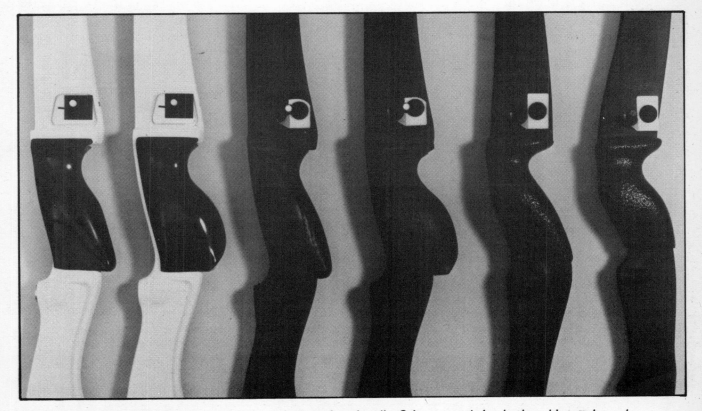

*Bow grips can be purchased separately to customize your bow handle. Grips are made in plastic, rubber and wood. While some are contoured to fit a larger hand, they also make the handle warmer to hold than a bare metal riser.*

# Chapter 10
# A LOOK AT QUIVERS

## Only One Arrow Can Be Held On Your Bow, So What Do You Do With The Others?

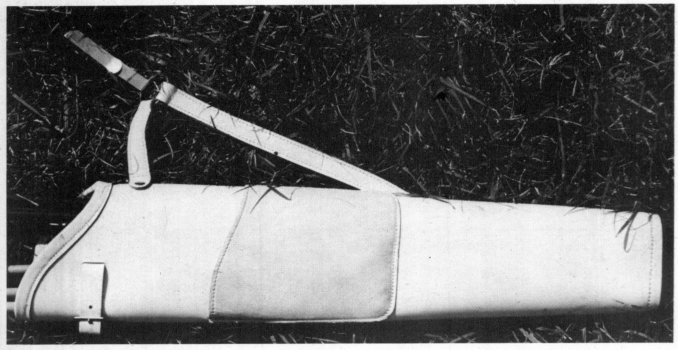

The side quiver hangs from the belt, with straps angling the quiver to a 30-degree slant to allow easier withdrawal of the arrows. Pockets attached to the outside provide a container for extra points, first-aid kit, other gear.

**W**HEN YOU take to the field or tournament range you usually take a more than ample supply of arrows with you. If the number of arrows totals a half dozen or more, you can be assured that the number of trips to the target to retrieve them will be fewer, the time spent in actual shooting much greater.

When you enter the field, there is one arrow that you need not worry about storing. That is the arrow that is nocked in your bow. You know where it will be — either in the target or on the arrow rest. But what do you do with the rest of your arrows? You put them in a quiver.

Although a quiver may not be considered essential, you'll find that even the most casual archer will have at least one.

Both simple and inexpensive is this side quiver that is made of vinyl. Its small size will handle about one dozen arrows as opposed to large capacity of other types.

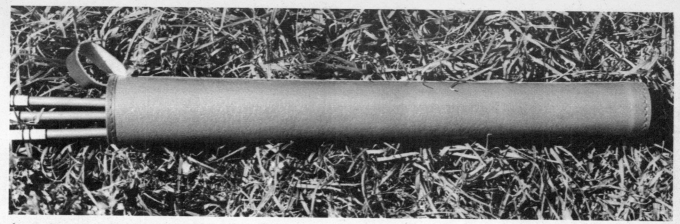

*A popular style for the beginning archer, this belt quiver is meant to hang vertically along the archer's thigh. The quiver is extremely economical insofar as price is concerned, yet will hold about twelve arrows with target points.*

When quivers first were developed is somewhat of a mystery, for all references made to archers throughout history show the use of a quiver. It seems they were developed within the same time frame as was the bow. Apparently it did not take long for these ancestors of Robin Hood to figure out the need for a case to transport and protect their shafts.

A portable case is actually all that a quiver is. It may have pockets added to the outside, ornate decorations and patriotic colors, but it is still nothing more than a case for arrows.

To decide which case is right for you then, you need only to determine where you will be using the quiver.

Quivers come in four basic styles: back quiver, side quiver, bowquiver and ground quiver. All have their intended uses and, although you might be able to use one in a shooting area for which it was not actually intended, you'll find that each far outperforms the others in its designated use.

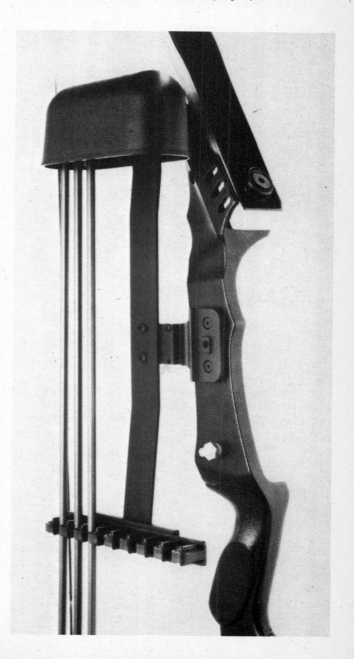

*The bow quiver mounts directly to the bow at the sight mount. Normally it holds six to eight arrows with broadheads. This QD model by PSE safely holds eight.*

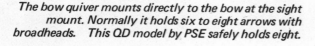

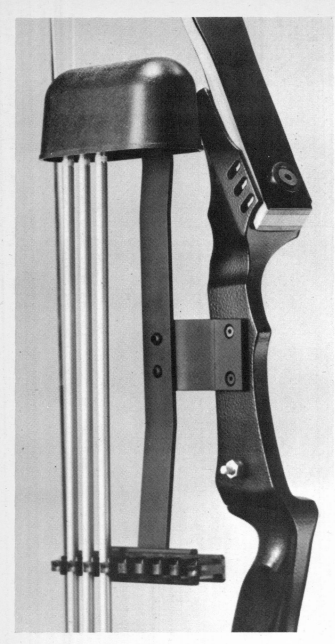

*In purchasing your bow quiver look for sufficient depth of the broadhead cover to protect the point from contact with your hands or fingers. A broadhead cut is dangerous.*

## BACK QUIVERS

The back quiver is possibly the oldest style or certainly the oldest for which we have visual proof, in the form of drawings and antique versions preserved in many of our museums. The back quiver was extremely popular in early archery, especially for the military bowmen. Lying across the back with arrow nocks extending beyond the shoulder, the quiver provided instant accessibility to fresh shafts when needed. In design it resembled an oversized, elongated feed bag, usually made of leather, with a strap that attached to the top and swung around to hook at the bottom, crossing the archer's chest. You could pack a large number of arrows into one back quiver; up to a couple dozen in most. Many styles included pockets attached to the outer side where one could store an extra bowstring,

*A favorite for school and youth groups is the ground quiver, a wire or metal ring suspended by one or two metal poles. Pushed into the ground, the rings hold the arrows. The ground quiver can be shared by two archers.*

arrow first-aid kit, pencil, money and whatever else might be needed. The back quiver could accommodate most anything, but it did have its drawbacks.

Because the quiver had such a large capacity, oftentimes an archer would find his half dozen shafts bouncing around inside the quiver. The bounce not only was noisy, it was distracting. And if one happened to be a bowhunter, it was downright discouraging. Many a deer waved farewell at the clatter of one arrow against another.

Withdrawing an arrow from a back quiver takes a little practice and always plenty of space. The arrow must swing in an arc from behind the archer to ahead of him, curving across his shoulder. Any obstacle, be it brush or bowman, within a yard's distance of him is apt to be hit by the sway of the arrow. And should that archer need to lean over to

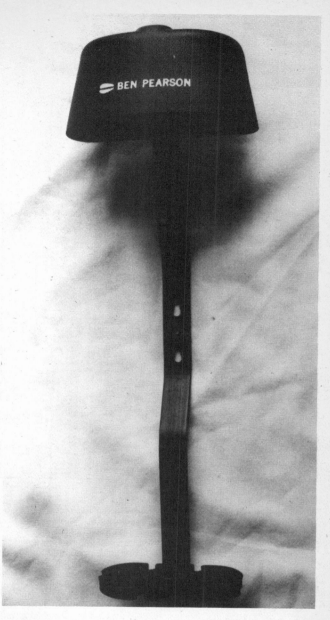

*Pearson's rugged but lightweight bow quiver also offers a quick-detach feature and six-arrow capacity. Quiver is held to the bow plate by means of a central screw, two mounting pins. It will fit any AMO standard bow.*

*Proline's quick-detachable bow quiver features a plastic mounting plate. Attached to the bow it allows quiver to be snapped into place or removed from the bow without the need of tools. The six-arrow quiver is of plastic.*

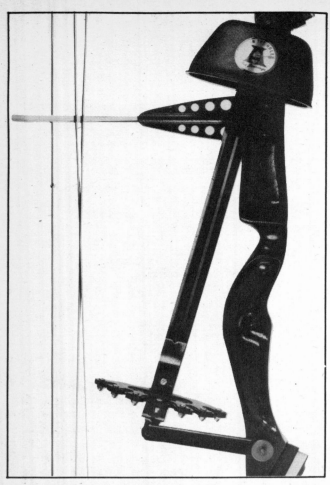

*Jennings' unique method for attaching Ace-in-the-Hole quiver slants the arrows toward the archer, allowing greater ease in withdrawing the shafts from the quiver shield. This quiver will easily hold up to eight arrows.*

## SIDE QUIVERS

Side quivers are any one of a variety of quivers that hang from the string side (right side for a right-handed shooter) of the archer. They may be classified as hip, side or belt quivers, depending on how they are attached. All are normally suspended from a belt, hanging down a few inches below the waist. Side quivers come in various circumferences and will hold from a half dozen to two dozen arrows.

retrieve an arrow embedded in the dirt or to check a game track, he will need to be additionally careful to avoid having one or more arrows fall from the quiver.

Although the back quiver was the most popular of quiver styles for many decades, it's difficult to purchase one today. Manufacturers no longer mass-produce them, and unless you happen upon a leather craftsman who can be talked into making one for you, the only way you may be able to obtain a back quiver is to make it yourself. Or you might contact some of the larger mail-order archery dealers. Some have back quivers that they have had in back supply and are still able to sell.

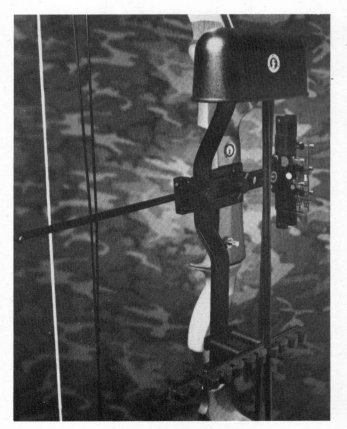

*Martin Archery offers this Model 3900 eight-arrow style. Fully loaded, the bow quiver offers stabilizing effect to the bow without a need for a separate stabilizer. The quiver is mounted to the sight screw mounting, but the bow still will accommodate a sight and cable guard.*

Add-A-Quiver from Martin Archery is a separate adapter that allows six more arrows to be added to the Model 3900 quiver. Author found it attaches quickly, solidly.

With the Martin QM-70 bracket the sight and quiver are mounted or unmounted quickly. The quiver mounts behind the bow. The 3900 and Kwikee Kompound Kwiver also may be bolted on permanently with the use of inexpensive model.

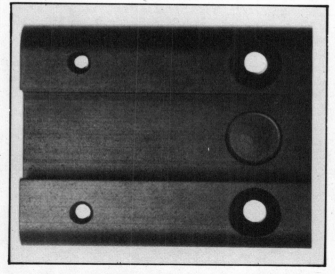

For true versatility look for a mounting bracket that will allow you to attach not only your bow quiver, but your bow sight. This QM-70 Martin bracket does that.

The hip or side quiver is an extremely popular style of quiver for tournament and field archers. The quiver hangs vertically from a belt, a few inches below waist level. The belt or side quiver differ in the angle in which they hang, with the side quiver angling to about thirty degrees behind the archer, while the belt quiver hangs straight down the archer's side.

A primary advantage to the side quiver is the ease with which the archer can withdraw his arrows. Because he can actually see what he is doing, he is less likely to drop or bounce his arrow against another arrow in the quiver. He knows exactly where his arrows are and how many he has remaining to shoot.

A disadvantage to the side quiver may be in the likelihood it offers for hangup in brush.

A stepchild of the back and side quiver is the pocket quiver, which snuggles into a rear hip pocket. A mini version of the back quiver, the pocket quiver will hold up to six arrows.

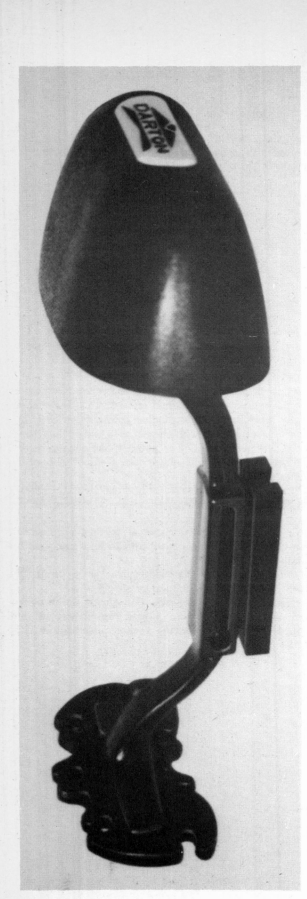

## BOW QUIVERS

Undoubtedly the most popular of quiver styles for the bowhunter is the bow quiver, whose unique design allows it to be fastened directly to the bow. Running parallel to the bow, the bow quiver normally is fastened directly to the side of the riser and serves not only to hold the arrows but to act as a stabilizer for the bow. Most bow quivers will hold six to eight arrows, with adapters available to double that number. Normally used with broadheads, the quiver comes complete with a padded shield that protects the archer from the razor-honed broadheads while holding the arrows securely in place. If you should choose to use a bow quiver, it is mandatory that you purchase one that includes a broadhead shield. The likelihood of cutting yourself severely with a broadhead is much too great without a shield.

Due to the placement of the bow quiver, mounted directly in front of the archer, he can withdraw an arrow while still keeping an eye on his target. Care must be taken

Outdoor writer and guide Judd Cooney (right) recommends a bow quiver for his clients who want to go after elk. He feels it is readily accessible for any fast action.

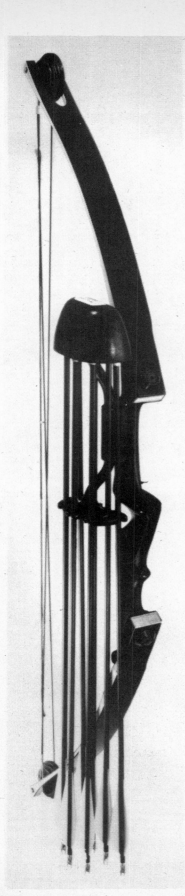

*The 12-inch Darton DBQ-7 model offers a snap-on mounting and will hold 7 arrows.*

*Separate holes in the quiver shield provide constant positioning for each broadhead so that they don't come in contact and thus dull themselves. In the case of the Proline quiver these pockets are of rigid plastic.*

when drawing the point free of the shield, however, as a tap against the plastic shield generally will send most game scurrying.

You also must be careful of the movement of the broadhead as you remove the arrow from the quiver and place it on the rest. More than one archer has accidentally cut his bowstring while attempting to nock a hunting arrow taken from a bow quiver.

## GROUND QUIVERS

Ground quivers are nothing more than a wire or metal ring with one or two legs that push into the ground to hold the quiver erect. Arrows are simply dropped inside the ring,

*The Catquiver attaches to the back of the archer in much the fashion of a light pack. The broadheads, pointed down, are not shielded; the arrows are easily withdrawn by reaching behind the back, pulling down for the release.*

*Depending upon the size of the hoops, the ground quiver will hold any number of arrows. Another advantage lies in the fact that it can be placed between a pair of archers and both of them can draw arrows from the same quiver.*

contained there by the ground and the ring.

Ground quivers are a popular choice for school archery programs and allow for use by more than one archer at a time. Provided the bowmen can tell their arrows apart, two archers can share one ground quiver by simply placing it between them.

Unlike the bow, side, and back quiver, the ground quiver is not portable. Although easily light enough in weight to be carried from one target to another, the archer must consciously do so. He also must be prepared to do a lot of bending if he intends on practicing for any period of time. With the fletching sitting about two feet high, the archer will need to bend down to get each arrow.

*The Jennings Ace-In-The-Hole bow quiver features a cup cushion made of soft rubber with arrow locating holes.*

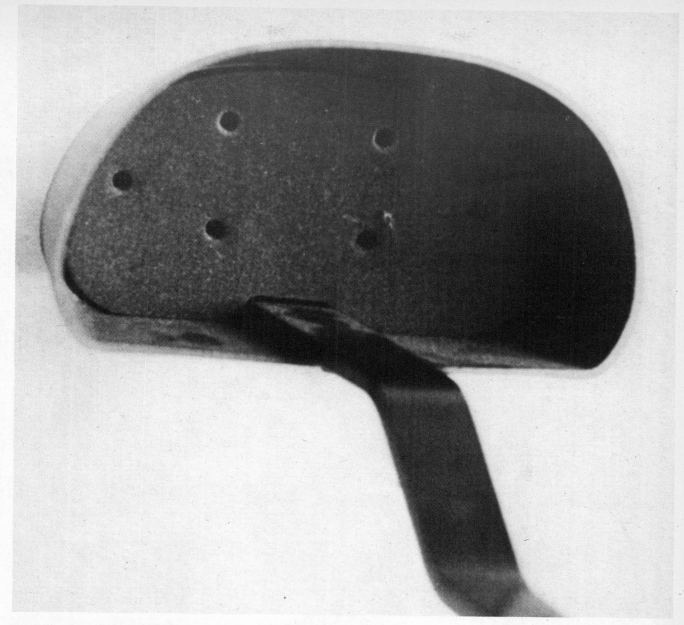

*The arrow locating holes in the cup cushion of this Ben Pearson bow quiver are in sponge padding for six heads.*

Because of the simplicity with which quivers are made, there is little or no maintenance. Bowquivers may need attention occasionally. The bowhunter must be certain that this type quiver is mounted tightly to the bow and that the rubber clips that hold the shaft in position are tight. If arrows begin to drop from the bow quiver it is normally a sign that the clips are beginning to loosen or spread. Clips may be replaced or bent to tighten them.

In purchasing a quiver look for one that will meet your needs. Consider whether or not it will hold all of the required arrows. If it is a bow quiver, will it mount to your bow? Can you control the quiver? Are you able to remove arrows quietly and easily?

You also will want to consider price. Side quivers may cost anywhere from $5 for a child's economy quiver to $30 for a deluxe target model. Bow quivers range in price from $15 to $35.

The quality of workmanship, the material from which the quiver is made, whether leather or vinyl, the addition of an outside pocket or dividers to separate the quiver into sections all contribute to the overall price of the quiver.

*Jim Dougherty, an archer for nearly three decades, came to favor the bow quiver early in his bowhunting career. Now the head of his own archery manufacturing company, he has tested most of the designs marketed over the years.*

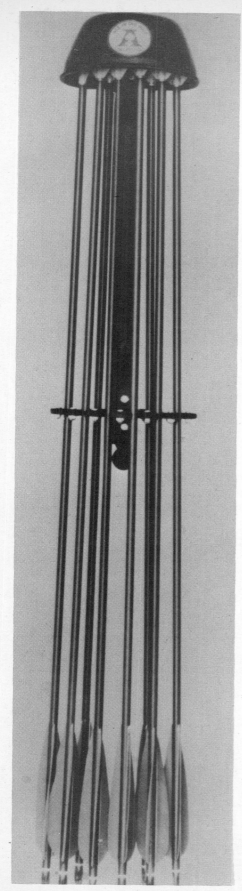

*Bear Archery's Hug Quiver is lightweight, yet sturdy. Featuring a quick-detach mounting plate, quiver will hold seven arrows, is designed to fit most compounds.*

In considering which quiver to purchase, realistically determine your needs. If you will only be shooting from your backyard or a controlled range, you may need only a ground quiver. If you expect to do a lot of walking from target to target, the ground quiver is impractical. Look instead to the field quiver, the hip or side quiver. If you expect to do most of your shooting during bowhunting season then you probably would be wise to purchase a bow quiver. Of all the styles, it is the only one that offers special protection for broadheads. Not only do the broadhead retainers keep the broadheads from possibly harming you, but they also prevent them from rubbing together and dulling each other.

Because quivers are so inexpensive, you may wish to have several styles on hand. Whether you have one or a half dozen, you will find both practice and serious shooting to be much easier.

*Bow quivers come in many shapes and sizes insofar as arrow capacity is concerned, but virtually all of them have the same basic design to protect the broadheads, as is the case with this Ace-In-The-Hole quiver model.*

For his draw of a PSE 70-pound compound four-wheel model,
Bill Fadala stands upright, bow in a vertical position.
Bow arm is straight but unlocked, hand released from
grip. Drawing hand uses three-finger grip, elbow high
above arrow line. Upon release archer attempts to
maintain position of both hands, arms and body.

# Chapter 11

# THE SOPHISTICATED STRING-GUN

*Some Tournament Archers May Not Agree, But Sam Fadala Insists The Compound Bow Has Made The Recurve Obsolete!*

THE COMPOUND BOW was not an overnight sensation like the Hula-Hoop or Silly Putty. First indications of a wheel-and-pulley bow came from the inventive mind of Dr. Claude Lapp of Washington, D.C., a physicist who built a few samples of mechanical bows.

Years later other minds expanded upon Dr. Lapp's basic ideas, and the person most responsible for the compound bow as we know it is H.W. Allen, who patented his version of the sophisticated string-gun in the early 1960s. During 1961-1962 Allen was working diligently on a bow that took advantage of the block-and-tackle principle. He first tried concentric pulleys, but by 1965 had changed to eccentric pulleys; this ingenious move aided both in performance and let-off, the reduction of the force needed to draw the bow to anchor point hold.

In 1967 Tom Jennings bought the first license from Allen to commercially produce a compound bow; and the race was on. Jennings personally promoted the bow by traveling widely and showing its advantages. His main concern was to convince the public of archers that the newfangled string-gun was not a threat to the basic tradition inherent in archery. One might think that every archer in the country immediately hot-footed down to the local shop to buy a compound. Not true; the bow of wheels and pulleys was good, but it was not yet perfected. It did not offer ballistics that much better than "stick" bows. And it was uglier than an alligator crossed with an orangutan. Tom Jennings and H.W. Allen had their work cut out for them. They had some selling to do.

Archery purists of the longbow school did not like the compound and they felt the mechanical bow would be in direct competition with the beautiful bow of yesteryear. Actually that never happened. If one looks at an archery magazine from a dozen years ago he will find a handful of longbow ads in it. If the reader looks at a current archery magazine he will find about the same number of ads for longbows. Sam Fadala, who researched this chapter for us, found room in philosophy as well as in practice for *both* bow types. The wonderful true longbow of narrow limb and thick core so loved by Howard Hill and his followers was in no danger of extinction. And if an archer does not believe that, let him order a true longbow from one of the master bowyers still making them. He'll wait longer to get

The four-wheel PSE compound mounts its quiver directly onto bow opposite arrow shelf, offering quick access to extra arrows. Archer shoots without sights or arm guard, although most compound shooters use some sort of sight system.

the bow than it takes to get an income tax refund. Such bowyers are busy; they have plenty of followers. And the good longbows of the day — the ones which are not flat-limbed "straight bows," but true longbows — have high performance with fine speed, tremendous stability, and plenty of cast and accuracy.

But another kind of bow is not alive and well. In the same archery magazines of the 1960s, the recurve was king. In those days the arguments raged between the longbow boys and the recurve fans over which bow style was best. Writers had more fun with that controversy than gun journalists over the .270 vs .30/06 battle. An archer could find bows in both styles that were light as a feather, strong as a lion, responsive as the steering wheel on a Formula I

race car, a joy to handle and to shoot. But the recurve went the way of the dinosaur. It's hard, in fact, to even find its bones lying around today. The compound bow sent the recurve to the Deep Six belly up.

In a current archery magazine my thumbing through found eight direct advertisements for the compound bow, three for the longbow and exactly zero for the recurve. Some would say the recurve deserved its demise. Others would not agree. The truth is some did and some did not. Fred Bear took a heap of game with a recurve bow. But we have to admit that the run of the mill recurve, while pretty, was flat-limbed, wide-limbed, about as fast as a turtle crossing a desert island, and probably should have been as defunct as last Saturday's newspaper, which it is. Be that as

The Jennings Forked Lightning is a newer two-wheel compound, using non-wood limbs, with hunting sights and cable guard attached. The John Schultz back quiver is large enough to hold hunting broadheads for big game, small game blunts and practice field-pointed arrows. A box of oatmeal placed in bottom of quiver holds arrows firmly and quietly in place.

it may, the fact looms clear — the compound is king and the longbow is queen. The recurve isn't even the ten of spades today.

"Comparing the first compounds on the market with today's sophisticated string-guns is like measuring a World War I biplane with an F16 jet fighter," Fadala reports. "Those first compounds were ugly as warts and as graceful as a hippo doing the tango. They were heavy. They were fat in the limbs. And performance was better in the advertisement than the field. All that has changed. As an example, a compound that exhibits the current state of the art is the Jennings Forked Lightning. The model I tested drew in the seventy-pound class with a mass weight of only four pounds and a total length of just 45½ inches.

"This bow exemplifies the trend in modern compounds, which is to small, light bows of high performance, mainly in the two-wheel class. The two-wheeler of the day has better performance than some of the previous four-wheelers, in fact. And it is the two-wheel compound that is enjoying the biggest market at the moment. Testing a fine four-wheel model, an Arrowstar, the velocity with a Lamiglass all-graphite arrow of 434 grains mass weight was in the 250-foot-per-second range, while the lighter and handier Forked Lightning drove the same arrow in the 240 fps

*Function of the cable guard mounted on Jennings Forked Lightning is to hold cable away from main bowstring during draw and release. Beeswax or other lubrication facilitates action as cable rubs along guard. Arrangement is intended to provide adequate clearance for arrow vanes or feathers, add to accuracy potential.*

*Somewhat different Jennings design mounts eccentric wheels from hangers, rather than through split limbs; simpler but with slightly less arrow velocity. Limbs are of rock hard maple and fiberglass, handle design is interchangeable. Thin, heavy stainless steel Fur-Long shafts offer deep penetration from 70-pound compound.*

*Wearing a camouflage face mask, the hunter draws an arrow from his back quiver, taking care not to raise his body above protective cover. Back quivers are not as popular with compound-bow hunters but offer large carrying capacity.*

domain. Statistically a three-foot-per-second difference is insignificant in archery. However, in the field such fine lines of distinction are hard to draw, and high performance in a lighter, handier bow is the goal sought."

The compound bow has used rather short, thick limbs with tremendous latent energy to take advantage of the block-and-tackle principle. The advantage is let-off. An average archer can now handle a stout bow because once he "breaks" the draw, the holding of the string is twenty-five, forty, even fifty percent less than the actual thrust of the bow itself in draw weight. So he can pull a sixty-pound bow and need hold back only forty pounds or even as little as

thirty pounds. The limb tips in the compound move very little as compared with the conventional bow, there being as much as two-thirds more bending in the old-style limb as compared with the new. And it is the eccentric cam that allows for the drop-off in actual holding force required to keep the bow at full draw.

"As long as we do not get totally carried away and relegate other bows — especially the better constructed longbows — to the ranks of the useless, it is correct to give the mechanical bow its due credit," Fadala contends. It does have advantages that exist in actual use, and not merely in a fancy advertisement. While being careful to

Part of the bowhunters' technique is to locate the game before the game locates him. Patience and a good pair of binoculars such as the Bausch & Lomb 9X35 held by Sam Fadala will help find the animal in question. The next step is to plan and execute the stalk to within arrow range. Most hunters will try 30- to 60-yard shots with compounds rated at sixty- or seventy-pound draw weights. Patience and careful stalking are essential.

recognize the fact that other bows are also good, we can examine some of the advantages of the compound bow.

## SPEED

The compound earned its reputation by advertisements that promised "Fifty percent more speed than a recurve." On the average this could be true, depending upon which compound and which recurve were selected to do battle in a speed race. And the same holds true for compound/longbow comparisons. Many of the flat-limbed recurves of the middle 1960s were lucky to achieve 150 to 175 fps with a hunting arrow. Some were much slower.

Fadala personally tested one recurve that gained a "muzzle velocity" of about 150 fps with an arrow that weighed 480 grains, and this was out of a seventy-pound-pull bow. Also, some of the longbows had dreary ballistics.

"I tested one longbow that earned a pitiful 125 fps with a 500-grain hunting arrow. Another, which the owner thought was faster than a cheetah chasing a zebra, got a whopping 160 fps with an arrow that only weighed 450 grains from a sixty-five-pound-pull bow. Therefore the claim of compound superiority in speed to the fifty percent level could hold up in some cases, but not in all cases. A seventy-pound longbow made by a master bowyer was

*Bowhunters buy more compounds than anybody else. Small as well as big game are popular targets, offering challenging shots for the careful hunter. Bill Fadala used a Jennings two-wheeler on this big Wyoming jack.*

chronographed at slightly over 200 fps with a 500-grain hunting arrow, about the same velocity enjoyed by the average compound at the time."

All bows are not created equal, to paraphrase the old saw. Why was the compound so fast? First, stored energy in the mechanical bow was high. Also, the way that energy was transferred to the arrow was important. High-speed photos show that an arrow from a conventional bow curves around the riser at the instant of release. The energy from the string transmitted to the nock of the arrow is released suddenly and inertia wants the arrow to remain at rest. Therefore the arrow tends to "buckle" around the riser of the bow, straightening out again to take its flight pattern.

Spine, or arrow stiffness, therefore has great effect upon arrow stability. After all, since the arrow has to whip around the bow, then get back on track, it must be just right in stiffness. The arrow, we say, has to recover correctly. In a longbow we use cedar arrows because cedar recovers quickly. When bent it returns to its original shape rapidly. However, in a compound bow the major thrust of stored energy does not blast the nock of the arrow at the instant of release. After all, the compound is "relaxed" by twenty-five, forty or even fifty percent-plus at full draw. The real power smacks the arrow when it is about half-way past the midpoint of the riser.

So what? The point is that a compound can use an arrow of less spine or stiffness, a lighter arrow, and since the

*Sam Fadala shows proper form as he draws Wing two-wheeler on a cedar shaft. Cedar is not as popular with hunters as aluminum or fiberglass but are inexpensive; good for small game practice.*

Fadala took this badger using Jennings four-wheel Arrowstar set at 70-pound draw weight. Premium grade Acme cedar shaft is in 80-pound spine class.

*Silhouetted hunter draws Jennings compound on javelina against rock wall. Razorbak-5 head tips aluminum shaft, feather fletching. At twenty yards, Razorbak-5 head completely penetrated javelina and knocked out golf-ball-size hole in granite behind the pig.*

arrow is lighter it follows that it will go faster than a heavier arrow given the same initial thrust of energy to propel it. The compound bow of sixty-pound draw weight firing an arrow spined for a forty-pound bow is bound to be fast, provided all mechanical factors of proper bow construction are in effect, of course.

## VALUE OF SPEED

We may tend to lose sight of the actual value of a fast bow, simply thinking that fast is better simply "because." In fact, all bows are turtle slow as compared with firearms. A so-called fast bow is generally considered one which will propel a hunting-weight arrow in excess of 200 fps. There are pellet guns that shoot faster than that. However, for at least two good reasons speed of arrow is vital to performance.

First, we have kinetic energy. While the kinetic energy of an arrow is minuscule, it still counts for something. Looking at a 500-grain arrow at a velocity of 215 fps, for example, we arrive at about fifty-one foot-pounds of kinetic energy. Even the tired old .45-70 rifle firing a 500-grain bullet at 1300 fps surpasses the 51 fpe mark by seven league steps to a figure around 1877 fpe. All the same, one factor in penetration is energy, and all things being equal higher energy means more penetration. Since penetration is the name of the bowhunting game, the more an arrow has the better.

Second, there is trajectory. A flat-shooting bow means a greater practical range limit. Not only will the arrow require less "Arkansas elevation" in order to strike the target, but its arrival on target as rapidly as possible may prevent the game from jumping the string or getting out of the way before the arrow actually gets there. A flatshooting compound bow can take advantage of sights, especially with pins set for twenty, thirty, forty and fifty yards. A practiced archer can claim a buck at fifty yards and more. Telescopic bow sights can add even more practical range to a bow, mainly from sheer visual advantage.

*Fadala recommends at least seventy pounds for hunting compound bow draw weight. In this case Fadala did not mount sight on bow.*

## LET-OFF

Let-off, or relaxation, is another advantage of the compound bow. In short, when a seventy-pound bow can be held at anchor point as easily as a forty-pound bow the archer has an advantage; for he can draw his bow and hold it as game comes toward him in the forest, plus he can hold at full draw longer for precise aim. His muscles will tire less quickly, too. In the field this means drawing the bow as that buck works toward the hunter and holding that draw until the best shot presents itself, which was hard to do with heavy conventional hunting bows, though some strong archers could do it.

Too much relaxation can be detrimental, of course, and some archers prefer a twenty-five percent limit. This much drop-off in holding force helps the archer control the bow,

but the tension on the string helps the arrow get away better with a smoother release possible. The heavier holding weight, in other words, lets the arrow "escape the string."

## ADJUSTABILITY

The conventional string-gun is set at the factory or bowyer and its draw limitations and poundage remain the same at all times. Sure, a longbow or recurve can be pulled back to shorter draw lengths for less poundage, but depending on the "stacking" of the bow, performance at partial draw may or may not be the best. Using our example of a compound bow, the Jennings Forked Lightning, the poundage range goes from fifty-five to seventy in that one bow. Not only that, but the "valley" is around two inches, meaning that an archer can achieve a draw length variation of as much as two inches without

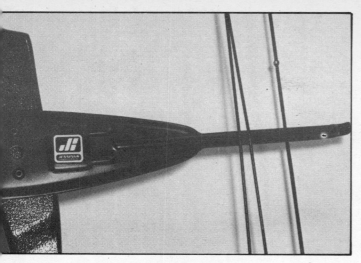

*Jennings cable guard as mounted on Forked Lighting offers a smooth shaft surface for minimum friction as cables ride along it. Arrows with large vanes are especially helped by the action of the guard holding cables away.*

*Razorbak-5 broadhead is designed and built for deep penetration. Test-shot into brick, head retains its original shape while chipping sizable hole in target.*

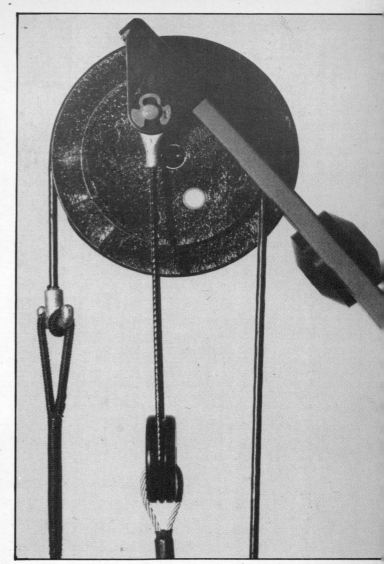

*Eccentric wheel on Jennings Forked Lightning shows new thin width; efficient but lightweight. Steel spindle acts as axle for eccentric, held on with circlip keeper. Note T-shaped retainer on which bowstring is mounted.*

performance loss. This means that exact draw length is not as crucial to point of impact as it is in the conventional bow.

Furthermore, the Forked Lightning allows the position of the valley to move by placing the cables into different slots on the tri-draw eccentrics. What happens is this: The poundage of the bow can be changed without adversely affecting the performance of the bow or the bow's draw length. By relaxing the limbs away from the limb platforms via an Allen wrench adjustment the change in draw weight is accomplished. Now we have several bows in one.

"Too much of a good thing can be bad and sometimes a bow will not react with full performance quality at the low end of its settings. In testing the Forked Lightning, better performance was achieved at sixty- to seventy-pound settings than at the fifty-five-pound setting, but at fifty-five

*Left: John Schulz, protege of famous archer Howard Hill, breaks wooden discs thrown into air; not recommended for amateurs. Cedar shaft is still visibly bent in flight as it leaves longbow.*

*For comparison: Longbow four-wheel compound and a recurve bow. Shorter overall length of compound design is another hunting advantage.*

the bow was still very operable. A wide range of draw weight can save the archer money," Fadala reports.

In the past the bow shooter usually purchased a fifty-pound model, instead of the sixty-five or seventy that he really wanted, because he had to work up to the heavier pull, developing his muscles for it. Today a compound can be purchased that ranges from fifty-five to seventy pounds pull and the archer can start at the fifty-five setting and work up to the seventy, all in one bow. When he is ready to drive heavy hunting arrows with the seventy-pound thrust he need not sell his bow and run to the store for a heavier one. He takes out his wrench and jacks up the power to match his new strength and mastery of the bow.

The compound bow has changed its image over the years in both physical appearance nad acceptance by the archery public. Never-ending interest in design and performance coupled with creative imagination has given us lighter, less complicated, high-performance models. The ungainly monster bow is gone. In its place is a sleek bow that

requires less tuning and allows for more flexibility in draw weight and length.

The two-wheeler is the order of the day, simple and high in performance. The four-wheelers also are lighter and easier to manage. Sufficient time has passed from the days of the first compounds for us to see a picture developing. In the picture is a bow of ever-changing dimensions. But while the compound may have put the recurve to pasture, the longbow remains, giving archers two different tools to enjoy — one ancient, the other a combination of an old set of rules in a new package.

The compound is the choice of the people. It has become the archer's standby. It shoots a variety of arrow styles; it adjusts over a wide range, fires its arrows with relative flatness of trajectory, drives heavy hunting arrows at high penetration speeds, puts target arrows in the gold with fantastic frequency, and allows the everyday bow shooter a chance to master a lot of power without having to hold all that power at the full draw anchor point.

With such credits no wonder it is a success.

# Chapter 12

# THE HOW OF SHOOTING

## Anyone Can Shoot Well By Following A Few Basic Steps

ANYONE CAN shoot a bow and arrow regardless of age or handicap. But to shoot any bow well, one should learn how to shoot it properly. Following a few basic steps will not only assure that you shoot to your best capabilities, but that you do not make archery physically difficult for yourself. Although the steps listed below refer to a right-handed shooter, if you shoot left-handed you need only to reverse sides for each position. The steps in shooting remain the same: stance, nocking, draw, anchor, hold, aim, release.

### STANCE

To shoot well one should be comfortable. Concern should be on the flight of the arrow and not on whether you will topple over when you release. Turn approximately ninety degrees from the target, allowing your bow arm (the left arm which will hold the bow) to point toward the target. Position your feet slightly apart, approximately eighteen inches, so you feel a good, secure base beneath you, the weight of your body equally distributed over each foot. Do not stand with your feet together at attention, or you will lose that secure support and find it difficult to hold steady on your target. Nor do you want to overextend your feet, causing you to fall or favor one leg over the other.

Stand straight, neither forcing your left hip (if you're a right-handed shooter) toward the target, nor pushing your shoulders away from the target. If shooting correctly the muscles of your back — not your arms — will be carrying the weight of the draw.

You may find, as many young archers in particular have noticed, that upon release your body wants to surge forward with the arrow. Hold your position until you hear the comforting *thunk* of the arrow hitting the target. Should you allow your body to move forward, you are apt to deflect the flight of the arrow dramatically, causing it to soar wide in any direction, dependent on where your bow arm went during your surge.

A common fault among novice archers is to use the hips to help force the bowstring back. It makes drawing all the more difficult. Good posture allows the large back and shoulder muscles to accept bulk of the strain.

*If your draw is correct you should be able to feel the shoulder muscles draw together in reaching anchor point.*

## NOCKING YOUR ARROW

Nocking an arrow sounds simple, but you must take care that you do it properly, especially if you are shooting in a line of archers. Keep your bow pointing toward the target, not at a fellow archer. Watch the tips of your bow so they do not hamper someone else's draw or shot. With your bow arm holding the bow, grasp the arrow shaft around the fletching area with your string hand (right hand), then guide it into place across the rest, sliding the nock onto the string.

Be sure that you have your hen or cock feather facing away from the riser. The cock feather is the odd-colored

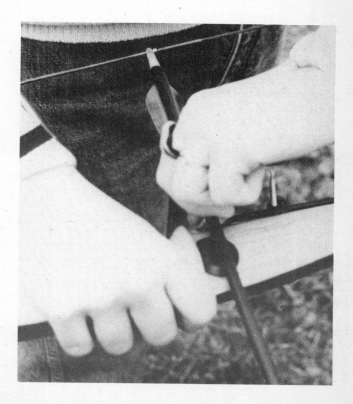

*Nocking an arrow without interfering with other archers on the line or dropping the arrow takes a little bit of practice. Keeping the bow in front of you, grasp the fletching of your arrow with the string hand, then slide it into place atop the rest and below the nock locator.*

The arrow nock must be seated securely against string or the arrow is likely to drop when released. Test the nocking position by pulling it into place with thumb and index finger. Don't be misled into attempting to draw the bow with fingers in this position, however, as the string is likely to pull free from your grasp.

Keep your little finger clear of the string. Due to the anatomical form of the smallest finger, to use it would require that your other three fingers bend acutely around the string, again making it hard to release.

The purpose of your three fingers is to draw the string back, not to hold the arrow in place. If the nock is properly secure on the string, you should feel a slight resistance and hear a soft snapping sound as it seats itself onto the string. The resistance should not be strong, an indication that the mouth of the nock is too tight and needs to be pried open slightly. Neither should the nock "fall" into place, with no apparent resistance whatever. This nock is too loose and

feather of a three-fletched arrow. If this fletching is nocked toward the inside of the bow, the arrow is apt to kick out as it passes the riser and fly wide to the right. With the thumb and index finger of your right hand, check to assure that the nock is tight against the string. If it is not you will hear a thunking sound when you release and your arrow will probably drop directly in front of you.

In shooting a bow one uses only the first digit of the first three fingers. The index finger is placed above the nock, the second and ring fingers below it. Resist the temptation to wrap your fingers tightly around the string. The more finger you place on the string, the more you must clear before the bowstring will release. During the draw you should hold these fingers perpendicular to the string, not wrapped tightly around it.

If nock tension on your bowstring is correct, you should be able to suspend the arrow from the bowstring without holding on, yet the shaft will sway around the string. If the nock is too tight, release of shaft will prove difficult. If too loose, it may fall off the string.

you will have to pinch the nock with your fingers to keep the arrow from staying behind when you draw.

Both novice and experienced archers occasionally feel the frustrations produced when an arrow begins to fall off the rest each time they draw back. Frequently the cause of this is pinching the nock between the fingers, combined with a tightening of the fingers which causes the arrow shaft to lift from the rest. The solution is to spread your fingers slightly, away from the nock, and let the hold of the nock bring the arrow back for you. And do not tighten your fingers around the string.

As you draw the bow back, you may notice a slight

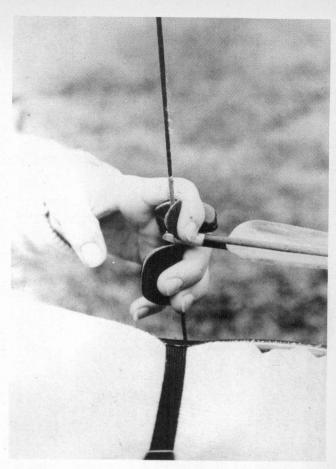

*Only the first digit of index, middle and ring fingers are used in drawing the bowstring. The fingers are held perpendicular to the string and shouldn't wrap around it.*

rolling of the string clockwise, this is normal. It is for this reason that right-handed archers must shoot right-handed style bows, and vice versa. Were a left-handed shooter to attempt to shoot a right-handed bow, he would find himself fighting the tendency of the arrow to fall from the rest as his fingers roll the string counterclockwise, pulling the shaft from the rest.

## THE DRAW

Drawing the bowstring to your anchor point should be a smooth, even pull. Extend your bow arm toward the target, arm fully extended and straight. Now pull the bowstring toward you. Frequently you will see an archer slip the index finger of his bow hand up over the arrow shaft as he draws to keep it from falling off the rest. If you position

*In nocking your arrow place the hen, or odd-colored, feather outward from the riser of the bow. This will allow arrow to pass the bow without possible deflection.*

The first step in the draw is to extend the bow arm up and out toward the target, then draw the bowstring toward you at shoulder level. Although the position of archer's bow arm and string hand are correct, grip on the bow is too tight. It should be more relaxed.

A common problem for even experienced archers is an arrow that seems to fall off the rest continuously at the onset or during the draw. Note tight clasp of index, middle fingers against the nock. It is this pressure that causes the arrow shaft to roll off the arrow rest.

your string hand properly and hold your bow upright, you should not need to do this; doing so can be harmful to your finger should you happen to overdraw or allow the finger to come in contact with the fletching during the release. You're better off to keep all fingers of the bow hand away from the rest and down on the handle where they belong.

Your bow arm should be at shoulder level throughout the draw, with the muscles of your shoulders and back pulling the bulk of the draw weight, not your arm muscles. You should actually be able to feel your shoulder muscles

moving together during the draw. Do not pull the bowstring back from a waist-high level, nor raise the elbow of your right arm up. In both positions you have effectively taken your back and shoulder muscles out of the draw, forcing you to use only the much weaker muscles of your arm to draw, a term we call "horsing" the bow.

In drawing, you may find the hand of your bow arm wrapping tightly around the bow. The rationale behind this is that you have to have a firm grip on the bow to keep it from flying back and hitting you in the face. In reality, this

*Although you may see other archers stabilizing the shaft with the index finger of the bow arm, this is an unwise practice that can even lead to minor injury if finger should remain above the bow handle during the release.*

cannot happen. The form of your hand prevents the bow from going anywhere at all. The placement of your thumb and index finger provides a natural V in which the bow rests, sitting in the webbed flesh between the two. The only way the bow could fly back toward you would be if you deliberately took your thumb away and that would be extremely difficult to do. You actually can open your hand wide during the draw with no ill effects, provided you remember to hold on during the release, otherwise you'll find your bow soaring off after the arrows.

Your hold on the bow should be loose, a good method of holding the bow suggesting that you run your fingers down the front of the riser. Positioning your fingers in this manner serves to turn your wrist slightly inward. In doing so you actually move the bow away from your bow arm, gaining more than enough string clearance. Since you must have control of the bow after the release, this placement allows the hold you need without being so loose as to allow the bow to fly forward or so tight that the bow jerks wildly to the side when you shoot.

mistake can be. Probably nothing has dampened the spirit of a would-be archer more quickly — often more completely — than a single string slap. Wearing an arm guard does not prevent the slap, but it does prevent the hurt.

## YOUR ANCHOR POINT

Your anchor point will vary depending upon the style of shooting you wish to do. Most field archers and bowhunters prefer the instinctive high anchor, also called a field anchor, with the index finger touching the corner of the mouth, wrist turned to position the thumb along the jaw line. This position gives a consistent anchor point, a reference spot when at full draw, allowing the archer to position each arrow in the same target area with each shot.

*Another common but incorrect method for curing constant arrow rest fall-off is canting the bow to hold the arrow on the rest, as demonstrated by left-hander Debbie Moore.*

In wrapping your bow hand tightly around the riser, you cause yourself unnecessary hardships. After a brief period of time you will find your bow arm tiring. The constant stress of that tight grasp will show quickly. You also are increasing the likelihood of string slap. String slap, as the term implies, is the slapping of the string against the inside of your bow arm as you release. Archers wear an arm guard to prevent this slap from hurting them, but if your grasp of the bow is correct, it never should hit you at all.

A wise archer wears an arm guard every time he shoots his bow, even though he knows how to shoot, because it only takes one string slap to let him know how painful his

*Most young archers grasp the bow handle in a death grip. This adds strain to the arm muscles of the bow arm and forces the bowstring to ride close to or against the bow arm. Ultimate result of this is string slap.*

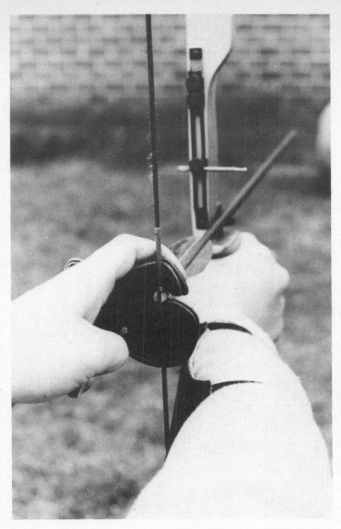

The tight, unyielding grip on the bow handle forces the bow arm to roll inward, placing the inner edge of the elbow and forearm in direct contact with the bowstring.

without the string, before you actually try to draw the bow, until the position feels comfortable to you. In practicing with the bowstring be certain you do not let go of the string without an arrow nocked in position. The energy that is normally transferred to the arrow to propel it will be transferred instead back to the bow limbs, causing unwanted stress and possible limb damage. This is termed dry firing and will rapidly cancel your bow's warranty.

A second style of anchor called the target anchor is common among tournament archers. This anchor point is frequently located midpoint of the chin, the bowstring crossing the nose and mouth. Also termed a low anchor, this position provides more distance to the arrow because of the lowered position of the nock end of the arrow.

To prevent a too-tight grip on the bow handle some will overcompensate by pulling their fingers away from the bow entirely. Bow must be grasped prior to release to keep it from following after the flight of the arrow.

Do not be concerned with the string hitting your face or mouth. It will not, unless you happen to have a heavy beard, in which case it may pull a whisker or two upon release.

Do not place your thumb high, above your index finger. Normally you cannot "feel" a specific spot on your face each time you shoot and may lose your consistency in anchor. Archery is a game of consistency, requiring that each step of the shot be identical in order to score well. Placing your thumb along the jawline provides that constant spot, since your jaw is not apt to change position.

Practice placement of your string hand several times

*Perhaps the best method of holding the bow is to run the fingers of the bow arm down the front spine of the riser. The bow then is held in a secure but light grasp.*

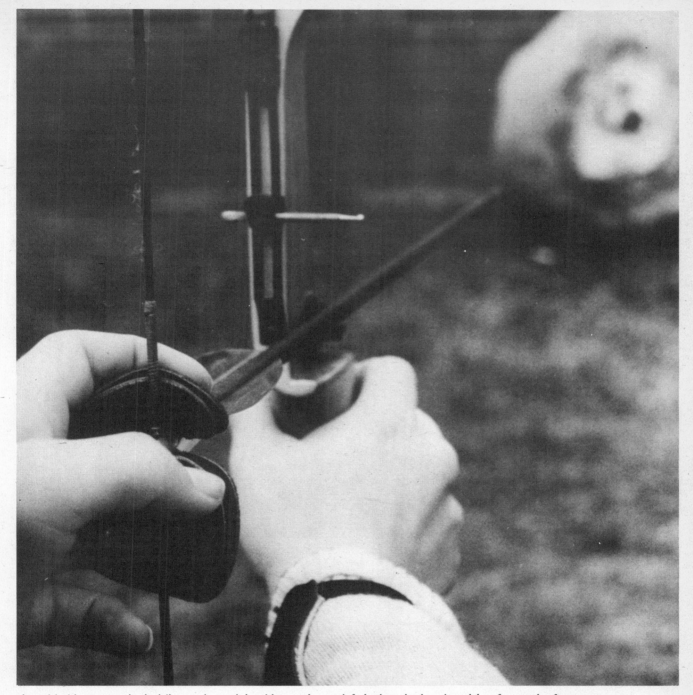

*An added bonus to the holding style explained in caption at left is that the hand position forces the forearm to rotate away from the path of the bowstring as the wrist is rotated inward and thus away from the riser of the bow.*

It does not matter which style of anchor you use, field or target. Both styles are equally effective, and you should use the one that feels most comfortable to you.

## HOLDING

Because you must take time to aim before you release your arrow, you must learn how to hold your draw. Most form problems occur during holding, especially if the archer is overbowed and must fight the weight of the draw or is limiting his draw to his arm muscles rather than his back and shoulders.

A frequent result is a slight "creeping" of the bow arm, the arm bending slightly in to ease the tension of the draw. If this happens, the archer not only will be reducing the draw weight of the bow but will be reducing the flight performance of the arrow.

Another problem with the hold occurs when the time span of the hold extends beyond the normal time period. Take your time in aiming, making sure to put the arrow or sight pin just where you want it before you release. However, you can spend too long in aiming, a fact that will

Shooting a bow from the waist may have been popular for Indian raids, but so was shooting from beneath a horse's neck. In reality it's hardly the ideal method of drawing a bow. The total draw weight of the bow would be shared between the arm muscles in this method rather than using the much stronger muscles of the back and shoulders to hold.

become apparent as the bow begins to shake or wave in front of you.

If this happens "let down." Ease up on the bowstring, without releasing the arrow. Rest a minute or so, then try again. As a matter of reference, you should be able to find your point of aim within twenty seconds of reaching full draw. A hold extending beyond thirty seconds normally will result in bow arm movement.

## AIMING

There are three general methods of aiming an arrow: instinctive, point-on (also termed gapping), and with the aid of a mechanical bowsight. Of the three, none has met with more controversy than has instinctive aim.

*Close but not quite right, Debbie Moore has overextended her elbow, removing the use of the shoulder and proper back muscles which should carry the brunt of draw weight.*

*Although a novice, left-handed Debbie Moore knows the first step to a successful shot lies in proper stance. Weight must be balanced equally on both feet, the spread of the feet providing a wide but comfortable support base.*

The term instinctive implies that the aim is done totally without thought or reason and is spontaneous. Throwing a baseball to a friend in the backyard is done largely by instinct. There is no careful planning and aiming before the ball is thrown. You simply throw it and allow your instincts to guide you in how far you must make it travel.

The instinctive archer draws, sights on his target and releases, all normally within a few seconds' time span. He does not concern himself with how far the arrow must go or what trajectory it must take, he simply looks and shoots.

A modified instinctive shooting method involves a quick glance at the end of the arrow to determine its placement on the target. This is an integral part of the point-on method of aiming, the reason most folks challenge the

claim of an instinctive shooter as being truly instinctive. If an archer spends any amount of time in aiming before he shoots, he probably is not shooting instinctively.

The point-on method of aiming requires that the archer use the point of the arrow as a guiding device. By practice he knows just when, at what distance and under what conditions he can place his point directly on the bull's-eye and expect to score. Also through practice he will learn how much he must adjust that point of aim as the distance increases or decreases between himself and the target.

*Favored by bowhunters and many field archers, the field anchor places the index finger at the corner of the mouth, thus bringing dominant eye directly over shaft.*

A good arrow release takes practice. Try it first without a bow, allowing yourself to become adjusted to the feel of the string fingers at anchor. The thumb should lie along the jaw line, providing reference point for draw.

Aiming time will be greatly increased over instinctive aiming because the archer actually is reasoning out each shot. He must learn to gauge accurately the distance between himself and the target and how to adjust for that distance. It takes a great deal of practice to be a point-on archer.

Undoubtably the most accurate of aiming methods for most archers is the use of the bow sight. A sight pin is added to the bow, and the archer needs only to line up his eye with the target, moving the bow until he has placed the pin directly on target before releasing. The addition of the sight pin functions much the same as a front sight on a rifle. For even greater aiming accuracy an archer may add a peep sight to the bowstring.

Although the addition of a sight makes aiming much more accurate, it takes a good deal of practice and experience to become proficient at aiming, for it is only effective if shooting form is correct and anchor consistent.

When you first begin shooting you may or may not have a sight on your bow. If you do have a sight it's a good idea to remove it until you have mastered the art of drawing and releasing the bow. The presence of a sight can prove a distraction to the novice archer, even though he soon will be relying on it as his primary aiming mechanism.

Use the point of your arrow as your aiming reference for your first few days of shooting. The shaft provides a ready guide between you and the target. At full draw, look toward the point of the arrow. Place that point directly in the center of the target. Depending upon how close you happen to be to the target, your arrow may go high or low on the target, but if the tip of the arrow is directly in the center of the bale, it will never go left or right, unless your release jerks it in one direction or another. The tip of the arrow gives a constant left or right reference and always should be used as such.

After shooting several arrows, you should begin to see a

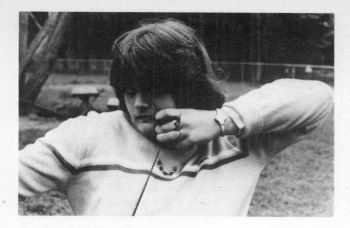

*Above: To release bowstring, Debbie Moore concentrates on target, maintaining her anchor until on target. (Upper right) The fingers are opened as the hand begins to move to the rear from the anchor point. (Right) Fingers of the string hand are swung rearward in the follow-through.*

grouping — all arrows in the same general area. You then can concentrate on moving that grouping toward the center of the target by moving your aiming point either higher or lower on the target, or by reattaching and using the bow sight.

If shooting field style you may find it advantageous to close your left eye and use only your dominant right eye. (This applies to right-hand archers. Reverse eyes if you are left-handed). You will find many archers ready and willing to challenge this suggestion, stating one should keep both eyes open. However, you may find that when both eyes are used, you subconsciously change from one eye to the other during your aiming. As previously noted in an earlier chapter, switching eyes can cause you to miss the target entirely, or shoot wild to the left. If you feel you can control your left eye, then by all means keep both eyes open if you wish. Otherwise you'll score better by closing

that non-dominant eye. In shooting target style you will want to keep both eyes open.

## RELEASING

Once you have your arrow on target there is nothing remaining but to release the bowstring. This should be easy, but there is no other single step in archery that causes more initial difficulty. New archers find it difficult to figure out just how to let go; instead, they wind up holding until the bow begins to shake and they must let down.

You will find archers suggesting that the best way to release the string is to quickly open your string hand. If you are having difficulty releasing the bowstring, that will certainly work and serves the purpose of getting that first arrow out of the way, something you must do before you can concentrate on improving your release.

The problem with simply letting go is that your release winds up being rough and jerky — anything but the

smooth and consistent release you need if you are to improve on your scores. A second method of releasing gives you that smooth release, and a chance to use your imagination as well.

When at full draw simply imagine your fingertips are the hinges of a door. They can swing but they cannot move away from your face until the hand has opened flat. To release the bowstring you must swing those hinged fingers backwards, straightening your hand out along your face as you do so. About halfway through your swing the string will glide past your fingers and release. Continue the flow of your string hand until it ends up directly behind you and alongside your head, maintaining a straight line between your hand and the target.

During your release resist the temptation to peek at the flight of your arrow. If you look too soon you are apt to jerk the bow to the left before the arrow has had a chance

*Above: Popular among tournament archers, the target anchor places the bowstring directly across the nose and lips, the line of the arrow directly between the eyes. (Below) Creeping is a common problem seen when the hold of the draw extends beyond physical limits. Archer tends to ease the weight of the draw by shortening the draw length. The result is poor arrow flight in virtually all instances; this technique also will greatly reduce arrow's distance.*

to clear it and the shaft will travel to the left of the target. Maintain your position, bow arm pointed directly at the target, your eyes and head the same, until you hear the impact of the arrow hitting the target. This is termed follow through, and prevents you from "porking" the arrow, jerking it down or left in your eagerness to see how well you shot.

To shoot a bow effectively, regardless of the style of aim you use, you must practice. There is no better way to improve your scores than to practice. Although most of your practicing can be done alone, it's a good idea to ask a knowledgeable archer to join you once in a while. Frequently the cause of a problem that is difficult for the archer to determine will be readily apparent to an observer. Then, too, shooting with a friend can be very enjoyable.

It may take many hours of practice to become an accomplished archer, but there is no reason why it cannot be fun.

*Left: Another typical problem for the novice is temptation to peek around the bow following release to see how well you have shot. Good follow-through dictates you hold your position until you hear the arrow strike the target.*

*Success is not always measured in how many golds the archer can score. Sometimes success means simply hitting a target.*

The bow sight has been frowned upon by some purists, but most tourney archers now depend upon its aid.

# Chapter 13
# TARGETS AND AIMING

## A Bow Sight Is No Guarantee Of Scoring Well — But It Might Help — Here's How For Some

TO THE TOURNAMENT ARCHER a six-gold — all six arrows in the bull's-eye — is the mark of success. To the novice watching such a demonstration of archery skills, such shooting may look easy. However, it takes only a few minutes of shooting to realize that hitting the target just exactly where you want to hit it is not as easy as it may appear. It takes a good deal of practice, and often some mechanical help; a bowsight.

A simple bowsight may be nothing more than a straight pin or small nail taped to the face of the bow so that the pin head extends above the arrow rest. Or it might be one of the deluxe-style multiple-pin bow sights with sliding tracks for color-coded sight pins and overall adjustments to move the entire sight setup if a new nocking point, string change or arrow weight requires it. There are a host of bow sights from which to choose. All work on the same basic principle, the sight pin providing a constant reference point between your eye and the target.

Whether your sight offers one sliding pin or a number of fixed pins — each one set for a specific distance — before the sight can be effective you must "shoot in" that pin, adjusting the pin as you shoot until it is on target.

Once the pin is set you can use it on any target at that same distance and score well. A sight pin set at twenty yards, for instance, should score a good hit on any target at twenty yards, regardless of the target's size or type.

To determine the proper setting of a sight pin you will need to shoot your bow in a controlled shooting area, one in which you know or can measure the distance from the target to your standing position. With that known distance you can then begin setting your bow sight.

*This simplified single-pin bow sight allows the archer to adjust for varying distances by sliding the bar up or down by adding more pins to the two additional pin clamps at the top of the bar. The pin is twisted in or out to make adjustments to the left or the right.*

What is the best way to set a sight? You could select a setting at random. Then, holding the sight on target, let fly an arrow to determine where it impacts. Eventually you're bound to walk your arrows onto the target, but the procedure is apt to be too time consuming. If you will allow your instincts to guide you, however, you can normally get fairly close with your initial setting. Simply draw on the target, and without using your bow sight, gauge where you need to aim by instinct. For most archers, their instincts will put them at least on the target butt, if not on the target itself.

Once you feel you have determined a reasonable aiming spot for your target, note the relative position of your sight pin to that target. The pin should be resting over the center

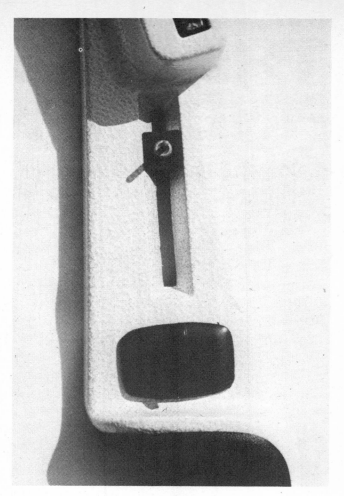

*An integral part of the bow's riser section, the sight accommodation for this Bear Mini-Magnum is built within the riser section and will allow for single-pin sighting.*

of the target. Adjust the pin until you have it sighting directly on the spot. Now release an arrow, using your best form to hold the sight pin on target. If the arrow hits the target or target butt, continue to shoot for several arrows, until you have a distinct grouping of the arrows on the target.

During this first phase of shooting-in, your primary concern is not so much where the individual arrows are impacting, rather that they are all impacting on the same general area. If you cannot group your arrows you are either altering your release or you are not properly using the sight. You must use it before the sight can be of any benefit to you. A tight arrow grouping is a good indication that the sight is being satisfactorily used.

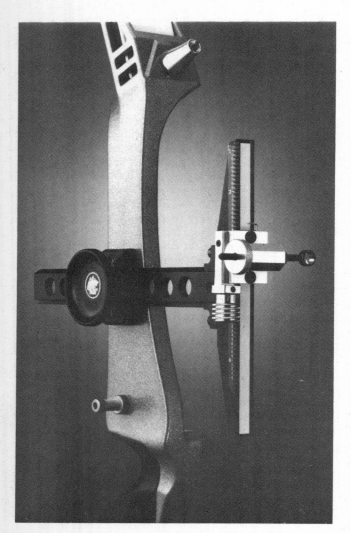

*Although a single-bar, single-pin Bear Accra-Sight is a tournament bow sight that has provisions for windage adjustments, micrometer adjustment, as well as a pin for yardage correction, it is hardly a simple sight.*

Once you have your arrows grouping, you may commence moving the spot of your sight to move the impact point closer to the desired target spot. To adjust your sight you must move the sight pin in the same direction as you wish the arrow to impact on the target. If your arrows are hitting left of the target, you will need to turn your sight pin out, to the left, for a right-handed shooter. By doing so you are actually moving the bow, itself, to the right. Adjustments for right, high and low hits are made in the same manner.

In adjusting your sight pin remember to move the pin in small increments, rather than twisting the pin in or out in a rapid, wide movement. A movement of the pin that slides the pin head a mere quarter-inch may move the impact point of your arrow six inches or more, depending on how far away from the target you happen to be.

*Bohning's Quiet-Tite hunter sight has four-pin, double-slotted capabilities, with a pin guard to protect pins against damage. Designed to meet AMO standards, this sight can be mounted on most hunting bows made currently.*

Once you have your pin set for the measured twenty yards, tighten the pin in position. As an added precaution against having to reset the sight, should it loosen and drop out of position, take an extra moment at this point to add a piece of tape to the side of the slide track — if there is no tape there already — and mark your settings on the tape with a pen and permanent ink. Should you find your arrows impacting off the target, you will want to check this tape indicator first to determine if the sight has simply slipped out of position.

If your bow sight is of the single-bar, single-pin type, in order to adjust your sight for varying distance you will need to slide the pin up or down the sight bar. Raising the sight pin will reduce the aiming distance, while lowering it places

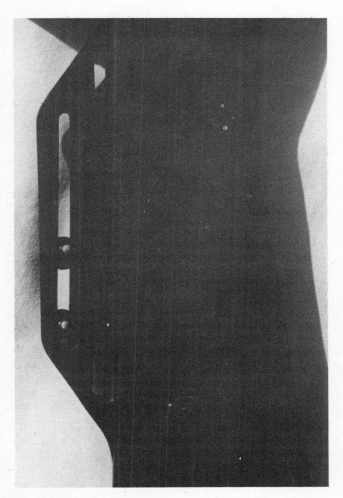

*A permanent part of the bow, the Indian Tracker double-bar sight will hold up to four pins. Closest and most distant pins are positioned on the longer, inside track.*

can be set without the need for time-consuming shooting. To set the remaining pins you will need only to refer to one of the many calibration charts offered by the archery manufacturers.

A calibration chart, as the term implies, is a sight graph with various distances calibrated for you normally in five- or ten-yard increments. The chart provided by PSE gives setting indications for distances from twenty to one hundred yards in ten-yard increments. Ranging's chart provides distances from fifteen to fifty yards in five-yard increments. Both provide removable tapes which mount directly to their sights, allowing you to shoot-in two distances and set your remaining pins for any other distances on the chart. A real time-saver, the charts work well with any multi-pin bow sight.

*Martin's one-piece hunter sight is double slotted, side mounting. It features four fluorescent-tipped pins for greater visibility in limited light. Double pin locking screws allow versatility for windage, elevation settings.*

the pin on more distant targets. A piece of tape beside the sight bar is a must for single-pin sights, as it provides instant reference for the various distances.

Most bow sights used today allow for the addition of several pins to the same sight, for marking various distances. These bow sights are called multi-pin sights, and normally have two or more tracks for the pins to slide on, and come complete with several sight pins, each painted a different color at the head to permit easy distinction betwen them.

If you desire, and have the marked distances to do so, you can set each for a different yardage by shooting them in the same manner in which you located your first pin. If you do not have several known distances to use as reference, look instead for just one additional distance. Although you will still have to shoot-in that pin setting, just as you did for your first pin, once you have the pin set all other distances

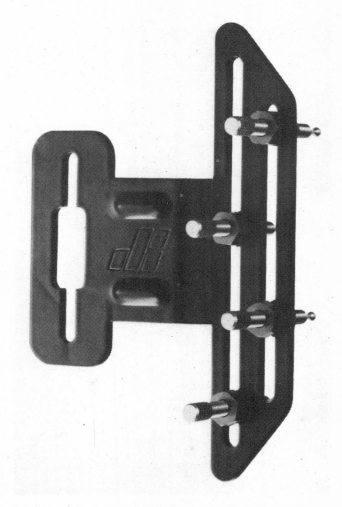

*Lock nuts on pins would allow one to adjust the windage without moving the elevation setting of the pin. The Jennings Deadshot hunting sight has these features.*

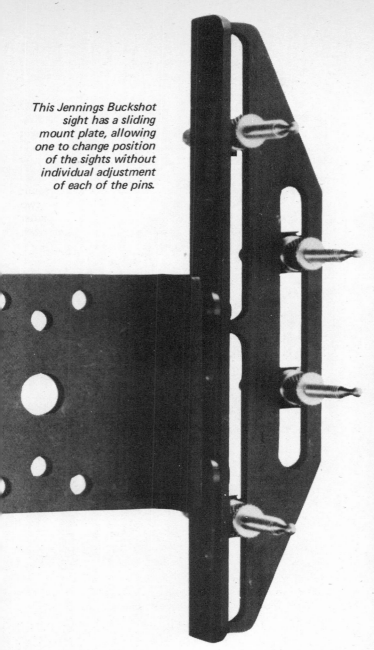

*This Jennings Buckshot sight has a sliding mount plate, allowing one to change position of the sights without individual adjustment of each of the pins.*

common is the change of a bowstring. By changing the string you will also need to change the nocking point. Unless your new nock is in precisely the same position on the string as was the previous nocking point — difficult to determine — your arrow impact is apt to change. Look for the sight setting to change each time you change bowstrings or otherwise alter the physical makeup of the bow in any way. A new rest, a change in anchor point or arrow weight — each can change the impact point of the arrows even though the bow and sight have not been changed.

When adding a sight to your bow great care must be exercised to assure that it is mounted properly and securely. Your sight will probably screw in to the outer side of the riser, the side away from the arrow rest. Most bows are pre-drilled and tapped for the addition of bow sights and require only the use of a screwdriver to attach. You will need to check this mounting periodically to be certain that the sight is still firm against the riser. A drop of Loc-Tite on each screw will ensure security.

For the most part you will probably not need to change the setting of your sight once you have it set. There are, however, variables that can change this. The most

*This economy hunting sight is the State I by PSE. It features a sight pin guard, dual slot pin positioning and a long sight bar offering hunter increased range.*

If your sight offers a sliding mounting bracket you will find adjusting for equipment changes to be both rapid and effective. A sliding mounting bracket allows you to adjust the entire sight at one time. Sights that do not have sliding mounting brackets may instead offer tracks in the mounting plate which allow you to swing the entire sight into position.

If a bow sight that has previously given you good impact suddenly seems to be poorly set, look to the sight itself, as well as to the environmental and external factors that may be temporarily altering your setup. Poor weather conditions

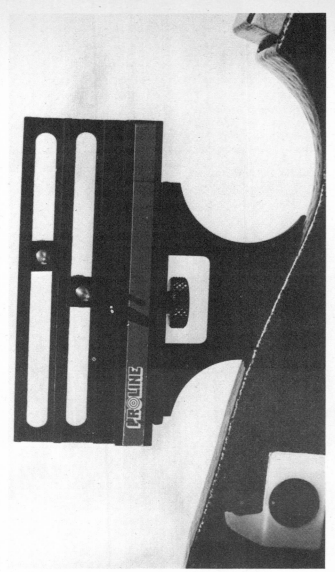

*Pro-Line's top sight is ideal both for hunting and field archery. It features multi-pin capabilities. The sliding sight mount offers the hunter increased range.*

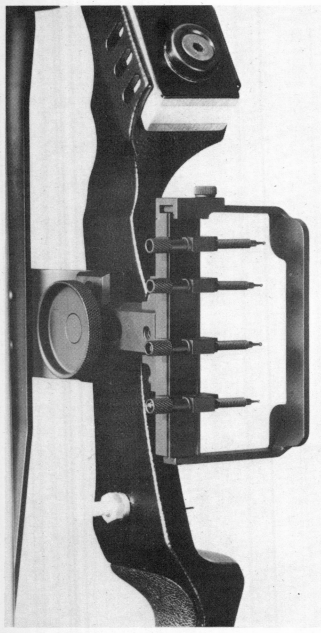

*PSE Elite line features three-way adjustability of the sight pin guard to protect the pins from damage, sight bar level adjustment, two-hole extension bar, as well as fully independent adjustments, for windage, elevation.*

are frequently a factor. High winds, rain, even high humidity may affect the impact of arrows even though the sight is perfectly set for normal shooting conditions. If such is the case you are better off if you change the target-aiming spot rather than altering the bow sight setting.

If several arrows impact perfectly, but you find yourself constantly losing one or more arrows, the problem is normally not the fault of the sight but of the archer. You may be altering your release or jerking the bow or perhaps shaking during your aim. If these are the problems do not change your sight. Work on correcting the shooting problems instead.

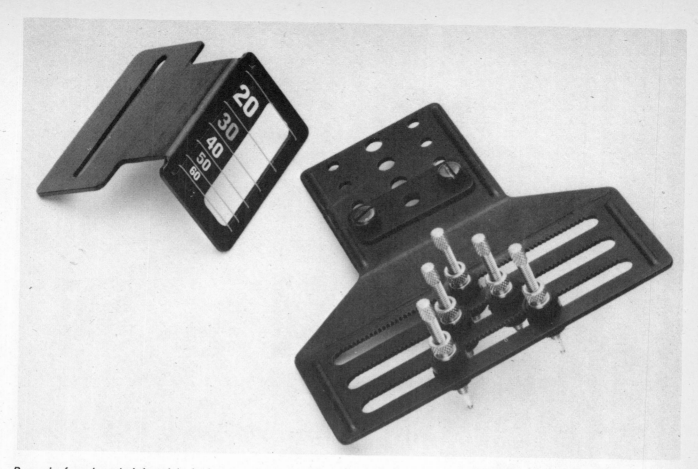

*Browning's rack-and-pinion sight includes a rangefinder. Constructed of aluminum alloy with annealed nylon gears, the settings are smooth and easy. The sight pins are micro-adjustable and have been shock mounted to prevent any damage.*

*Martin's Hawkeye scope gives rifle sighting capabilities to a bow. The addition of a scope forces concentration by the archer on the target pin and image much as the rear sight of a rifle forces alignment of the front sight on the target. For added capabilities a peep sight may be added to the bowstring. The peep sights have a large aperture for hunting and a smaller choice for target shooting. They allow another reference point.*

*An integral part of accurate sight shooting is determination of the target distance. Rangefinders such as Ranging 50 offer immediate distance readings, thus allowing archer to select the proper pin for the distance he will shoot.*

*Martin's series called the Deerslayer features a rangefinder plate for determining distance from the target to the archer.*

*Dust & Dawn is single-pin sliding sight. It features a luminous pin for low-light sighting.*

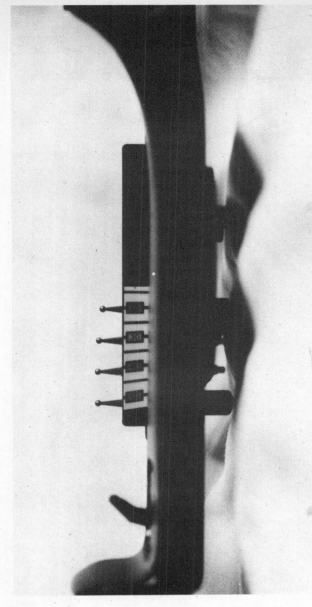

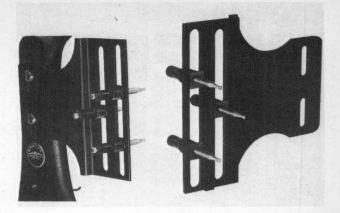

The Darton S-80 has two-slotted, three-pin sight mounts for the Darton bow. Construction is of anodized aluminum. The sight is dually adjustable for both windage, elevation.

*Gaining popularity among archers is a calibration chart on the sight bar. The chart allows the shooter to set two of his pins, then use the chart indicators to set the remaining pins. It has proved a success.*

There is little in terms of maintenance that needs be done for bow sights. The sight is normally left in place on the bow and requires no lubrication or servicing. An occasional check to assure that the mounting bracket is tight is about all that is required. Check the condition of the sight pins. Should a pin be bent, the impact of the arrow when using that pin will generally be off, since the bend has altered the direction of the aim.

Whether you shoot with or without a bow sight hitting the target is still a matter of calibration. You must know how far away from your target you are and where you need to aim in order to reach that target. Gauging distances is perhaps the greatest difficulty an archer faces. Unless the target distances are premarked for you, you must be able to accurately determine these distances if you hope to score well. Gauging distances takes a lot of practice.

Some folks never are really accurate at determining shooting distances. For them, as well as for any archer who wants to be sure of his judgment, the rangefinder is a distinct advantage.

A rangefinder is similar in nature to an adjustable-focus camera lens. The archer sights through the eyepiece of the finder, turning a focusing dial until the target is in good focus. He then refers to a chart on the focusing wheel to tell him just how far away his target is. Once he knows that distance he is then able to select the proper sight pin and take his shot. Probably the most popular rangefinder for archers is the Ranging Eagle-Eye 50; size and weight are comparable to that of a pocket instant camera.

In selecting a bow sight look for one that offers a sufficient number of adjustments to match your shooting needs. If you will be shooting tournament rounds only, a simple single-bar, single-pin sight may perform well for you. If you expect to be shooting at varying distances and will have little time to adjust your sights you will probably want a sight that offers several settings.

If you wish to use the same sight on several bows look for a unit that offers an adjustable mounting plate, so that you can move the position of the entire sight with one motion.

And finally, look at cost. Bow sights vary in cost from as little as $10 to $75 or more. Although the highest-priced sights are superb in performance, they may not be what you require. If you are content to be an occasional weekend shooter a less expensive model would probably be the better choice. If you intend to win shooting medals or will be relying on your bow to provide the bulk of your meat supply for yourself and your family, the more expensive models can easily be justified. Be realistic in your needs and your financial capabilities and you will be able to enjoy your bow sight to its fullest extent.

# Chapter 14
# WHERE TO SHOOT

## For Some The Real Challenge Is Locating A Suitable Place To Shoot Arrows

*The venerable Fred Bear pauses during a hunting trip to discuss proper bowhunting areas with other enthusiasts.*

**A**RCHERY REQUIRES distance. Not a lot of distance; as little as ten yards will provide sufficient distance to learn the basics of form and release. But eventually you will begin looking for more room, greater distances, a larger challenge. Where, then, does the novice archer go to find shooting facilities? What requirements must be met before an area becomes an acceptable "range"? How does your town go about getting a range of its own if there is not one currently available? *Where does the novice archer go to find shooting facilities?*

As a matter of fact, 1976 gold medal Olympian Luann Ryon conducts all her practice over the back part of her driveway. For safety she uses tough straw butts; she continues working on her championship form at home.

What about your own backyard? Most yards offer more

than ample room for shooting safely, provided local laws don't prohibit archery. Some cities frown on backyard shooting, and before you venture into your own yard you would be wise to check with local authorities.

Backyard shooting requires that sufficient clearance be given both behind and on either side of the target. *Your first concern must be safety.* Position your target so that it is impossible for anyone, of any age or size, to get between your arrow and the the target, or to be injured by an arrow that passes through the target. It's a good idea to set your target low to the ground, to restrict the distance the arrow might travel if it misses the target. You do not need a large target. A target butt the width of a hay bale will do nicely for most novice archers, while more experienced archers may prefer even smaller target butts.

Bowfishing is a sport that can be undertaken in almost any area where there is water and a supply of rough fish. While it may be nice to have a boat, it certainly isn't needed. Many bowfishermen use waders or shoot from shore.

The type of target butt you use will determine the exact placement of your target. If the butt allows the passage of arrows through it, as is the case of a hay bale when meeting compound-shot arrows, you must either place the target in an area that gives wide clearance behind the target butt or add a retaining wall to catch wayward arrows. An old cotton blanket often works well, as does a discarded mattress. Cotton batting will stop most arrows quickly and effectively.

To prevent arrow passage, purchase one of the many portable target butts on the market that prevents arrow passage. Two especially effective butts are the Promat and the Calmont Supertarget. Promat offers a tightly woven nylon backstop that catches field points from bows as heavy as seventy pounds without allowing penetration

Basic archery instruction can be given in almost any area that affords shooting room, backstop for safety.

*If it's hunting practice you are after, a field archery course can be set up in any wooded area or in hills to offer the type of terrain and environment that one will find afield. Targets usually are at unmarked distances.*

through the screen. The Calmont Supertarget features a cotton-packed center core that also prevents arrow passage. So effective is the Supertarget that even with half of the cotton missing the target butt can still stop arrows shot with a fifty-pound compound bow without arrow penetration through the butt.

It is *imperative* that you be able to see clearly on both sides of your target butt. Consequently, you will not want to place your target alongside or in front of brush or low bushes. Although your sidewalk or wall hedge may not be of sufficient height to prevent you from noticing a human being approaching, it may hide an approaching pet or small child.

A home that features a brick privacy wall or a solid back wall offering admission by only one clearly visible means makes an excellent backstop, although it can be rough on arrows. Lay a discarded mattress up against the wall and you will give your arrows excellent protection.

If you do not have a safe area in which to shoot in your backyard consider the possibility of shooting into your garage. You must be certain that you are not surprised by an unexpected visitor inside the garage. The addition of a

sliding lock which you can secure from inside the garage will normally provide all the security you will need. Standing outside the garage you can normally obtain a shooting distance of ten or more yards with little difficulty.

Whether you are shooting in your backyard or into your garage, be sure that the area you are shooting into is well lighted. You should be able to see anyone or anything approaching within a twenty-yard circle of the target area.

If local laws prevent it or your facilities do not meet the needs for shooting in your backyard, look instead to property near you. Often a local farmer will allow you to practice on his land, provided you get his permission *prior* to shooting, and notify him each time you intend to use his land. He'll be able to tell you what areas will be free of livestock and accessible to you. Never use another individual's land without his specific permission or you are likely to ruin the chance of you or anyone else ever using the land again. Once a landowner has decided against allowing you to use his property you will find it difficult to get him to change his mind.

When shooting on private land remember to limit your shots to those in a straight or downward direction. Never

*In field archery shooting using animal targets from a commercial source or those made by individuals can add challenge or a touch of realism to informal competition.*

shoot up, either straight up or into a tree. There is no way that you can accurately determine where an arrow will come down if shot straight up. As for arrows shot into trees or high walls, an embedded arrow high in a tree or wall makes an extremely poor impression on non-shooters, and is apt to cost you your shooting privileges.

There is an abundance of natural targets in the wild. Dead tree limbs provide a soft, yet retarding target for bowhunting practice. Be sure that the bark on your intended target has softened or you are apt to bend your aluminum shaft, or shatter fiberglass and wood shafts.

A natural target that provides the best safety is a cleared

hillside. Pick out a wild flower or an unusual clearing as your target, and allow the hill to be your backstop.

If you cannot shoot on private land you will need to look for archery clubs within your shooting or commuting area. There are state archery organizations in every state in the United States. A call or letter to one will quickly tell you what local clubs might be available to help. Private hunting preserves may also allow you to shoot, if only on paper targets. Ask them. The worst answer you can get is no.

*Requirements For An Acceptable Range.* What does an area need in order to become an acceptable archery range? First, and always foremost, it must offer safety. An archer must be assured that his arrows will not harm anyone or anything when practicing. Most public ranges position their targets so that safety is built in.

Signs should be posted notifying non-archers of the fact that this area is used for archery to prevent them from climbing over retaining walls just to see what is going on. If your range has limited space try to position your targets so that they are backed by a natural backstop such as a hillside. Keep targets out in the open where there is ample opportunity to see behind and on both sides of the targets.

You will find most public ranges post sets of rules they expect you to follow when you shoot their ranges. Some rules may vary, but you will always find regulations regarding the hours the range is open and the type of field arrowhead you are permitted to use. Frequently broadheads are forbidden. This is not an apparent attempt by the governing body to deter bowhunting. Restriction of broadheads is based on the possibility of lost arrow shafts, and the chance of an unsuspecting individual locating the lost shaft for you. Broadheads are made to induce bleeding, and will cause as much harm to a person as they do to the game for which they are intended.

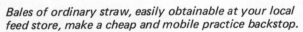

*Bales of ordinary straw, easily obtainable at your local feed store, make a cheap and mobile practice backstop.*

*Layers of corrugated cardboard, laid on top of each other in such a way that the edges form the backstop, make an excellent target butt for backyard archery practice.*

Although the center of this Supertarget has been hit so often with arrows that it is missing nearly half of its filling, it still stops arrows from 50-pound compound.

If you are participating in an NAA or NFAA club you will find the national organization dictating specific range requirements. The purpose of these requirements is to allow you to compete on a national level, although shooting at your local range. Your range meets these minimum requirements to assure that the tournaments you participate in are recognized as official tournaments should you desire to progress to the national competitions.

To shoot a nationally recognized round you must have nationally recognized targets. There is a variety of targets that may meet this requirement.

If you are not concerned with national participation almost anything will do as a target, provided it is mounted to a safe target butt. A paper plate makes an excellent bull's-eye, as does a balloon. Balloons are much more fun to

*Your own backyard is the first possibility for practice shooting after checking that it is not in violation of any law. The shooting area must be highly visible behind and on both sides of the target butt. Area also should be free of foliage that might tend to hide any animal.*

Balloons can heighten enjoyment of target practice, as they can prove an elusive target on a windy afternoon.

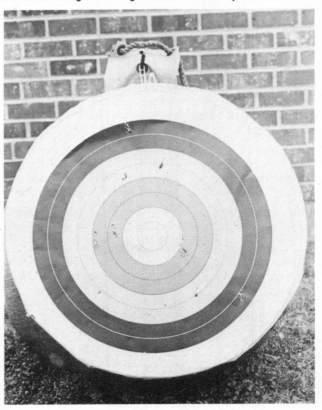

shoot at than are the paper plates, however. A deck of cards, a poster, or one of the numerous manufactured paper targets also make excellent targets.

You will find that many archery manufacturers carry a large line of paper targets, both for tournament shooting and bowhunting practice. There are targets for NAA and NFAA competition, as well as specialty and novelty targets.

Most popular among archery clubs is the ten-ring target, so named because of the five sets of colored rings that make up the face of the target. Should an individual tell you that he has just shot six-gold he means that he has just shot six arrows into the centermost ring of a ten-ring target. Scoring of ten-ring targets is based on a ten-point count, with the innermost gold ring counting highest, working out to the outside white ring with a score of one point. When shooting a ten-ring target the recognized rule is that any arrow that breaks the black line separating two rings will count for the higher score.

Shooting a field tournament or range you may see one of three popular target faces. The NFAA black hunter target features three scoring rings on a black background. Only the inside ring is white. Scoring is done on a three-point schedule, with the white ring counting highest. The design of the dual color target forces the archer to concentrate on the inside ring, tending to improve concentration.

For indoor shooting the NFAA encourages the five-ring target, similar in design to the three-ring outside target but adding two additional rings. Scoring is based on a five-point system with the inside ring again scoring highest.

*Animal targets come in various sizes and styles. Some are available in life size, others in full color. All feature scoring lines designating kill and wound areas.*

*With animal targets any hits inside the inner circle count the highest, while hits scored outside the outer circle mean a deduction of three points from the score.*

*Animal targets shown all are approved by the National Field Archery Association and have been manufactured to the organization's specifications for competition.*

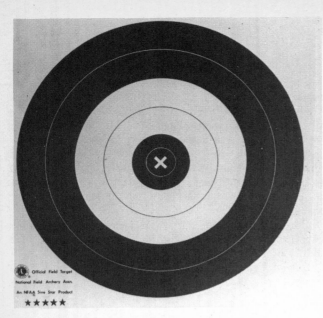

The five-ring NFAA official target face is designed to offer a focusing point heightening one's concentration.

Bowhunters find the wide variety of animal targets of particular interest, especially those that are printed to life size. The targets not only give reality to the practice but include scoring rings to emphasize fatal shots as opposed to those that might only wound the game. Scoring on an animal target is normally based on a 3, 1, minus-3 basis, with arrows striking the kill area being worth three points, while those that hit outside the outer ring deduct three points. The animal target emphasizes the need to pick a spot on the animal before releasing and penalizes poor shooting.

If shooting a "novelty shoot" you may be surprised to discover targets fashioned in the shape of cartoon characters or Western motifs. In a recent tournament intended to benefit the American Cancer Society archers shot at targets shaped like bed pans and hypodermic syringes. Like the animal targets, scoring was based on a 3, 1, -3 basis, with participation proceeds of the tournament going to the cancer-fighting foundation. You'll find archery clubs actively supporting such organizations, providing a service to the organization while providing themselves a reason for another shoot.

*Building An Archery Range In Your Town.* Although the drastic reduction in federal funds for recreation makes it unlikely that such funding will soon be available for the construction of local archery ranges, plans for such ranges can still be obtained, as can advice on funding. Through the American Archery Council local clubs throughout the United States are able to glean information on building their own ranges. The AAC currently offers three basic designs in archery ranges, with blueprints for each available by writing directly to them. The costs of constructing the

ranges are said to be less than that of lighting for a baseball field or the construction of a double tennis court. So eager is the AAC to help in constructing your own range that they will also provide a scale model of the range on loan to you while you present the construction project to your local government organization, and offer the assistance of one of their members in explaining how the range works and the actual costs of building such a range.

To aid you in funding for your range you may wish to write to the Superintendent of Documents, U.S. Government Printing Office, Washington, DC 20402. The Superintendent has copies of a digest called "Federal Outdoor Recreation Programs and Recreation-Related Environment Programs" which, although the lengthy title may tend to turn you away, is well worth the $1.35 mailing price. The digest lists over 290 federal programs that are designed to assist organizations seeking to develop outdoor recreational programs. The digest explains the purpose and function of these organizations and explains how you can obtain assistance.

*How To Put Some Fun Into Your Practice.* Although archery should routinely be enjoyable, it is not always fun, especially if you happen to be shooting poorly. Novelty targets are a means of turning an otherwise poor shooting day into a day of enjoyment. Adding movement to your targets is another diversion.

There are a number of targets that provide movement to your shooting. A balloon swaying in the wind gives movement, but can only be relied upon if the wind blows. For more consistent movement consider the swinging or catapult targets.

Moving targets give motion to your target and dramatically increase both the level of difficulty and enjoyment of shooting. An easy moving target to construct requires the use of a fulcrum and a weighted target. A tire with a target positioned inside the center hub can provide a swinging target. Make sure the helper initiating the tire movement is safely away from the target before you begin to shoot. By suspending the tire from a rope and attaching another lengthy section of rope to the side of the tire your helper can pull the tire into activity then safely back off before archers begin their shots.

To provide side movement to your target consider positioning it on a hillside using a guideline to roll the target downhill as the archers try their luck.

Or for even greater levels of difficulty try shooting at aerial targets. This requires the use of flu-flu arrows; specially fletched arrows that will fly only short distances before falling back to the ground. You may construct a simple catapult with an expansion of elastic, or find a "volunteer" to toss the target into the air for you. Empty milk cartons make excellent targets for aerial shooting and can easily be obtained from club members.

You need not spend a large sum of money to make your shooting diversified and challenging. In fact, you need not spend any money, provided you have the aid of creative friends and some scrap material on hand. Old tires can normally be picked up from tire stores at little or no cost. Targets for them can be nothing more than a piece of

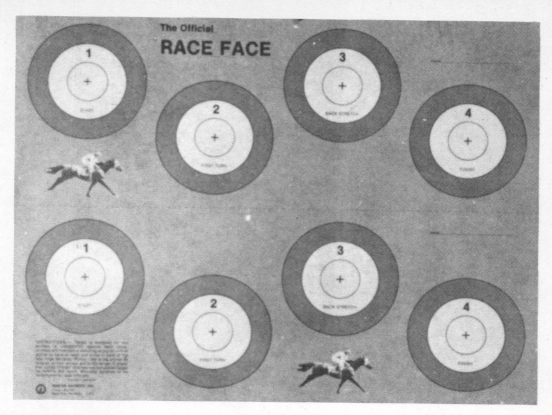

*Novelty targets come in a variety of styles to challenge novice and experienced archers alike. Games such as this race face allow to archers to pit their skills against each other while both are able to improve techniques.*

posterboard taped to the center of the tire. Milk cartons for aerial targets require only the willingness of a housewife or two to rescue them from the trash. And if you desire practice in shooting from tree stands or elevated ground, you can add height to your otherwise flat backyard shooting by doing your shooting from the top of a secure foot stool or ladder.

In planning your practice shooting insist that safety be the overriding requirement. If you are certain that you can shoot safely, both in terms of living beings and personal property, then allow your imagination to guide you in making practice sessions versatile and challenging, and put a smile into your shooting.

*Although this NFAA target has three scoring rings, the archer sees only the center ring. All-black target is meant to concentrate archer's attention on the center.*

# Chapter 15

# FINISH YOUR OWN CUSTOM RECURVE

## Takedown Recurve Kit Bow Offers An Excellent Introduction To The Recurve

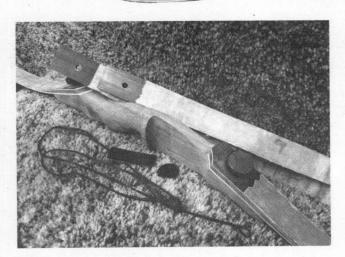

You can order a duplicate set of limbs or those of a different weight. They are rigged to fit the riser, which means you can have a backup or a target system with only one riser. Arrow rest, string are included.

Left: Bob Learn nocks an arrow to the bow that he has just completed. As always, the quality of such work is determined ultimately on how well it launches an arrow.

THE COMPOUND is in the driver's seat as far as popularity of target and hunting archers today. It has many good features, but there are many archers who still prefer the longbow and more who favor the recurve bow.

If you like to shoot the recurve bow and wish to buy a new one you might be surprised at the lack of availability. There aren't many companies making the recurve today. You can buy them from a few custom shops, but they cost as much as, if not more than, a high-priced compound. On the other hand there is at least one source of new recurves that is attractive to the recurve archer who wants a three-piece take-down for under one hundred dollars.

For a look at this style of bow, long popular with archers, we asked Bob Learn to conduct some research on the Bingham Projects takedown recurve bow. Bingham's semi-finished recurve kits are challenging, satisfying do-it-yourself, learn-as-you-go projects, sold at reasonable prices. The results, declares Learn, are highly satisfying for the archer. Here is what he reports:

Bingham Outdoor Recreation Projects, Inc., has been in the business of making semi-finished bows for more than twenty years. Based in Ogden, Utah, they produce several bows that you put the final finish on. Want to make a bow from scratch with laminated rock maple, fiberglass face and back and all the tillering and other work that goes into it? Bingham sells the kits and the instructions for you to do just that, if you have the necessary shop equipment, says Bob Learn.

They make recurve bows in the basic shape. This is a bow that is laminated; the limbs are tillered. The builder cuts out the riser section; a block of wood glued to the limbs with the pattern scribed on the riser, and you can make any shape you want. You do need a bandsaw and a variety of power sanders for this project.

The custom models are Learn's favorite bows. These are made in standard recurve patterns of various lengths and draw weights. They are tillered, the riser is shaped and all you need do is sand out the riser, sand the limbs and spray a finish on. This was more Bob Learn's speed so he ordered one of the custom models from Bingham. It should appeal to more archers interested in a do-it-yourself project, he felt.

The three-piece takedown bow listed in Bingham's catalog is called the Mt. Verde Custom Hunter. It is fifty-eight inches long and may be ordered in any limb weight for draws up to sixty-five pounds weight. If you want more draw weight than that they are available, but cost an additional five dollars.

Another advantage of the takedown system, believes Learn, is that you can order an extra set of limbs to either match the pair you ordered or one lighter or heavier, as you like. Learn ordered one riser with a set of limbs at sixty

The riser comes equipped with knurled knobs that hold the limbs to the riser. The nylon washer is meant to serve as a buffer between the knob and the bow's limbs. The entire bow can be assembled, finished in a few hours.

pounds. This makes an excellent hunting weight and one he can handle. All bows have different characteristics and one bow at sixty won't feel the same as another. The difference is all in the limb design and amount of reflex and deflex, according to Learn. For an additional fee Learn ordered the second set of limbs at a light thirty-five pounds. This lighter bow would be good for beginners. Most of Learn's bows are fifty pounds or heavier, so when someone showed an interest in shooting, he had nothing they could pull. This

also is a good lightweight bow for some types of target shooting.

Prices are subject to change, but Learn's basic riser and one set of limbs ran seventy-five dollars at the time. The extra set of lighter limbs cost thirty-five dollars, so for just a bit over a hundred dollars, you can have two bows.

Learn estimated the limb wood is probably shedua, an exotic imported hardwood. At any rate, the wood has good color and grain. What Learn liked about the riser was the grip. He likes to grip the handle of a bow till his knuckles turn white. Some bows you can do this with and others you can't. When Learn gripped this riser his first finger of the bow hand just met the thumb; just what Learn prefers in a grip shape and size.

The attaching bolt, shown with knob and washer, has been epoxied into the riser. The short pin acts as locator.

Tools for this project are simple. It can be achieved with grades of sandpaper, but a rasp makes it faster.

A preliminary check by our reporter proved that Bingham had filled the order as placed. He had one set of limbs at sixty-three pounds, good hunting weight, and one set for thirty-three pounds. Those would be finished out later for target work. There was a black dacron bowstring, a Mohair arrow rest and similar backplate for the sight window. Learn prefers to shoot from the shelf so would use these units. The builder may mount a side rest on the window if preferred. This bow could be shot just as it arrived. The riser is rough from the heavy sanding grits used at the plant but it was preshaped. The takedown system comprises a knurled nut or knob about 1½ inches in diameter, which acts as a locking system to hold the limbs on the riser when assembled. To assure proper alignment there is an alignment pin on the riser that fits a predrilled alignment hole in the limb base. You can't force the limbs out of alignment even if you wanted to.

One problem that arose was to determine which limb went on top and which went on the bottom of the riser. A quick call on the phone gave an easy reply. Bingham makes the limbs with equal tiller so it makes no difference where you put either limb. In the past some limbs were made with the lower limb a bit stiffer than the upper to allow for the two fingers under and one finger over the arrow nock point. Most archers today use a release device, so tiller is zero on this model.

The first phase to finish the bow was to strip off the tape covering the fiberglass on the face and back. This is simple and removed by one long pull. Learn offers a word of caution here. The limbs are tillered but the edges are still in the raw state. There are slivers of fiberglass that make nasty, inflamed sores if you run them into your hand. Don't run fingers down the limb edges, and don't try to brace the bow until the limbs are sanded down.

The attachment area of the riser should not be touched. Some roughness will not hurt in achieving a bond between the riser and the limbs. Sanding could create problems in match-up and the area is sealed by the final finish.

There are few tools required to finish out the bow. Learn used a wood rasp to make the limb edges smoother. Start the rasp at the limb base, rasping toward the tip of the limb. If there are any fiberglass slivers they will be cut off and not strip out. If you rasp the other way and pick up a sliver you could run out a strip of glass the length of the limb.

The limb tips have a white fiberglass overlay that enhances the looks of the bow as well as adding strength to the tips. They are sanded and square. Learn over-sanded a bit and rounded both tips.

Learn used fifty-grit sandpaper on the riser section. He liked the rough feel of the grip as it came from the plant, feeling that it aided in gripping and holding the riser. This would equate to checkering on a custom rifle stock.

One section of the riser not touched is the flat end section where the limbs are attached. This is already sanded as smooth as needed and any more work might change the way the limbs fit the base. Learn left that area entirely alone.

After working the riser section over with fifty-grit paper he moved to eighty, then to 150, and finally to 220-grit finish sandpaper. One grit of finer paper removes the sanding marks left by the former grit until you have a finely sanded and good-looking finish. You can work forever on the sanding if you are a perfectionist, says Learn, but while he wanted the bow to look good, he was anxious to get into the field with it.

*The edges of the limbs are of rough fiberglass and can be mean if you get a sliver in your hand. Take special care in rasping the edges as illustrated. According to Learn, only a light touch is needed for smooth-up work.*

*In using the rasp one should take extreme care not to alter the basic shape to any marked degree or one might weaken the riser. The purpose of the rasp is to speed up the process, not to change the style of the riser design.*

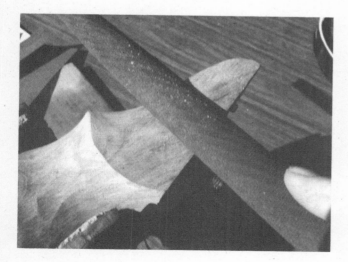

When you finish with the 220 paper on the riser, use the same paper to rough up the surface of the fiberglass on both sides of the limbs. The limbs need light sanding to remove any releasing agents from the tape or the finish might not stick. Sand lightly and wipe clean.

Bob Learn cautions that there are a few things you should be careful with during your finishing project: Don't change the sight window by cutting it in deeper. Don't cut the grip area deeper, either. It is made to withstand heavy bow weights, but if you alter these areas you might make the riser too weak. When sanding the limbs take care not to go too deep. If you rasp the edges, do it lightly. A bit too much with either and you could change the tiller of the limbs. They could possibly twist and throw a string. These

*The base of the limb must be well cleaned in the area of the laminations, sanding edge, hardwood to remove marks.*

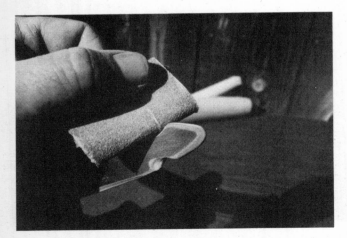

*Craftsman uses sandpaper to remove sharp edges on the string nocks at the ends of the limbs. By this means one is able to make certain they won't cut, fray string.*

are wide limbs, measuring 1¾ inches, so you would really have to be careless to do any damage to the tiller. Rasp and sand lightly to remove edges, not to alter the design.

Another point to consider is that fiberglass is itchy stuff. Use a shop apron to keep the glass sandings from your clothes. Learn prefers to sand with the object in a wood vise for the heavy work, then switch and sand with the unit in his lap wearing an old shop apron.

One other area of possible concern is the string nocks that are cut on each limb end. These have been cut to give the proper string depth and tiller. They need to be cleaned up with the 220-grit paper, Clean them, but don't sand too deep or you will end up with a seesaw battle trying to get them trued again.

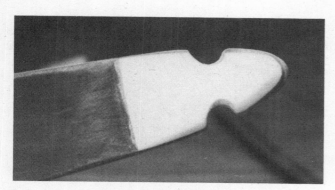

String nock with the tip overlay has been finished and the overlay sanded to bevel into the glass of the limb.

A few hours' sanding is all that is required to finish out your Bingham Mt. Verde takedown bow. The choice of finish is up to the individual. Some will want to use a two-solution epoxy finish currently on the market. Learn prefers single-phase polyurethane as it goes on fast, clean and seems to last forever. Regardless of what is used, the wood and limbs must be sealed from moisture. Lacquer or shellac will work. Behr brand polyurethane satin finish is one favorite. It is available in spray cans.

To finish, dust the riser and place the knobs on the bolts. This protects the threads from spray finish. The substance wouldn't hurt them but the knobs are a handy

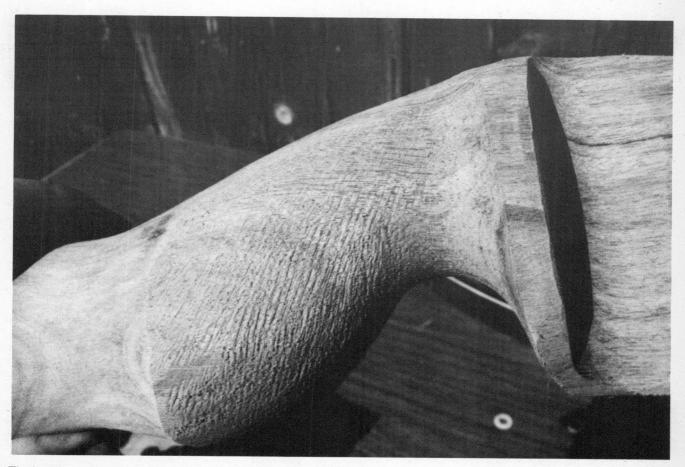

The handle section of the riser has rough production sanding grooves. Learn felt they aided gripping and only smoothed them down a bit, although they can be removed completely with the diligent application of sandpaper, elbow grease.

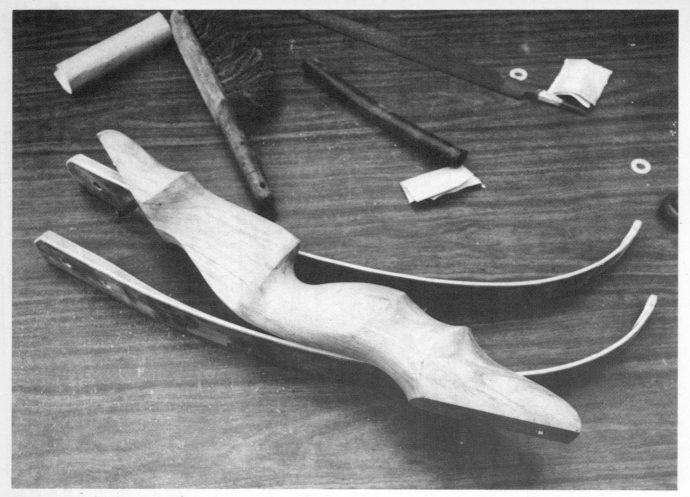

The riser and one set of limbs have been sanded and are ready for finishing. One should wipe the sanding dust from all sections of the bow. Paper towels work well for this, but take care that no paper residue is left on surface.

The finished riser is sealed with satin polyurethane, the mohair side plate, arrow rest are glued in position.

way to hold the bow while finish spraying. The holes in the limb base sections make good hanging spots, too. Learn used three clothes hangers, bent them so they would go over the rod that tightens the garage door and slipped the limbs on the hook. The riser knob was used to bend the third hanger to make a fast, nifty hanging system.

Spray carefully to avoid running the finish, cautions Learn. This project got three coats of satin polyurethane that didn't run. It looks great and the satin results in a good non-glare finish.

After the unit had spent two days curing to be certain there would be no mars in the finsih, the bow was weighed on Learn's bow scales. It trued out at sixty-three pounds at twenty-eight-inch draw.

Bob Learn next did some test shooting. The string that came with the unit was nocked with a nocking point at one-half-inch above the right angle to the rest. The rest supplied by Bingham is a mohair style that glues to the window shelf. There is a sideplate of the same material which works well for shooters like Learn.

Two shaft spines were used: the 2020 Easton aluminums and a set of 2018 XX75s. Learn used a three-finger release on the initial shots to get the feel of the bow. An arrow was nocked, the distance paced at about twenty yards and the Bingham takedown sent the arrow cleanly and with authority to the expanded styrofoam butt. Not only is the bow fast for a recurve, but it is whisper quiet. There is a bit of noise from any bow, but recurves are consistently quieter than any compounds. What little string noise that comes from the recurve can be further reduced with string silencers.

The rough section left on the grip area proved satisfying for Learn's style of shooting. The bow felt solid in the hand, and the grip may be smoothed down later if needed. One problem with gripping the handle is bow torque. Shooting with a loose bow hand should eliminate the problem of torque, but some archers prefer the white-knuckle style.

The poundage on this recurve isn't too much for lots of shooting and is heavy enough for big-boned game such as elk or bear, or for deer and other thin-skinned varmints.

The last phase is to finish out the extra set of limbs ordered. These cost $35 up to and including sixty-five pounds draw, and if you prefer heavier limbs, to seventy-five pounds, they are available by adding five dollars to the cost. If you should break or damage one limb you can replace it with additional matched limbs. In the past one limb would be stiffer, have higher tiller, but these Bingham limbs are made with zero tiller.

An extra set of limbs was placed on the riser and the knobs turned down to see how they fit. These limbs are all preset by a jig system at the plant and it makes no difference when you order your extra limbs, says Learn. His short hunter model at fifty-eight inches shoots great, feels even better in the bow hand and puts out a fast arrow.

Bingham Outdoor Projects has been making semi-finished bows for over twenty years. Learn has finished out a number of them from longbows to compounds and has been happy with each. Bingham offers a guarantee with the unit against manufacturing defects.

Archers who prefer shooting with sights might find the sight window a bit short with its four-inch length. But those who practice instinctive shooting will find this bow satisfactory.

Many archers today have never shot a recurve bow, says Learn. They buy a compound and stay with it for all phases of archery. There is nothing wrong with a compound, but you can do a lot with a recurve you can't do with a compound. Learn likes to feel the tug of the draw weight building up as he draws a recurve. He can snap shoot the recurve at any point in the draw. Snap shooting may develop some bad shooting habits but many have done it for years with no ill effects.

If you go to a flight shoot or your club has a distance shoot at the end of a tournament, you can do things with the recurve you can't with a compound. Using a full-length thirty-two-inch fletched arrow it is possible to overdraw the recurve, get more poundage, and probably outshoot the compound bows in the same weight class. You can't overdraw a compound so your competitors might never know how you outshot them. A thirty-two-inch arrow might place the draw behind the ear but it works great and really confuses many archers who don't know the capabilities of the recurve.

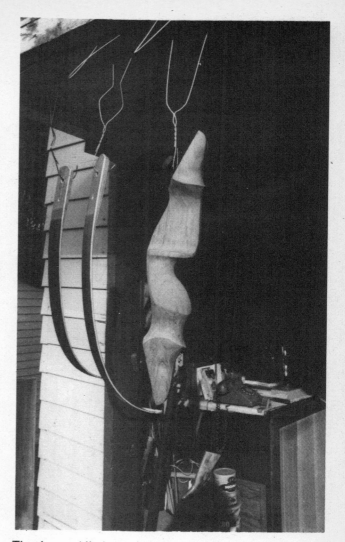

The riser and limbs are held by coat hangers while being sprayed. Pick a quiet, windless day, if possible, or you may end up with dust in the finish. Apply several coats.

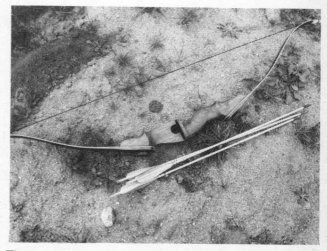

The completed Bingham take-down bow is braced and ready to shoot. It has clean lines and performed beautifully.

# Chapter 16

# IS BOWHUNTING FOR YOU?

*More Than Two Million Bowhunters Took To The Field During The 1981 Seasons — What Attracted Them May Attract You*

WHILE WE MAY never know the total number of archers there might be in the United States, we can accurately gauge the number of bowhunters, for we know that nearly 2,000,000 of them purchased bowhunting licenses in 1981, and the total is growing each year. What is it that makes bowhunting so appealing?

For the gun hunter who wishes to increase his time in the field, in some states bowhunting offers a means of doubling that time. Granted, hunting with a rifle seems a good deal easier, and the chances of success are much greater. A bowhunter can expect to take game only about twenty of every one hundred times that he hunts. The remainder of the time he is left with empty game bags, tired feet, wonderful memories, and stories of what might have been.

Of even greater appeal than the increased time in the field that archery provides, is the greater challenge of hunting with a bow and arrow. A rifle marksman can sight and down his deer from as far away as a hundred yards or more. The bowhunter must get within an average of forty yards before he will even attempt a shot. No self-respecting deer is going to stand around waiting for a hunter to close to within forty yards of him, and more often than not the bowhunter is left with the vision of a white flag bounding as the deer takes off, long before he has even had a chance to nock an arrow.

To take an animal with a bow and arrow requires the bowhunter to sneak, crawl and squirm to within forty yards or less without alerting the animal to his presence, without causing unnatural noises that would scare the animal away, and without succumbing to target panic when he finally

*There is great satisfaction in the proper placement of an arrow for a one-shot kill, as well as filling a freezer with good venison steaks.*

*Left: In bowhunting one requisite is to be certain draw weight is heavy enough to take the game being hunted.*

does get within shooting distance. It's a tough task, and many a bowhunter has returned home empty-handed and more than a little dejected.

What does it require to be a bowhunter? Persistence. It matters not whether you are male or female, aged or still in your early teens. Most states will allow you to bowhunt from the time you are twelve years of age, and in several states there is no age requirement for small game. In bowhunting the emphasis is not on how old you are, rather on how knowledgeable you are.

In order to bowhunt you must be capable of shooting a bow that can be expected to down the animal with one shot, quickly and effectively. For small game that may require the use of a bow no more than twenty-five pounds in draw weight. For big game you will want your bow to draw a minimum of forty-five pounds. Gone are the days when to shoot big game required excessively heavy draw weights of seventy, eighty or more pounds. A fifty-pound compound will send an arrow completely through a deer unless it should happen to hit a bone on the way.

In some states you will find that archers must be able to cast their arrow a specified distance before obtaining a bowhunting license. The purpose of this regulation is to assure that lightweight bows, which might only be expected to injure the animal, are not used. With the let-off capabilities of today's compound bows there is little need

*While a going-away shot may be the only alternative in some cases, it is more likely to wound than to kill game.*

*A number of experienced bowhunters favor short bows with a heavy draw, as they are easier to handle in the brush.*

*A tree stand, no matter how crude, can be a big asset in those areas where the bowhunter has checked out the game trails and is reasonably certain of game traffic.*

for such light bows. The average thirty-five-pound draw weight compound bow will cast an arrow as far as two hundred yards or more, five times the recommended forty-yard shooting distance.

In many states bowhunters are seeing the implementation of bowhunting safety certification courses. Occasionally these courses are taught specifically for bowhunters, but most of the time the course is simply included as a part of hunting safety certification, a course for both gun and bow hunters. During the course the instructor may or may not refer to bows, depending generally on whether or not he is, himself, a bowhunter. The emphasis is on safe hunting, however, and the rules of safety pertain whether the hunter is using a rifle or a bow.

While some hunters take up the bow to increase their hunting time, others will drop the rifle entirely in favor of the less assured bow. It is difficult to deny the increased challenge of stalking an animal in its home environment, in an area where he knows all the tree roots, and you are apt to trip over each of them. There's no denying that the animal definitely has the advantage in these situations.

Some gun hunters take to archery because it opens up lands that would otherwise be closed to them. The percentage of landowners who permit bowhunting on their property is far greater than is the number who allow gun

*There are areas of the country, especially near desert, where a horse can be used to get close to game, doubling as a pack animal in getting the downed deer or elk out to civilization once the telling shot has been made.*

*The die-hards of bowhunting will do almost anything to accomplish their goals, including a bit of plain-and-fancy rock climbing. This is unusual, however, as few species are found in vegetation-free wilderness area.*

*In the off-season from bowhunting, field archery ranges offer the bowhunter a chance to maintain his techniques.*

hunting. The archer must get so close to his quarry there is little likelihood that he will mistake his animal for one of the landowner's prize herefords or hogs. In fact, many of these landowners are themselves bowhunters.

Folks who are concerned about the effect that hunting has on animal population breathe much easier when confronting a bowhunter. With little more than a twenty-percent success ratio overall, the bowhunter is not apt to seriously affect the population balance of any one game animal. Conservation officers realizing this will frequently extend hunting seasons to bowhunters before and after the normal hunting season has closed.

## EQUIPMENT REQUIREMENTS

What equipment is needed for bowhunting as opposed to tournament or field shooting? The type of gear will vary little; the major difference being in the tone of that gear. Bowhunting equipment is normally muted in color, often verging on dull. Shining silver side plates and gloss-painted risers are conspicuous by their absence, replaced by dull green or black paint, perhaps painted in a camouflage pattern.

The archer himself is often dressed to resemble his bow; dull and inconspicuous. The average bowhunter about to

*If a bowhunter is especially sharp, he will plan his hunt long before opening day. One route to success with game-getting is to talk with anyone who knows the terrain and game.*

*In the hunting field, most bowhunters attempt to resemble trees with legs. Camouflaged from head to foot, they also dull their bows by using bow socks, tape or camouflage paint.*

*When things are slow in the hunting fields, excellent practice may be achieved by stump shooting or by shooting at other items at unknown distances in order to coordinate eye with bow, learn range estimation.*

take to the field greatly resembles a tree with legs, wearing camouflaged trousers and top, boots, a hat of some sort to cover his hair, often also of a camouflage material. If he is going after big game even his face and hands will be camouflaged, with makeup or cloth to hide light-reflecting skin.

Broadheads, normally forbidden in field shooting, are a must for bowhunting, and can be expected to be honed to razor sharpness. Also honed to a razor's edge is the bowhunter's shooting and hunting abilities. Prior to the opening of hunting season he will have practiced his hunting techniques long and hard. If he expects to shoot from a tree stand he will have practiced from tree stands, or from a ladder used to simulate a tree stand. He will probably have scouted his hunting area before the season ever began, plotting the route he will take, noting game signs, likely watering spots, sources of food. He will have read all the latest information he could locate on his particular game, and if he is especially sharp he will have talked with his local game conservation officer and landowner.

Working with a conservation officer provides the bowhunter with expert information about feeding habits, movement, probable herd size, etc. The bowhunter may learn where to hunt and where not to go. Up-to-date information on food sources and watering holes will also be available to him. The conservation officer also gains from this exchange of information, learning what the bowhunter has seen, and perhaps after the hunt, what techniques brought the bowhunter success. If the conservation officer wishes to know about a particular problem in the bowhunter's area he need only mention it to the bowhunter and reasonably expect the bowhunter to return from the hunt with the information he was seeking. Working together the conservation officer is able to study the population of his animals while the bowhunter enjoys his time in the field.

# Chapter 17
# CHOOSING YOUR GAME

*Different Techniques And Tougher Challenges Face The Bowhunter, But The Game Are The Same As For The Gun Hunter*

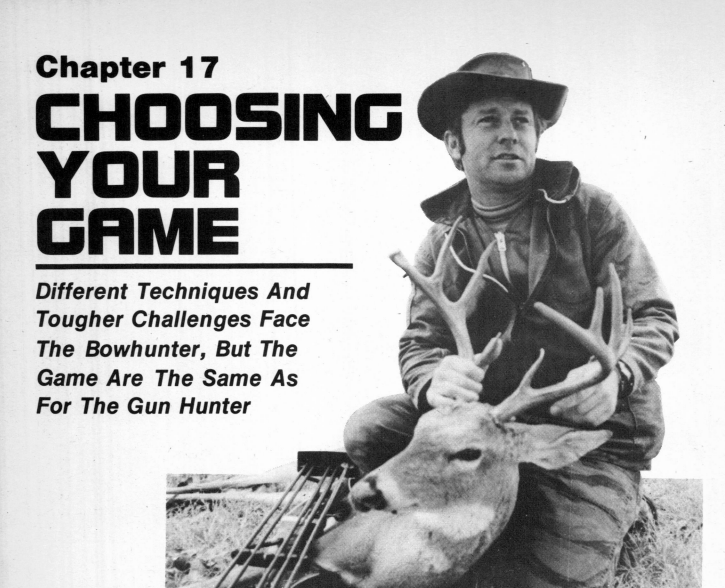

*Jim Dougherty passed up other bucks before this one came along to be taken with bow.*

WHAT GAME CAN BE hunted with a bow? Any game you can hunt with a gun, and even one additional type: fish. From small game to big game, snakes to elephants, you may take the animal with a bow, provided the bowhunting season is legal and you know how it is done. There are, of course, some game more popular with bowhunters than others. Undoubtedly the favorite target of the bowman is the deer.

## DEER

Were someone to discover that you are a bowhunter, the first question he might ask of you is "How many deer have you bagged?" To the bowhunter the deer is the game to hunt; not only because it is a reasonably attainable goal, but because properly cooked venison can provide some of the tastiest eating in existence.

Due to its abundance throughout much of the eastern United States, the whitetail deer is the most sought after. There are more than a dozen subspecies of whitetail deer in the U.S., with one or more species being found in all states except California and Nevada. Averaging 135 to 165 pounds for a mature buck, the smallest of whitetail is believed to be the Florida Keys deer at about fifty pounds, while the largest, the northern whitetail, may weigh in at more than two hundred pounds.

Normally reddish brown during the summer months, the whitetail changes to a dull, gray coloring in the wintertime. At least one part of its body never changes color, however, and that is the bright white coloring of its tail. It is the underside of the whitetail deer's tail that is colored white, however, and you are apt to see it at about the same moment you realize that you have missed the shot you were trying for. When frightened or alarmed the tail of the whitetail raises straight up, flashing the white underside as a white flag as it bounds away to safety.

Described as homebodies, whitetail deer prefer to stay within a limited area, and unless frightened or forced away will normally spend their entire lives within a mile or so radius of their birth spot. Look for this wary creature in heavy foliage, wooded areas with occasional open flatland.

Larger in size than the whitetail is the mule deer, averaging about two hundred pounds, with some bucks

*A tree stand in a good position often affords one the opportunity to get a good look at his trophy buck before launching an arrow. Through heavy brush it's harder.*

*The venerable Fred Bear looks over a trophy ram taken on one of his hunts. He waited until right shot was presented.*

easily exceeding three hundred. Like the whitetail the mule deer has its featured physical characteristic that gives it its name: oversized ears. The ears act much like radar receptors, providing the animal with an especially acute hearing capability.

The whitetail and mule deer can be compared to brothers, and as brothers are totally different in nature and habit. Whereas the whitetail deer likes to stay around the homefront, the mule deer is a wanderer. Born with itchy

feet a mule deer is apt to travel a hundred miles or more in search of better food, fairer weather conditions, or simply because he feels the need to move on.

In contrast to the heavy foliage favored by the whitetail deer, muleys prefer open terrain broken by an occasional forest. Although the nature of the animal is to roam, the geographical location of muleys is more restricted than is that of the whitetail. Mule deer can be found in an area of the United States bounded by western Canada, south to

Mexico, and from the Dakotas to the West Coast. The presence of mule deer in the eastern half of the U.S. is an extreme rarity.

The bowhunter who spooks a mule deer is not apt to see a white flag waving at him as the animal retreats, for it is the characteristic of the muley to tuck his tail when frightened, rather than raise it. Bowhunters refer to this as *low tailing*.

Although the blacktail deer is actually a subspecies of mule deer, most bowhunters consider it as a separate category of deer due to its abundance, accounting for nearly twenty percent of the total mule deer population.

The blacktail deer, like the whitetail, gets its name from the coloring of its tail, dark brown or black in color with a limited amount of white on the underside of the tail.

Blacktail deer are a favored game of California bowhunters and can be found along the Pacific coastline from British Columbia to central California. In size the blacktail averages about 150 pounds, smaller than both his whitetail and muley cousins, but large enough to offer plenty of venison for the freezer and dinner table.

For the bowhunter seeking admittance into the Pope & Young Club of trophy game hunters, the size of a deer's antlers is normally the greatest concern. The antler is used

*Judging from the thickness of this buck's neck, he may be in rut, but this certainly doesn't harm trophy value.*

*This big brown bear was taken with a take-down bow in thick woods; streams where they feed on fish are good areas in which to find a bear, although a number of states currently allow bowhunters to use baits to lure them.*

to judge the trophy qualifications of deer. All deer pass through the same development pattern in growing to their adult status. Beginning as button bucks the deer aged less than a year can be expected to show only small knobs at the base of the crown. These deer are referred to as button bucks. During their second year deer antlers begin to show some length, extending straight out in a single, horned fashion. Such a deer is called a spike buck. During their third year bucks begin to show the characteristic branching of a whitetail or muley. General herd health, food and

water quality and availability, and genetic factors all affect antler size and shape, however, and the age of a specific buck may not always be determined by counting the number of tines carried.

The antlers of a whitetail deer feature a single main beam, curving off each brow, with points growing along its length. Mule deer antlers tend to fork off into two branches, these in turn branching off to form a series of Ys along the length of the antler.

Depending on whether or not you are using an eastern or

*The pronghorn antelope of Wyoming and surrounding states is wary and speedy, but often can be lured by curiosity.*

western count, the same deer may be labeled as a four or an eight-point buck. The term "point" refers to the spiked knobs growing off the antler. To be counted the tine must measure a minimum of one inch. If you are using an eastern count you will count the number of points on each antler and add them together. If yours is a western count you will give only the total count on one side.

In terms of attrition the bowhunter rates very low in population effect on the deer, coming far below that of nature, automobiles and dogs, domestic and wild. Winter snows can produce a devastating effect on entire herds of deer, leaving countless numbers to starve to death or trapped and easy prey for other wild animals.

In hunting deer you will need to take advantage of every hunting aid available. Although deer are thought to be color blind, they have superb eyesight and will note the movement of an eyelid from many yards away. They have excellent lateral as well as forward vision. Their greatest sensory capability may be that of smell, and they are especially adept at picking up the scent of man. A number

*Shooting a variety of game birds allowed by law presents a special challenge.  Special arrowheads are made for the sport.*

of scents and lures are offered to cover up human scents, and should be considered when bowhunting deer.

Three basic styles of hunting are used in seeking out deer: the drive, ambush and still-hunt. A drive requires the use of a group of hunters, most of whom have fanned out and attempt a slow, quiet driving technique, forcing the deer toward one or more bowhunters positioned in a known area.

Ambush requires that the bowhunter set up some type of cover from which he can hide while he waits for the game to come to him. Ambush is only effective if the deer are in the area and will pass by. Preseason scouting is especially important if you are to use this type of hunting technique.

Still hunting is probably the most difficult of hunting techniques, in that it requires you move among the deer's natural terrain, holding your movement to a snail's pace, while you attempt to locate and stalk an animal. Complete camouflage from head to toe is a must. You must know a great deal about your game's natural habits to be successful. Knowledge breeds success for the bowhunter.

## OTHER BIG GAME

Although deer are the most popular of big game animals sought by bowhunters, they are hardly the only game to fill

*This bowhunter has strapped himself to trunk of tree so there will be no danger of falling during his shot.*

*Some game such as wild goats can be taken in the open as they browse. This photo was taken on Santa Catalina Island.*

This snowshoe hare photographed in upper Michigan has nothing to do with Easter and goes great in a stew pot.

a game bag. Elk, moose, caribou, antelope, sheep, goats, bear and cats are also favored targets. The bowhunter who favors big-game hunting can be expected to spend a good deal of time in preparation long before he takes to the field in search of his animal. To successfully hunt any big game animal requires that the hunter be thoroughly familiar with that animal's sensory and physical capabilities, the type of food it prefers and where that food might be found; preferred habitat. Shelves of books have been written on bowhunting big game, and should be studied prior to any hunt. The more familiar the bowhunter is with his game, how it can be expected to behave, and what methods of hunting have worked for other archers, the more likely he is

to fill his own game bag. You'll find bowhunters to be a talkative lot generally, and although they may not tell you precisely where they downed their trophy animal, they will more than likely be happy to tell you how they downed it.

## SMALL GAME

Nearly all small game may be hunted with a bow, from snakes to prairie dogs, birds to fish. Rabbits are an especially popular small game target, as are squirrels. Both, when properly prepared, offer excellent eating.

A typical list of small game suited for the bow and arrow include: rabbits, snakes, raccoon, ducks, prairie dogs, squirrels, rock chucks, groundhogs, birds and fish.

*Bowhunter at right in this photo is almost hidden in the reeds by his camouflage. He is shooting over his decoys, but one should check state and national game laws carefully to determine seasons and legalities regarding waterfowl.*

*Bohning makes arrowheads to fit almost every bowhunting need from bowfishing to big game in Black Copperhead line.*

Because of the reduced bow weight needed to bag them, small-game hunting is a good way to introduce the young archer to bowhunting. Although most small game, particularly rabbit and squirrel, abound throughout the United States, getting to within shooting distance of them may be somewhat of a task. Small-game hunting offers the veteran bowhunter the opportunity to teach the novice each of the steps in a hunt, from how to determine a good hunting area to tips on game's habitat, stalking and tracking skills, and how to care for the meat once he has downed the animal. The same stalking techniques that allow a bowhunter to approach within shooting distance of a rabbit will get him within shooting distance of a deer. But should he fail to get a shot off, the sight of a rabbit in safe retreat is much easier to accept than the sight of a trophy whitetail in the same mode.

*Bow reels for bowfishing are made by most major makers, but this model made by Ben Pearson features a mounting bracket that allows one to use any bow for this sport.*

*There are those who insist the carp is a wily creature and that it is necessary to wear camouflage if you are to creep up on his pool without sending him away in a hurry. Other bowfishermen may hunt in swimming trunks!*

## BOWFISHING

There is at least one quarry for which the bowhunter has the advantage over his gun-hunting comrades: fish. While you're not apt to see hunters using rifles on fish, you may often see them using bows and arrows. Although most states will allow you to bowfish, few will allow you to try your luck on the popular edible breeds of fish. Bowhunters generally hunt what is referred to as trash fish, those fish that only the specially seasoned fish lover might eat, and only after lengthy, specially prepared cooking.

A typical list of fish that might be considered acceptable species for bowfishing include the eel, sand shark, goblin shark, herring, red mullet, bowfin, blackfish, most types of garfish and carp. However, you will need to check your local fishing laws before taking your bowfishing rig into the waters.

What is a bowfishing rig? It is nothing more than a combination of bow, fishing rod and reel merged into one

unit. The bow is any bow you choose to use, although longbows are seldom used for bowfishing. Most archers seem to prefer the recurve bow because of the reduced cost factor in replacing it should it wind up in the ocean or river. But compounds are also popular.

The rod part of your fishing rig is a straight section of tubing, threaded to fit the stabilizer recesses on your bow, with a single eye at the end to guide the fishing line. The addition of the rod allows you to actually work the fish much as you would with conventional fishing equipment. It is not necessary that you have a rod, but it does offer the added dimension of working the fish. Without a rod you will want to attach your reel directly to the face of the bow. You may purchase special bowfishing reels, or use a conventional closed-face reel. All work well. Most reels are simply taped to the face of the bow, to allow for easy removal when the archer changes to dry-land shooting.

Line for bowfishing will be the same type and style as

Gale Brown proves that ladies can do well at bowfishing. She took this 9-pound carp with 40-pound Bear recurve and Zebco 808 reel, 72-pound line.

you might use if you were fishing with a regular rod and reel. The major differences will be in the type of hook you use, and the manner in which you "cast."

To catch a fish you must hook it. You cannot simply shoot it with a regular field arrow and expect to land your fish. Without some sort of hook apparatus at the end of the arrow shaft the fish would simply slide off and be lost to you. Fish hooks for archery are called fish points; sharp-ended, bullet-shaped points with streamlined bodies, normally of steel, with a finger or barb functioning as the hooking element. Depending on the style a fish point may have either one or two barbs. The barbs may be attached in a fixed position or may be retractable for easier withdrawal from the fish once you have landed it.

Once you hook your fish you will need to reel it in. The design of the arrow shaft makes this easier, and allows you to retrieve your arrow on those occasions when you miss your fish. Arrows for bowfishing are normally made from fiberglass, which provides them flotation capabilities. Your bowfishing arrow may or may not have fletching. If there is fletching it will be of rubber or plastic material. Due to the short shooting distance in bowfishing you will not need to concern yourself with the length of the arrow shaft. Everyone shoots the same length fish arrow, and does so with the same success as any other bowfisherman.

You do not actually cast your line in bowfishing; you shoot it, just as you might any other arrow, remembering that the fish you see in the water is not actually where it appears to be. You will need to allow for water reflection, the false image given to the fish by the bending of light rays passing through water. To hook your fish you will probably need to shoot just beneath the fish. How far below you aim will depend on how deep in the water the fish lies.

In bowfishing there are some basic safety rules to consider that will not be faced in any other type of archery. You must remember that your arrow is attached to a line. That line normally runs from the nock end of the arrow to the riser section of the bow, where the reel is mounted. Normally the line is slack, and may rest over your bow hand. Take care that your hand or fingers do not get wrapped in this line, or a release may leave you with a nasty cut.

Be sure to check your local fishing regulations regarding types of fish you may seek with your bow, and the limitations on those fish. And don't forget to try your luck on frogs. Gourmet diners know the exquisite taste of frog legs. You'll find them served in many of the finest restaurants throughout the world. You can have that same quality eating from the comfort of your own dining room. Bowfishing rigs make it easy. Many states allow bowfishing for frogs. If your state is one of them, take advantage of the opportunity. It's a lot more fun than gigging them, and the dinner you'll enjoy makes it well worth the effort.

Ken Brown took this 80-pound alligator gar taken on the Trinity River in Texas with a 50-pound Bear recurve bow.

*Stephanie Fadala uses open sights on Barnett Wildcat crossbow to hit relatively large target at close range. Crossbows require considerable familiarization and practice before the shooter becomes proficient with them.*

# Chapter 18

# THE EXOTIC CROSSBOW

## Steeped In History, The Crossbow Combines Rifle Stock And Bow Limb To Thrust A Speedy Bolt

**T**HERE WAS a time when the crossbow was considered the epitome of weaponry, capable of casting countless arrows without even tiring the shooter. But that was before the introduction of gunpowder. Today the presence of a crossbow shooter is a rare and intriguing treat.

The crossbow is a mating of gun with bow. Shot in much the same manner as you would shoot a rifle, thrust for the abbreviated arrows — called bolts — comes from the energy

of the bent bow limbs. Although effective at a far shorter distance than the rifle, it still is unique among armament. Drawn into a shooting position the riser section of the bow is held firm to the front plate of the stock, while the bowstring draws back to lock in place over the trigger mechanism. A channel running the length of the stock provides a resting place for the short arrows, measuring fourteen to eighteen inches in length. When the trigger is pulled the locking mechanism on the string drops forward, allowing the string to slide freely past it. The thrust from the string as it hastens to relax the bend on the bow limbs propels the arrow to the target.

Although archers who favored the crossbow during the Middle Ages lacked sights and a knowledge of physics to provide them the best shooting mechanism available, history tells us that their crossbows were extremely effective and known to be both accurate and deadly. Today use of the crossbow is limited largely to paper targets, although there have been modern-day military experiments. Only about half of our states allow bowhunting with a crossbow, largely because they are unsure as to how to classify the tool; whether to be guided by gun hunting seasons or bowhunting seasons. In most of these states game is limited to unprotected species, with use in hunting

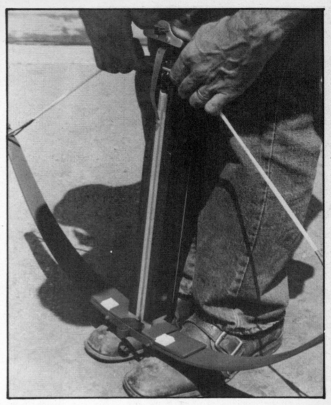

*Most crossbows are built with some sort of foot brace to hold the bow steady while drawing string into cocked position. Effort is considerable, extreme care required.*

*Carol Pelosi uses somewhat different hold on tournament crossbow. Note placement of shooter's left hand on grip.*

often limited to the "primitive weapons" season. The crossbow typically shares this season with the black-powder rifle.

Currently all but one state allow the use of a crossbow for target shooting; that one exception is West Virginia. Why the crossbow should be outlawed in West Virginia is a mystery. However, current laws of that state forbid the use or possession of any style of crossbow.

Shooting technique for a crossbow is much the same as that for the rifle, with the major difference in the procedures required to "chamber" an arrow. To load a crossbow bolt, one must draw the bowstring back to a position just behind the trigger mechanism where it will lock into place, thus holding the bow at the ready until you squeeze the trigger.

One will find that drawing a crossbow limb takes a bit of effort. The bow is designed to withstand great shooting strains and, as such, is somewhat difficult to bring to full draw. The crossbow generally is placed with the nose of the bow stock touching or pointing toward the ground. Bracing

*Front portion of Barnett crossbow is massively built nose and housing. Prod is set into housing and held in place by turning bolt. Too much force may cause damage to prod.*

Although crossbows now being sold include a safety lock for use in the field, great care must be taken to prevent an accidental release. A bolt shot from a crossbow is capable of speeds up to 190 feet per second. The crossbow is not a toy and should never be treated as one.

If interested in shooting a crossbow one should have little difficulty in purchasing one. Most larger sporting goods stores carry them. You may, however, have difficulty in finding a place to shoot. The crossbow, once the darling of English soldiers, has been given an unfair reputation, which it is forever trying to outlive. The crossbow not only is extremely accurate, it is also quiet. Consequently it makes an excellent poaching weapon and was used excessively for that purpose several years back. Many individuals began blaming the crossbow itself for the poaching, rather than the unethical hunter using the bow. Therefore, the crossbow has had to prove itself as a bona fide target and hunting tool. The climb back to popularity is extremely slow, but appears to be a steady process.

Much of the credit for renewed acceptance of the crossbow must go to the three major crossbow organizations in the United States. The National Crossbowmen, a Maryland organization, is believed to be the oldest known crossbow club in the U.S. Each year the National Crossbowmen conduct a tournament in search of that year's reigning crossbow champion. Often as not the winner is a woman.

Because of the ease of shooting a crossbow many women have taken up the sport. The women sight every bit as

the stock against his stomach muscles, the bowman then draws the bow back to lock.

Because the crossbow trigger is normally extremely sensitive to the archer's finger, one must be certain not to dislodge an arrow accidentally before ready to shoot.

Fletching for crossbow bolts, like that for full-sized arrows, consists of three fletch, with one feather or vane as the hen feather. Unlike shooting with a traditional-styled bow, the cock feather of a crossbow bolt is placed toward the bow stock, where it rests in a channel groove extending the length of the bow stock. This groove is designed to give the arrow guidance as it is released.

Positioned with the butt of the bow stuck snug against the shoulder, the crossbow is aimed like a rifle. A sight pin, if attached to the front of the stock, provides a sighting mechanism for the bow. Many commercially made models now on the market also include a rear sight to better tune the sight image.

*Dick Benedict of Chatsworth, California, demonstrates one of his own crossbows. His stocks are constructed of fine laminated hand-rubbed walnut with 140-pound-draw limbs.*

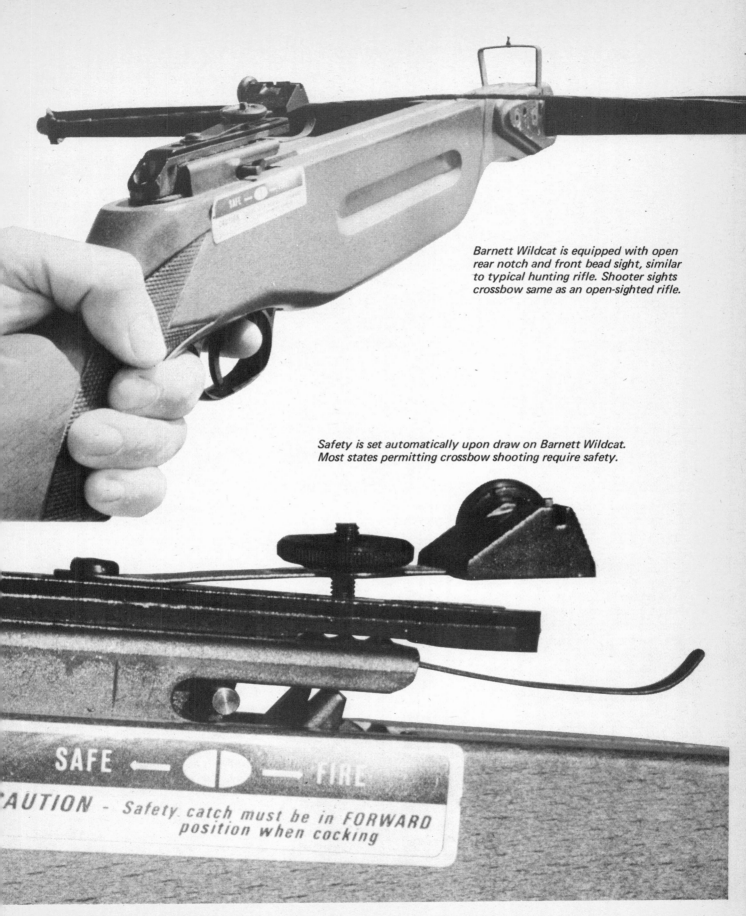

*Barnett Wildcat is equipped with open rear notch and front bead sight, similar to typical hunting rifle. Shooter sights crossbow same as an open-sighted rifle.*

*Safety is set automatically upon draw on Barnett Wildcat. Most states permitting crossbow shooting require safety.*

SAFE ← ▭ → FIRE

CAUTION - Safety catch must be in FORWARD position when cocking

Almost as complicated as a modern competition target rifle, this Benedict model features massive limbs, custom-fitted thumb-hole stock, rifle-type telescopic sight. Standards draw weight on this Silver Knight crossbow is 140 pounds.

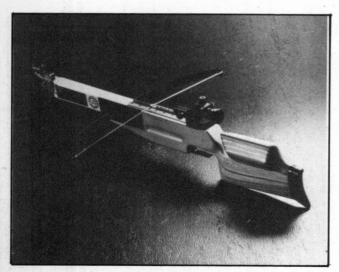

Newly introduced, produced in Germany, the Wenzeler/Feinwerkbau 10m crossbow is intended for competition work, retailing in the $1000 range. Bow is said to place its 4.5mm bolts through same hole time after time. Imported by Beeman's, much of design is credited to European crossbow champion G. Wenzeler and air-gun manufacturer Feinwerkbau.

accurately as their male counterparts and, with the aid of a cocking mechanism such as a stirrup, cocking lever or windlass, the most difficult part of crossbow use — cocking the bowstring into a ready position — is removed. There is no recoil to the bow when the arrow is released, no expensive cartridges to purchase. As in traditional-style archery, the bolts are shot over and over again, unless lost to the underbrush.

If you participate in crossbow shooting you will find yourself being encouraged to join the National Crossbowmen or one of the other two organized crossbow clubs: the American Crossbow Association and the National Crossbow Hunters Association, Incorporated. Membership in these clubs aids one in keeping abreast of changes in shooting laws and availability of new equipment. Regulations regarding the use of the crossbow change frequently and you will want to be made aware of these changes as soon as possible. To contact these crossbow groups write to them at: National Crossbowmen, 200 Laytonsville Road, Gaithersburg, MD 20760; American Crossbow Association, P.O. Box 72, Huntsville, AR 72740; and National Crossbow Hunters Association, Incorporated, 201 Citizens Bank Building, Wadsworth, OH 44281.

*Bernard Horton downed this 1150-pound cow moose in British Columbia with one of his own Safari Magnum crossbows produced in Scotland, imported by Precision Sports, Ithaca, New York. Horton shot first 15½-inch bolt from 60 paces, second pass-through bolt from 50 paces. Bow weighs four pounds two ounces with polypropylene stock.*

# With The Basic Components, Skills And Tools The Amateur Bowyer Can Build A Shootable Crossbow

*The basic homemade crossbow may be constructed from a rifle stock, trigger assembly, prod, a forward grip handle from an old recurve, aluminum strap, aluminum channel, short piece of angle aluminum, heavy bowstring.*

**T**HE CROSSBOW was justly regarded as a truly formidable military weapon in the days prior to the adoption of gunpowder. At the peak of its development the crossbow could deliver more punch than a hand-drawn bow since some of them employed systems composed of levers or a small windlass for cocking. This enabled crossbows to muster pulls well beyond the power of the strongest men. It seems probable that the crossbow was held in favor by some for a considerable interval after the early firearms came on the scene.

In modern times few would see much use or need for such magnum versions of the crossbow, but there are archery enthusiasts with an interest in getting acquainted with the crossbow for the sake of its historical aura, as well as for the specialized capabilities it offers.

Bob Learn is one of those incurable do-it-yourselfers who believe — perhaps rightly — that making something can

be at least half the fun. He addressed himself to the project of assembling his own crossbow from component parts either made or purchased from various sources. The following account and accompanying photos enable the reader to follow him through the steps to completion.

Crossbows, Learn concedes, are a weird hybrid between conventional bows and rifles, quite apt to stir distaste in rifleman or archer, alike. It's a natural assumption that one can pick up a crossbow and fire it with expert accuracy from the start. Such an assumption does not prove correct, with few if any exceptions. In actuality, accurate use of the crossbow is considerably more challenging than a conventional bow. Each step of cocking, loading and shooting the crossbow must be carried out with total uniformity; if not, results will be extremely erratic.

Many modern crossbows allow the string to ride along what might be termed the barrel of the stock. That results

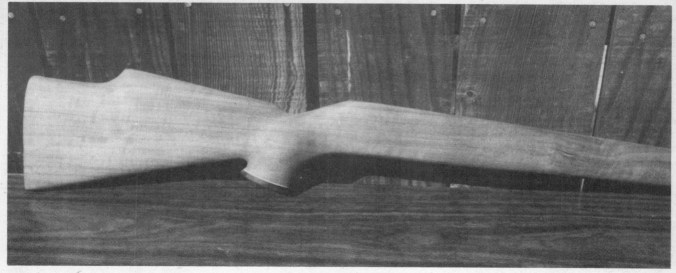

*Rollover stock comb has been removed from stock; some lightening is achieved and comb will not be needed for crossbow work. In the condition shown, stock has been thoroughly sanded with relatively rough 80-grit sandpaper.*

*Although the chosen stock shows some cracks in trigger assembly area, strength here is not as important as it would be for absorbing modern cartridge recoil.*

in friction that depletes the potential energy to a serious extent, likewise causing serious wear on the string.

There are a few minor differences in nomenclature between crossbows and conventional archery tackle that should be noted for the sake of clarity. The bowlike device at the front of a crossbow is termed a *prod*. The arrows are called *bolts*, sometimes quarrels.

Amateur crossbowyers have made use of assorted approaches in constructing the prod, including leaves from old automobile springs, suitably reshaped with a grindstone. It is apt to pose quite a challenge to convert such raw material into a really satisfactory prod, since the spring action tends to be quite a bit more powerful than most would desire.

Checking around Learn found that there are commercial sources for ready-made crossbow prods that can be much better suited. Companies that sell the Barnett system, for example, usually offer replacement parts including the prod, trigger group and front assembly sections. Bingham

Projects, Incorporated, Box 3013, Ogden, UT 84409, is one such supplier.

The trigger mechanism for a crossbow must be capable of holding the considerable force of the cocked prod, meanwhile releasing it without undue effort. Designing and making such a system from scratch offers more challenge than most builders would feel they needed. Learn concurred with that and bought an assembly from Martin's Archery Company, Route 5, Box 127, Walla Walla, WA 99362. The unit he bought incorporates a safety catch, which he viewed as important, mindful that some of the states that permit use of the crossbow for hunting decree that it have a safety on the trigger system.

The prod that Learn used was one he purchased several

*The trigger assembly is carefully measured, the stock marked to the rear and center of what would be the action area of a rifle stock, then marked for inletting.*

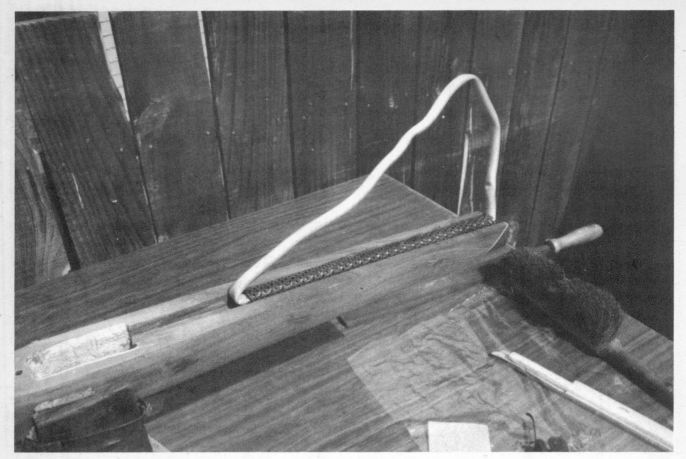

The stock needed to be channeled out in the area that would have accepted the rifle barrel. Lacking more sophisticated tools, Learn fashioned a modified wood channel rasp with an aluminum tubing handle, as shown.

After the channel had been rounded out with the modified rasp shown above, a regular flat-edged wood rasp was used to square the bottom corners. Wood removal should be done slowly and carefully, using the cut-and-try method.

years ago when an archery company went out of business. The cost was modest and he stored it away, pending the time when he'd accumulated all the other needfuls. The prod he used is made of fiberglass laminated to a core of maple in a technique similar to those used for modern recurve bows, except that the prod is much shorter and stronger in pull.

Another needed ingredient is the stock and, again, you could design and construct one. Learn felt that most of the crossbows he'd seen looked rather weird. He wanted one that would be reasonably normal in appearance, if not downright handsome. He visited Royal Arms, 1210 Bert Acosta Street, El Cajon, CA 92020, and bought one of their factory-second stocks in claro walnut. It had some cracks and blemishes that rendered it unsuitable for use on a rifle, so the cost was down about forty dollars, but the defects posed no problem for Learn's intended purposes. Moreover, it was not inletted, which was all to the good, since a stock inletted to fit the barreled action of a rifle would be quite unsuitable for use on a crossbow.

With all the basic parts procured and laid out on the work bench for contemplation, it was obvious to Learn that the completed crossbow was going to be somewhat different from conventional examples of such things. The stock had a rollover comb in the Monte Carlo pattern with respectably good grain and coloring in the wood. The prod had a gray fiberglass facing, front and back, with an unstrung length of thirty-six inches from nock to nock. It had a one-inch hole drilled through the riser section, making a keyhole center-shot bow system. That seemed desirable to Learn in terms of his envisioned design.

The trigger assembly as purchased has a sight system built in, but Learn planned to use a telescopic sight originally made for use on .22 rimfire rifles by Bushnell Optical Company of 2828 East Foothill Boulevard, Pasadena, CA 91107. That would involve some modification of the original sight system as supplied.

As the first step Learn sanded down the stock to a preliminary finish, removing the surplus amount of rollover from the off side in the process. That reduced the weight and removed the tooling marks left by Royal Arms' rough-forming operation. He used 80-grit sandpaper, moving on to finer grits after the desired form was achieved. The upper part of the forend — what would become the barrel of the finished crossbow — was left flat, but was trued up and sanded smooth. There was a rosewood forend tip and pistol grip cap, and he left those as they were, at least for the starting phases.

With the stock more or less formed and sanded to his conditional satisfaction, Learn turned attention to installing and fitting the trigger group. At first it appeared the trigger would be too long, but he was able to work that out to his satisfaction. He located the trigger assembly at the back of the stock, but slightly farther forward than it would have been on a rifle. The reason was to afford a flat surface for the screw that holds the back of the trigger unit. Locating it slightly forward provided the needed flat surface and saved a lot of sanding at the same time.

Learn marked out the length and width of the relief opening for the trigger group and installed a router bit in the chuck of his drill press for the actual wood removal. He found that approach both simple and effective. Lacking such equipment the same chore could be performed with a wood chisel, perhaps with starting holes made by use of an electric hand drill or brace and bit.

It's possible to rough out the inletting for the trigger, leaving the final fitting until a later stage. The important thing to keep in mind is that it's always easier to remove wood than to replace it. Should a bit too much be removed, however, it can be replaced by plastic steel during the final fitting.

A hole was drilled down through the stock so that the trigger could project from the lower surface of the stock at that point. The hole should be drilled with care, so that the trigger will be centered properly. The upper portion of the trigger group well must be inletted so that the

*With inletting complete, the trigger assembly and the Delrin track are protected by plastic kitchen wrap and placed in the stock. The plastic wrap acts as a release agent for the plastic steel with which the parts are to be coated, forming a perfect fit. Plastic steel was liberally applied with trigger in place, allowed to cure.*

Base of the prod attachment device may be formed by first cutting and grinding out a keyhole that will match the prod. An aluminum strap is then cut and fitted to span over the riser of the prod, as illustrated above.

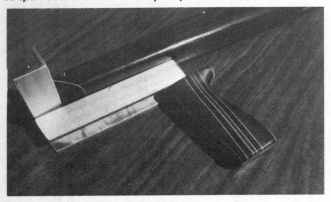

Ready for mounting are the aluminum base channel below the stock, right angle at its position, and forward grip which will be assembled at the rear of the channel.

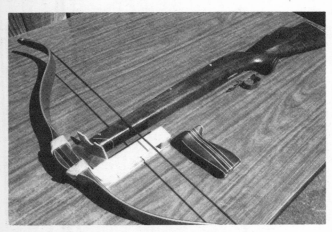

All components of the homemade crossbow are set in correct positions, ready for final assembly, above.

string-holding components are at the desired level when the trigger group is secured in place. Learn moved forward on that operation slowly, utilizing the cut-and-try approach, removing a bit of wood here, another bit there, until the trigger group fitted snugly and in its proper location.

With the basic stock inletting completed Learn covered the trigger group with thin kitchen plastic, of the general type represented by Saran Wrap, to serve as a release agent. He then applied a liberal amount of plastic steel to the inletted opening, positioned the protected trigger assembly carefully, removed the surplus plastic steel, and set the assembly aside to cure up.

That done he addressed the problem of the bowstring. There was no clue as to the draw weight of the prod, so that had to be determined. He took the shortest string he had, put it over the nocks and installed it on his bowscale system. That incorporates a system of pulleys for weighing bows and it worked quite well for checking the weight of the prod, since it is nothing but an uncommonly short bow.

From the point of initial tension on the too-long string Learn pulled the prod into the scales for a distance equal to a draw of fourteen inches on the stock. At that point the draw weight was indicated as eighty pounds. This is rather heavy by standards of conventional bow, but somewhat light in terms of typical crossbows. The state of Wyoming, as Learn recalls, allows the use of crossbows for hunting, but specifies a minimum draw weight of ninety pounds. Crossbow prods with a draw weight of 130 pounds or more are by no means uncommon.

As noted the unstrung length of the prod was thirty-six inches. Utilizing standard string-laying techniques Learn made up two strings of twenty strands apiece at a length of thirty-three inches.

The prod has a set of false nocks, as well as the working set; that is, two nocks at each end. The false nocks are the inner ones, intended for use in bracing the bow. Typical bracing procedure is to install a string long enough to span the distance between the false nocks, after which the bow is drawn rearward on the tackle system of the bowscale, or perhaps by cocking it after installation on the crossbow, itself. That gets the primary nocks sufficiently close together so that the regular bowstring can be worked between the loops at the ends of the first string to be slipped over their outer nocks. At that point the tension of the bracing string is eased off, guiding the regular string into its nocks as may be necessary.

Since the prod seemed safe at a fourteen-inch draw Learn marked the barrel of the stock measuring fourteen inches ahead of the claws of the trigger unit, the point at which the string would be held in fully drawn and cocked mode. Once the stock was marked at that point the excess wood ahead of it was cut off and trued up squarely.

Since it was a standard rifle stock the forend tapered upward toward the front. The top of the forend was flat, but the lower surface was not; a factor that must be taken into account when cutting it off at the front.

By this time the plastic steel had cured around the trigger assembly, so that was removed for purposes of inletting the channel down the upper surface of the barrel. It was necessary to inlet the barrel to accommodate the Delrin track on which the bolt would ride. Delrin is a remarkably hard synthetic material, similar to Teflon but somewhat harder. It offered a low coefficient of friction, along with good potential for resisting long-term wear. A piece was purchased in a plastic shop a bit over fourteen inches long, one inch wide and one-quarter-inch thick. This was split down the center to obtain a piece one-half by one-quarter-inch in cross-section that would make up the rail. It remained to inlet that into the barrel.

Those who customarily work at bedding rifle actions may have appropriate inletting tools for such chores, but Learn lacked such facilities. An alternative possibility might have been a router, but that was not available, etiher. By the time a jig could have been made up to enable routing the channel with a router bit in the drill press, Learn felt the job could be performed by hand, so he chose that approach.

A quick trip to a nearby hardware store produced one of the wood rasps called a Surform. One proved to be available in one-half-inch diameter, round in cross-section, so Learn bought the rasp without handle. He improvised a handle to suit his needs, bending it from aluminum tubing, as illustrated in the accompanying photo.

He scribed a line down the center of the barrel, with two more lines equidistant on either side to mark the boundaries for the inletting, and proceeded to rasp out the channel. The Surform rasp removed the wood quite quickly, proving reasonably easy to control within the scribed lines. Since the bottom of the channel was semicircular in cross-section, he used a flat wood rasp to square the bottom of the channel to fit the length of Delrin. The inletting was stopped at a point where just a small amount of the Delrin still protruded above the surface of the channel, so that it could be sanded down flush, or left for a slightly high center.

With the trigger group fastened in place, the barrel or upper forward surface of the stock was completed by drilling guide holes and using wood screws to hold the length of Delrin securely in the channel. Learn found that it was impossible to glue the Delrin, nor would any other adhesive material — including two-solution epoxy — achieve a useful grip on the stuff. The top of the channel between the wood and the Delrin was smoothed with sandpaper and a thin layer of plastic steel was used to fill in the gaps. After curing that was worked down to leave a friction-free but durable surface.

Further sanding of the stock with progressively finer-grit papers left its surface in good condition for the final finish, which consisted of several coats of Tru-Oil stock finish,

*Before mounting under stock, trigger guard was sprayed with flat black enamel to reduce glare and reflection.*

*Bushnell four-power .22 telescopic sight is mounted atop trigger unit. Visible screw head just forward of scope mount helps hold Delrin track in place.*

each hand-rubbed and allowed to dry before the next coat. Other finishes might work equally well, but Learn felt pleased with the results thus obtained.

One item lacking in the trigger group as received and installed was a trigger guard. Although a crossbow delivers little or no detectable recoil, Learn felt it best to provide a butt plate to protect the wood of the stock at that point; more a matter of appearance than function. A trip to a nearby gun shop turned up a hard rubber butt plate with a white line spacer, along with a rusty old trigger guard from some unidentifiable make and model of black powder rifle.

The trigger guard was cleaned up and sprayed with flat black paint before being installed. It and the butt plate were put in place while the final coat of finish was curing on the stock.

With the stock essentially completed it remained to secure the prod to the front of the project. A section of one-inch aluminum channel was used as the base unit, being attached to the stock with a pair of heavy-duty wood screws through the metal and into the wood. The channel extended above the level of the bolt rail to the dimension of the riser section of the prod.

To attach the prod to the stock Learn took a piece of 1½-inch aluminum angle, four inches in length. That was centered on the prod and the keyhole area was ground even with the base of the riser hole. The fletch of the bolt must pass down the channel and out the end or it will flip the bolt in almost any random direction. A clean path for the bolt and fletch is mandatory.

*An old black-powder rifle donated its rusted and pitted trigger guard to the project. New mounting screw holes have yet to be drilled in hammer-wrought metal guard.*

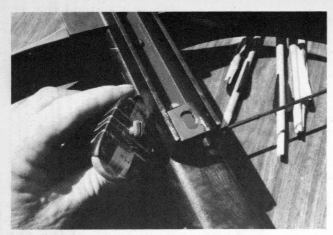

*Attaching forward handle is simple. Builder Learn first slotted the aluminum prod mount as shown, then turned a large-head screw into handle. Sides of screw are ground flat to approximately match prod mount slot. To install handle, match screw to slot, twist half turn.*

*Metal parts were given three spray coats of flat black enamel before final assembly. Forward handle acts as support and rest for prone or bench crossbow shooting.*

*Royal Arms stock was equipped with white line spacers at butt plate, at grip cap and rosewood forend section.*

The piece of aluminum angle was bolted to the section of aluminum channel that was attached to the stock. When the prod was placed on the angle it fit with just a slight amount of down-pressure on the channel with the bowstring. In subsequent fine-tuning the pressure of the string against the Delrin rail was relieved to provide a straightline path for the string, with minimal friction against the rail.

Two holes were predrilled into the riser of the prod and used to attach the prod to the aluminum angle with aluminum strap. Strap or band iron could be used, but at the expense of increasing the weight. Holes were drilled through the vertical metal arms and the prod was held to the stock with two bolts passing through the riser and metal before being tightened. A pilot hole was drilled to accommodate a sheet-metal screw going through the metal base and into the riser. The prod is thus secured at its midsection by the arms, along with the screw at its base.

To adjust the height of the string on the barrel of the stock, Learn shimmed the prod for the base with some brass shim stock until the string barely skimmed along the Delrin rail. Final adjustments were made and the securing hardware was torqued to its final tension.

There is a potential hazard in shooting a crossbow built on this type of stock. The forend is both narrow and shallow in comparison to typical crossbow designs. Thus it would be a strong possibility that unwary fingertips could edge upward to get in the path of that sizzling bowstring. That could provide a memorable, if not traumatic, lesson.

By way of preventing such mishaps Learn chose to provide a foregrip that would project downward from the forend, rather in a manner reminiscent of the legendary Thompson submachine gun. Foraging in his scrap pile he turned up an old bow that had delaminated to an essentially useless status. The riser remained intact so he cut the shaped handle grip from the limbs, intending this to serve as the foregrip. It was sanded, sprayed and attached to the back of the aluminum channel by means of a simple approach.

A pilot hole was drilled down into the top of the foregrip section of a diameter equal to the minor diameter of the sheet metal screw that was selected to secure the foregrip. The head of the screw was ground to provide a pair of parallel flats, resulting in a screw with a narrow, two-sided head. The metal channel at the back of the forward mounting system was drilled and filed until the hole in the metal matched the screw head.

To fasten the foregrip to the stock the screw is put in its slotted hole in the base, whereupon the lower tip of the screw is started into the hole drilled in the top of the foregrip and the foregrip is turned upward into snug contact with the metal. Learn found that this worked extremely well and with the forward hand thus positioned there was zero risk of getting a fingertip zapped by the bowstring.

That terminated the construction phase, leaving the tuning and testing to be done, not necessarily in that order. Along with the other operations he had made up a few bolts, sixteen inches in length, some with feather fletches, others carrying plastic vanes, with the intent of finding which worked the best. They were made by cutting a full-length fiberglass arrow shaft in half, adding the nock at one end and capping the other end with a fired empty case from a caliber .30 GI carbine cartridge. It is a burden of the crossbowman that bolts are recovered rarely, if ever, and usually in a poor state of repair even then. Nevertheless they must be as uniform as possible if there is to be any pretense of accuracy.

The Bushnell .22 scope of four-power magnification was attached to the dovetail grooves that remained on the top

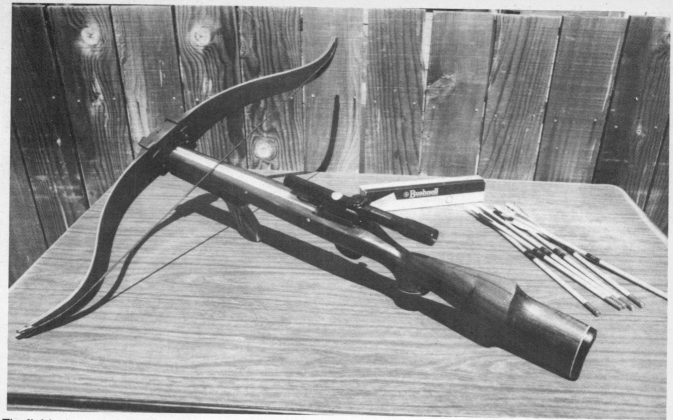

The finished crossbow ready for testing. With the most accurate bolt as a guide, the scope sight is adjusted for point-of-impact shooting. The prod string just touches top of white Delrin track inletted into stock.

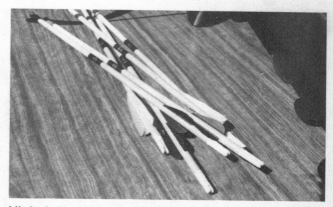

All the bolts assembled for the project were tipped with .30 caliber Carbine empty brass shells. Some were fletched with three-inch feathers, others with short plastic vanes.

of the trigger group after removal of the open iron sights provided. There was absolutely no way to boresight the installation, short of trial and error. Zeroing would have to be accomplished via the scope adjustments, on a basis of directing the scope reticle toward the observed point of impact.

The cocking operation is performed by placing the front of the crossbow on the ground and pulling upward on the string with both hands until it is engaged and held by the claws or dogs on the trigger assembly. The bow is then at full draw and will remain so until the trigger is pulled to shoot it or release the string for uncocking. The latter operation, it should be noted, fairly well requires availability of at least three hands and some amount of cautious skill. Naturally it would be quite damaging to the crossbow to shoot it without a bolt in place, so that should be avoided.

A cardboard box was placed against a bank to provide a generous area of safe backstop. Learn stepped off fifty paces, cocked the prod, placed the bolt beneath its leafspring hold-down clip, brought the crossbow up to aiming position, put off the safety and a surprisingly light pressure on the trigger sent the bolt briskly downrange. It missed the box, but not by a great distance, perhaps by six inches from a dead-center hold.

Employing a judicious amount of Kentucky windage for the second bolt sent it sizzling into the box. Five out of six test shots hit the box, which Learn judged was close to the size of a coyote's vital area.

The first test session left a few minor improvements to be done, such as sanding down the Delrin bolt rail to lower the bolt by a fine fraction of an inch. The scope needed to be brought into perfect alignment with the rest of the system, but Learn regarded those as minor chores and part of the fun of the project.

# Chapter 19

*Bowhunters' silhouette courses may be set up in limited spaces, such as athletic fields, park lands. Silhouettes take less room than most field archery tournaments, provide spectator interest.*

# BOWHUNTERS SILHOUETTES

## *Following The Lead Of Rifle And Handgun Shooters, A New Aspect Of The Sport Is Born*

THE SPORT OF ARCHERY has long cast about for an aspect that would capture the imagination and support of spectators and participants alike. To the uninitiated, watching a long target archery tournament may seem a boring activity. Even the more exciting outdoor bowhunter target shoots are not designed for the spectator, although participants are sure to enjoy the matches. Archery golf and other variations have been tried, but have not caught on as popular sports.

Early in the decade of the Eighties, a new aspect of the sport emerged in the West; Bowhunters Silhouettes International. The sport is the brainchild of David Myers and Harvey Naslund, two Californians with extensive outdoor and archery experience. If the initial interest shown by archers is an indication, the sport is sure to grow in popularity and significance. Bowhunters silhouette shooting may have the same impact on archery as has rifle and pistol silhouette shooting on firearms competition.

The silhouette targets are patterned after the rifle and pistol silhouette game, but constructed of special foam.

With the round completed, competitors retrieve their own arrows from targets, above.

Rifle and pistol silhouette shooting has grown to hundreds of meets per year with thousands of participants and industry support in a relatively few years. Why has the sport gained so much, so fast? Most agree that it is because of the action involved; when a shot is fired and the target hit, something happens that all can see. The target falls down!

Bowhunter's silhouettes are an adaptation of this fast-growing shooting sport. Bowhunters Silhouettes International (BSI) is an organization specifically for bowhunters, formed to provide competition and fellowship among bowhunters by utilizing and developing the skills and equipment used in bowhunting.

The possibilities to be found in silhouette shooting are endless. The benefits of silhouette shooting are much the same for the archer as for the firearms buff; i.e., the targets and distances are representative of actual hunting conditions; the targets respond immediately to a solid hit by falling over; and spectators as well as shooters can share in the excitement of the sport.

In the rifle and pistol sports, four basic silhouettes are

At right, still-standing targets attest to the skill required to score well at this new archery sport.

*Women and men compete equally at bowhunter silhouettes. Foam animal targets must be knocked over to count on score.*

employed: chicken, pig (javelina), turkey and ram. The targets are made of steel; grade and thickness depends on the type and caliber of ammunition used. For bowhunters, Myers and Naslund have developed special arrow-receptive ethafoam silhouettes built to international standards of shape and dimension.

Why not different silhouettes for the bowhunter? The silhouette shapes are based upon international acceptance and standardization of the existing four silhouettes of chicken, pig, turkey and ram. For the bowhunting sport to grow and hold an international position, Naslund and Myers believe there must be crossover from the rifle and pistol sports. A bowhunter walking into a gun store wearing a lapel pin of a ram is immediately recognized as a silhouette shooter by those engaged in the rifle and pistol sports.

The scoring is simple. In a National Rifle Association-sanctioned rifle match, for example, forty rounds are fired at forty silhouettes for score. One point is scored by the shooter for each animal down. Pistol matches, sponsored by the International Handgun Metallic Silhouette Association (IHMSA), are scored similarly.

For the bowhunter, twelve targets are set up, three chickens, three pigs, three turkeys, and three rams. A

*Central California county fairground was site of this early BSI match.*

bowhunter steps to the shooting line with twelve arrows and shoots an arrow at each silhouette. After twelve shots he has finished a round and his score is recorded. In a normal match, the archer will shoot three rounds for a total of thirty-six silhouettes and a possible perfect score of thirty-six.

The next consideration was to develop the type of competition that would serve to develop and improve the skills of the bowhunter. Furthermore, the program must be designed around the equipment used by the bowhunter in his hunting pursuits.

It has long been apparent that the bowhunter quickly grows weary of shooting paper targets set at predetermined distances.

Additionally, the equipment used by the most successful target archers to shoot paper targets is generally not suited to the bowhunting sports and does little to improve a bowhunter's skills beyond a basic level.

Every sport needs a set of rules allowing the competitors to compare themselves with one another. In early 1982, BSI published its first rule book. The book is comprehensive and simply written, aimed at the uninitiated bowhunter or archery club member who has had no experience with the sport to conduct or participate in a silhouette meet. With the permission of Bowhunters Silhouettes International, portions of the handbook are included here:

''To represent the bowhunter's needs, BSI has incorporated numerous features in its silhouette program to represent field conditions. This approach allows maximum

*As the silhouette shooters step to the line, each has a scorekeeper standing behind to record targets hit or missed.*

*One of the early promoters of bowhunter silhouettes is Harvey Naslund. His experience with handgun and rifle steel silhouette shooting prompted interest in new sport.*

utilization of bowhunting equipment and serves to improve the skills of the bowhunter. These field conditions include: a mixing of known and unknown distances, repositioning between shots, shooting time limits, life size silhouettes, familiar animal shapes, and the use of hunting bows and arrows equipped with field points.

"When a BSI bowhunter steps to the line he faces twelve silhouettes (three of each series, chicken, pig, turkey, and ram) set at distances ranging from approximately twenty meters to seventy meters. Only four of the silhouettes are at known and marked yardages. Number 1 Chicken (twenty-five meters), Number 1 Pig (thirty-five meters), Number 1 Turkey (fifty meters), and Number 1 Ram (sixty-five meters). The rest of each series are placed at the discretion of the match director just prior to the match. Once the silhouettes are placed for a match, practice rounds are prohibited.

"The bowhunter is allowed two minutes to shoot twelve arrows. Additionally, he must move laterally to the right or left between each shot, as outlined in the BSI Official Rules. The time limitations, unmarked yardage silhouettes and requirement for the bowhunter to move between each shot all contribute to simulate the field conditions of a BSI format."

Those who are accustomed to equipment restrictions or

*A typical hillside silhouette target range with white lines marking shooters' lanes. Only one of each target is at a known distance, according to BSI rules. The remaining eight, two of each series, are placed at unknown ranges.*

classifications based upon equipment used will find such regulations unnecessary in BSI competition.

"Whether you choose to compete or just to observe a BSI bowhunter silhouette match, you will have to agree that finally the bowhunter has a competitive sport all his own. To successfully play the game, he must learn to move, think, and shoot in a matter of seconds. And when he knocks the animal flat — those watching will immediately recognize and share in the elation of a bowhunter getting his animal.

"Certainly the average bowhunter/archery club will not be prepared to put as much promotion behind their club matches as is required to promote a regional BSI match. Neither should the club be expected to spend as much money on trophies, or award expensive equipment as prizes.

"The idea of shooting silhouettes is to afford the members an opportunity to compete against each other, while at the same time enjoying individual awards and recognition (pins) and sharpening their skills for the next hunting trip."

BSI suggests the clubs host their matches in conjunction

*Nearest silhouette target, the chicken, is placed at 20 meters, the farthest, the ram, is placed at a distant 65 meters. The bowhunter must learn to move, think, and shoot in a matter of seconds.*

*Association's rules provide for use of any hunting bow in competition, as witness this more traditional archer. Time limit for round — two minutes — may favor the longbow or recurve shooter. Competitors move with each arrow.*

with other shoots to gain maximum exposure, participation and attract new members to their organizations.

"Your club range is not the only place that a BSI match may be conducted. Limited facilities, inclement weather, type of terrain and other considerations may cause you to find a temporary (or permanent) alternative in selecting a match site.

"In every county in the United States there are fairgrounds to be found. Most of these have facilities that are ideally suited to the hosting of silhouette matches with large outdoor arenas and spectator seating. Most are adjacent to the metropolitan areas, and served by well traveled thoroughfares. Little League baseball fields, football fields and civic parks also offer alternatives to the club range. When one considers that the silhouettes are easily transported and the entire range sets up in a short period of time, the match site possibilities are almost endless."

Space requirements for your own silhouette range are minimal. You need an area about eighty yards long and wide enough to accommodate four lanes or more, each five yards wide. Thus a typical four-lane bowhunters' silhouette club range would measure approximately eighty by twenty yards.

There are a few considerations that should be kept in mind when planning your range. The first is the direction of the prevailing winds. Wind is the nemesis of all outdoor silhouette sports, big bore rifle included. It is virtually impossible to create a silhouette that will stand up under a strong gust of wind, yet fall when hit by an arrow or bullet. With this in mind, plan your range so that the prevailing winds come in at a ninety-degree angle to your silhouettes. This will eliminate most of the problems. Be aware, however, that occasionally you will be plagued by unfavorable breezes that will cause delays, alibi rounds, and in some cases, even a cancellation of the match.

The type of terrain is quite important. Gravel, cobblestone surface, or even scattered boulders can cause

*Before shooting begins match director checks out targets to see that each is properly set up for the upcoming round.*

*Participants must remain within their assigned lane while shooting, and must shoot only their own twelve targets.*

severe damage to arrow shafts. A grassy turf is desirable. The grass should be cropped as short as possible, as arrows have a way of losing themselves in the high grass.

The range does not have to be on level ground. In fact, a gentle upward slope is ideal, as the shooter and spectator alike can get a clear view of each silhouette when the lanes run up the slope.

Little equipment is needed in laying out a BSI range. A few pointed stakes, a one-hundred-foot tape measure, string and a chalk cart. The use of the chalk cart helps identify the boundaries of each lane and serves to enhance the appearance of your silhouette range.

Some points to remember: Make sure that ample room and allowance is made for spectators behind the shooting line, to allow them a clear view of the match and falling targets. At the same time insure that the match officials and necessary tables, scoreboards, public address system and speaker's stand are positioned at the rear, right corner of the range, permitting the director to look across each lane.

"Once your range has been laid out to proper specification, you can now put the finishing touches to it. Remove scattered boulders, mow the tall grass, and weeds, and put in known yardage stakes. On the left side of each lane you should drive four stakes at the following distances: twenty-five meters, thirty-five meters, fifty meters, sixty-five meters. These stakes will provide permanent reference points in placing the Number One animal of each series.

"Once these tasks have been completed, you are ready to host an official BSI match. It won't be long before the revenue generated from official practice rounds and official BSI matches will be enough to build a classy looking scoreboard and a permanent set of bleachers for spectators.

"The placement of the silhouettes in each lane just prior to the official match can be almost as much fun as shooting at them. Other than the four standardized distances; (twenty-five, thirty-five, fifty and sixty-five meters for chicken, pig, turkey and ram) you can place the silhouettes anywhere you want as long as they are within the boundaries of the assigned lane and one series does not overlap another. If your most distant chicken placement is thirty-two meters, you must not place a pig any closer to

Typical close-cropped grass of an athletic field makes locating missed arrows easier; not all hit the target!

Competitors shoot each of three rounds on a different lane, under a different scorekeeper; targets are reset for each round.

the line that slightly more than thirty-three meters. Obviously you would not set one animal directly behind the other. Each lane is set up a little differently than any other. This keeps the shooters on their toes, and requires them to adjust their thinking and techniques when required to change lanes."

BSI has established a classifications system that will enable affiliated clubs to host matches in which the novice shooter will be able to compete on a level with his peers and be given the opportunity to share in the awards structure with the more proficient and experienced bowhunter.

"Classifications are based upon scores achieved in a three round match (thirty-six possible) as follows:

B Class:          0 to 10 points
A Class:          11 to 17 points.
AA Class:         18 to 23 points.
AAA Class:        24 to 30 points.
International Class: 31 to 36 points.

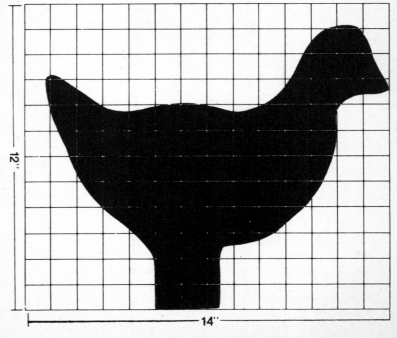

**BSI**
**BOWHUNTERS**
**SILHOUETTES**
**INTERNATIONAL** ™
POST OFFICE BOX 6470
ORANGE, CALIFORNIA 92667

27"

33"

**RAM: 65meters~70.85yards**

**CHICKEN: 25meters~27.25yards**

12"

14"

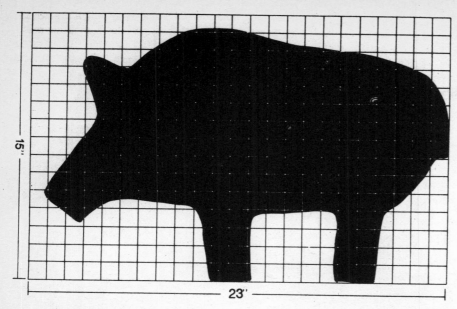

**PIG: 35meters (38.15yards)**

**TURKEY: 50meter (54.5yards)**

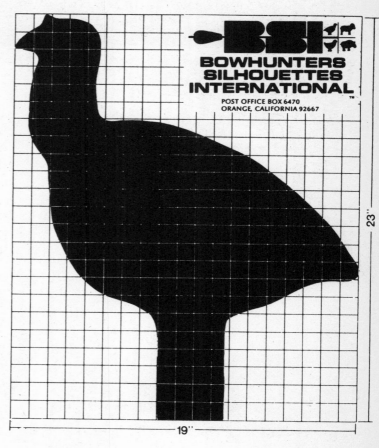

**BSI**

**BOWHUNTERS SILHOUETTES INTERNATIONAL** ™

POST OFFICE BOX 6470
ORANGE, CALIFORNIA 92667

"To establish class: Average two previous match scores achieved in official BSI practice rounds and/or official BSI match. Exception: To achieve International class, the bowhunter must achieve International scores in three consecutive official BSI practice rounds and/or official BSI matches.

"To move from any higher to lower class, the bowhunter must shoot scores reflecting a lower class in three consecutive matches."

Those interested in learning more about this new sport or who may wish to become members of the BSI, may contact Bowhunters Silhouettes International, P.O. Box 6470, Orange, California 92667. Membership includes a subscription to the club's publication.

*Shooters are permitted use of either a stabilizer or a bow-mounted quiver for stabilization, but not both.*

## OFFICIAL RULES
### Bowhunters Silhouettes International
### SILHOUETTE PROGRAM

1. SPORTSMANSHIP — All contestants will adhere to the basic rules of sportsmanship while competing in the contest. The use of belligerent or vulgar language will not be tolerated at any time. Excessive drinking or the actions as a result of drinking will result in disqualification.

2. ENTRIES — Contestants may only enter the Bowhunter Silhouette matches on a team basis. Each team member agrees to serve as scorekeeper/target setter for a time equal to that spent in competition.

3. EQUIPMENT REQUIREMENTS — The bowhunter may use any style or type of equipment generally suited to the bowhunting sports; however, field points must be used on all arrows. Crossbows are strictly prohibited. A shooter may not approach the line with more than one dozen (12) arrows in his/her possession, with the exception of those arrows used in lieu of a stabilizer in the bow quiver.

4. EQUIPMENT INSPECTION — The match director may at any time ask a competitor to submit his equipment to the match committee for inspection. Failure to comply will result in automatic disqualification.

5. PLACING OF TARGETS — Silhouettes will be placed at the discretion of the match director with the exception of the standardized distance placements; No. 1 chicken: twenty-five meters (27.5 yards); No. 1 pig:

*An uphill range makes silhouette targets easier to see, but not easier to hit. Shooter must judge unknown range.*

*Opposite page: Competitors may use any equipment normal for hunting but are permitted no more than twelve arrows.*

At right, Naslund uses heated blade to cut special heavyweight ethafoam into silhouette target shapes.

David Myers, below, finds production of bowhunter silhouettes to be a backyard operation at this point.

Target bases are made of same ethafoam material to save weight. While unaffected by most weather conditions, strong winds will blow silhouettes over.

*Silhouette targets for a large match may be transported in the back of a pickup truck or small trailer, as above.*

*Experimentation with several kinds of foam lead BSI's Dave Myers to develop a special arrow-receptive type of ethafoam for targets, built to specifications.*

thirty-five meters (38.15 yards); No. 1 turkey: fifty meters (54.5 yards); and No. 1 ram: sixty-five meters (70.85 yards). Under no circumstances will any of the silhouette series overlap another in vertical distance from the shooter.

6. SHOOTING SEQUENCE — The bowhunter must shoot one arrow only at each silhouette in proper sequence (left to right) starting with chickens, pigs, turkeys and rams in that order.

7. SHOOTING POSITIONS AND MOVEMENT — The bowhunter may shoot from any stance he/she chooses. However, all shooting must be from a position relative to the silhouette that causes the arrow flight to be parallel to the boundary lines of his/her assigned shooting lane. Thus the bowhunter is required to move laterally (left or right) between each shot.

8. SHOOTING TIMES — A maximum of two (2) minutes is alloted each bowhunter to shoot twelve (12) arrows at twelve (12) silhouettes.

9. SHOOTING ASSIGNMENTS — Each team member will be assigned a relay and a lane number. In most cases the lane number will be the same for both members of the team, but the relay numbers will be different, as one member of each team will be utilized as a target setter and scorekeeper while the other member is shooting. In no instance will one team member score and set for his teammate.

*In case of blow-over, the match director may allow the shooter a maximum of ten seconds for each alibi shot.*

*Silhouette shoots are intended to provide fun for spectators and competitors. Flying milk cartons with flu-flus or other diversions offer relaxation between rounds. Sponsoring bowhunter clubs may add several such events.*

To score a perfect round a competitor must knock down every silhouette in his lane, in the proper order; twelve targets within the two-minute time limit. The archer must be fast as well as accurate with his arrows.

10. SKIP OR RICOCHET HITS — Skip hits count only if the intended target is involved. If the shooter is shooting at No. 2 chicken and misses, but knocks down one of his pigs, he loses the shot and does not get credit for the animal down. However, should his arrow skip or ricochet into the competitor's lane and knock an animal down, the shooter loses his shot, while the competitor gets credit for the animal down.

11. ALIBI ROUNDS — An "Alibi" request may be made by the competitor when his target was knocked down by the wind denying an opportunity to shoot. The shooter will be allowed ten (10) seconds to complete each alibi shot. In no case will alibi shot be allowed for a claimed "pass-through" shot.

12. SCORING — One (1) point per target knocked down. The value is the same for all targets. Hits are reflected by placing an "X" in the appropriate box on the score card. Misses are marked as a zero (0).

California's Ben Lewis established himself early as the man to beat in bowhunter silhouette matches.

13. SCORE CARDS — Each competitor will be furnished a properly filled-out score card which he will present to his scorekeeper when approaching the shooting line. Upon completing each round, both the shooter and scorekeeper must initial the score card before turning it over to the silhouette committee for tabulation.

14. Ties are to be broken by high ram count. Should two teams be tied at 9 points, the person who scored the most ram hits would be declared the winner. In the event that the ram count is also tied, then turkeys will be counted to determine the winner — then if necessary the pigs and the chickens.

15. SHOOT-OUTS — Only in a dead heat, after all animals are counted, should a match be prolonged by shoot-outs. However, should this occur, the two teams involved will stage a shoot-out at six chickens, each set at fifty meters. The team scoring the highest score out of a possible six count would then be declared the winner.

16. AWARDING OF SILHOUETTE PINS — "Six" (6) and "Nine" (9) animal pins are incorporated into all BSI awards structures. Numbered pins are earned and awarded for consecutive hits within consecutive rounds only. (A six-chicken pin is earned if the bowhunter scores six chickens in two consecutive rounds.) Note: Ram twelve pins are awarded for a "lane sweep" — the knocking down of all twelve (12) silhouettes in a lane. A "Ram-36" pin is awarded for a "Grand Slam" — a perfect score of 36.

17. RE-ENTRIES — Re-entries to be allowed at the discretion of the match officials. However, the initial match score stands, regardless of scores earned as a re-entry. (However, the bowhunter may earn additional "animal pins" as a re-entry.)

18. PROTESTS — A competitor may protest the equipment used, the manner in which another competitor conducted himself, or the recording of scores at any time. However, such protests must be put in writing and presented to the match director within thirty minutes following the conclusion of the match.

# Chapter 20
# ARCHERY ORGANIZATIONS

## *Where Are They And Why? What Have They To Offer And What Can You Give In Return?*

AAC

AMO

BOWHUNTERS WHO CARE

NAA

JOAD

IF YOU are into archery for any period of time, you will begin to wonder about the organizational aspects of the sport. Are there clubs you can turn to for guidance? How about national organizations? What place is archery holding in the realm of sports today? Can you expect the sport to grow or is it, as you may have heard some of your friends expound, an archaic, passe sport, to be practiced by a perpetually small number of enthusiasts?

Archery is rapidly gaining a strong following in outdoor sports, largely because of the impact it has on hunting, and because of the opportunities for individual growth and challenge that it offers.

Archery has been termed by the manufacturers of sporting goods as a "recession sport," placing it in excellent company with camping and fishing. In 1978 more than 1.25 million Americans were involved in the active practice of bowhunting, providing more than four million dollars yearly to the Pittman-Robertson Federal Excise Tax funds established by the state wildlife management programs to develop and maintain conservation programs within the states.

That's a lot of dollars, and a lot of archers, and yet it is far less than half the number of archers now in the United States. Not taken into account are the many thousands of young archers participating in Junior Olympic Archery Development (JOAD) programs, the scores of college and high-school students involved in school archery programs, the Scouts and youth groups that practice archery during camp programs or the adult archers who restrict their shooting to tournament archery or backyard shooting. Although you may not hear a great deal about archery and its growing multitudes, the fact remains that it is gaining ever constant numbers of participants. To help these new as well as the experienced archers to practice their sport to their ultimate ability, a number of national and state organizations have been created. Perhaps the foremost of these, and certainly the most renowned, is the National Archery Association

## NAA

The National Archery Association (NAA) is the oldest national sports organization of any kind in the United States. A nonprofit corporation, the goal of the NAA is to promote the advancement of archery through establishment of uniform codes of shooting ethics and competition. Founded in 1879 the NAA is the recognized governing body for archery in the United States and represents this country in worldwide archery involvement, including Olympic and international competition.

From its home base in Pennsylvania the NAA reaches out across the U.S. to meet the needs of its members, providing advice and national sanction to local organizations in their scheduled tournaments and, if needed, daily maintenance guidance and problem-solving suggestions. Those interested may write to the NAA by addressing their inquiries to National Archery Association, 1750 E. Boulder St., Colorado Springs, Colorado 80909.

## JOAD

Recognizing the need to develop a training program for young archers who might someday represent the United States in world competitions, the NAA developed JOAD.

The Junior Olympic Archery Development program is the nationally recognized training program for young archers, whether they be bent on international competition or simply wish to learn how to shoot a bow for their own, personal enjoyment. The program revolves around a graduated series of development skill levels, seeking to take the archer from novice to Olympian. Involvement in the program allows a member national recognition of his achievements wherever he might reside.

A JOAD member may be any boy or girl under the age of 18. To form a local club and obtain national chartership requires a minimum of six youngsters wishing to participate in the program and one adult leader. Although the leader does not have to be an expert with bow and arrow, he or she should be familiar with the basic techniques of archery. The primary function of this leader is to assure that national rules and regulations are being adhered to, as outlined in the Junior Archers Handbook, available by writing to the National Archery Association, 1750 E. Boulder, Colorado Springs, Colorado 80909.

## NFAA

Not to be confused with the NAA, the National Field Archery Association also is a national organization, but developed for the promotion and advancement of *field* archery, or outdoor archery, as opposed to the primarily indoor archery of the NAA.

The functions of the NFAA and NAA are quire similar in that both provide guidance on formation and behavioral responsibilities of local clubs. Both provide guidelines for tournaments which allow a competitor in Michigan to match his skills equally against a competitor in Washington state or any part of the United States between. The basic differences between the two are in the makeup of the tournament facilities.

For NAA tournaments you can expect to see level ground and ten-ring targets set at specified distances which you will know before you shoot them. In NFAA tournament play the grounds will probably be anything but level. You may find yourself shooting at targets above or below you, between trees or over brush. One particular international tournament had competitors straddling logs spanning a creek while they shot, but that's an unusual occurrence.

The idea behind the field tournament is to place your tournament shooting in the realm of bowhunting. Shooting in the outdoors means shooting where you are likely to run into a tree or two, climb a hill or cross a stream. And you can be sure that if those items are anywhere among the grounds of the tournament area you'll face them at some time during the tournament.

Targets for field tournaments often will vary as well. You may shoot at a ten-ring, but more than likely your target will be a three-ring, five-ring, animal or novelty target. All are appropriate and recognized targets for field tournaments, with the scoring for these tournaments determined prior to the tournament's beginning.

As for known distances on a field tournament, you may or may not be given this information. Targets at unknown distances are extremely popular among field archers, requiring the competitor to gauge for himself, without mechanical aids, the distances he will be shooting.

For all tournaments, NFAA or NAA, you will find strict regulations regarding shooting safety. To our knowledge, there never has been an archer injured by another archer during a nationally sanctioned tournament, and credit is due to these strict safety regulations. Members of the two organizations are extremely proud of their safety records and intend to keep them intact.

Membership in the NFAA, as in the NAA, is open to all archers, novice and experienced of all ages, with family rates available at a considerable savings. Competition is divided into categories based upon the age and equipment of the archer, with categories for those who shoot with all accessories (from sights to stabilizers) to those who shoot barebow style (with no mechanical aids).

For information on the NFAA, direct your questions to the National Field Archery Association, Route 2, Box 514, Redlands, California 92373.

## AAC

The American Archery Council (AAC), based in North Palm Beach, Florida, functions as a sounding horn for the national archery organizations. Direction comes not only from the national organization leaders, but from the major archery manufacturers as well. The purpose of the AAC is to organize and represent *all* phases of archery as a single entity. The organization strives to promote coordination of efforts and assistance among the different state and national bodies, while providing a single responsible body to deal with problems between archery and outside groups.

A primary interest of the AAC is the development and distribution of educational materials relating to archery and bowhunting. Members of the group are likely to appear at National Rifle Association meetings, state and national fish and wildlife conferences, governmental meetings in which archery and hunting in general are being challenged. During 1979 the AAC distributed more than 50,000 copies of their newsletter advising fish and game departments, organized bowhunters, archery dealers, and other interested parties on the status of archery in the United States.

While the AAC may not be able to handle every single archery-related problem fielded to it by individuals and local groups, it offers a referral service of names and addresses of individuals and groups who can help.

For more information on the AAC, how it can help you and how you can help archery, you may write to them in care of the American Archery Council, 200 Castlewood Road, North Palm Beach, Florida 33408.

## AMO

The Archery Manufacturers Organization (AMO) is a trade organization for the archery industry, including in its membership all major manufacturers of archery products, from bows to nocks. Although AMO serves the primary function of coordinating and directing relations between the many manufacturers, it serves an even greater service to the individual archer.

Through its influence AMO has been able to initiate a voluntary industry-wide standards program whereby a single archery item may be identical in basic design to that of any similar item, regardless of the manufacturer. This means that the bow quiver manufactured by Bear Archery will fit not only a Bear bow, but any other bow being made, provided both items carry the AMO logo on them so indicating. The screw-in point of any Saunder's small game point will fit any other arrow shaft adapter carrying the AMO tag. Bowstrings, regardless of who might make them, are identical in size and basic composition to those of any other bowstring.

Since its introduction of the voluntary standards program in 1968, the AMO has standardized such items as bow lengths, bowstring lengths, cable lengths and design, bow weights, arrow spine selection charts, bow sights, stabilizers, draw lengths, broadhead and field arrow fletching standards, and archery nomenclature. Manufacturer's products that meet these voluntary standards are permitted the use of the AMO logo on these items, telling any archer that the product has met their specific criteria.

Any archer desiring to receive a copy of the most recent AMO standards may obtain a copy by sending fifty cents, to cover the costs of materials and postage, to the Archery Manufacturer's Organization, 200 Castlewood Road, North Palm Beach, Florida 33408.

## BOWHUNTERS WHO CARE

A relatively new guy on the national organizational block, Bowhunters Who Care is a nonprofit corporation organized to promote and preserve bowhunting in the United States. Although organized as recently as 1979, Bowhunters Who Care has already made great strides in the development of bowhunting. Bowhunters Who Care concentrates on developing a high level of communication and cooperation between the individual bowhunter and landowner. It does this through mass publication of the bowhunter's code of ethics, and by actively seeking solutions to bowhunter/landowner conflicts. The

# STATE ORGANIZATIONS

**ALABAMA ARCHERY ASSOCIATION**
3900 Wooten Drive
Birmingham, Alabama 35241

**BOWHUNTERS OF ALABAMA, INC.**
Star Route 6, Box 128-D
Guntersville, Alabama 35976
Phone: (205) 582-8158
Membership Fees: $2 per year
Approximate Membership: 1300
Contact: George F. Leath, III, President

**ARIZONA BOWHUNTERS FIELD ARCHERY ASSOCIATION**
1517 East Coronado Road
Phoenix, Arizona 85006
Membership Fees: $16 per head of household; $4 per family member (maximum $25 per family)
Contact: Arlene Bunten

**ARKANSAS STATE ARCHERY ASSOCIATION**
P.O. Box 102
Lamar, Arkansas 72846
Phone: (501) 885-3353
Membership Fees: $20 (includes NFAA membership)

**ARKANSAS BOWHUNTERS ASSOCIATION**
P.O. Box 9902
Little Rock, Arkansas 72219
Phone: (501) 562-0273
Membership Fees: $7 — individual; $10.50 family; $3.50 — non-resident
Approximate Membership: 450
Contact: Harold Hile, president; T.E. Thompson, secretary/treasurer

**BRITISH COLUMBIA ARCHERY ASSOCIATION**
39 - 8th Street
New Westminster, B.C. V3M 3N7 Canada
Phone: (604) 524-1674
Membership Fees: $10
Approximate Membership: 600
Contact: Jim Wiebe, Membership Chairman

**STATE ARCHERS OF CALIFORNIA**
445 South Del Sol Lane
Diamond Bar, California 91765
Phone: (714) 595-9368
Membership Fees: $5, adults; $2.50, under 18; $8 family
Approximate Membership: 190
Contact: Karl B. Radde

**COLORADO STATE ARCHERY ASSOCIATION**
c/o Marjorie Evans, Secretary
1507 East 1st Street
Pueblo, Colorado 81001
Phone: (303) 524-7739

**COLORADO BOWHUNTERS ASSOCIATION, INC.**
2085 Nome Street
Aurora, Colorado 80010
Phone: (303) 757-7052
Membership Fees: $7
Approximate Membership: 2200
Contact: Larry O. Baker

**CONNECTICUT ARCHERY ASSOCIATION**
19 Fairland Drive
Huntington, Connecticut 06484

**DELAWARE STATE ARCHERY ASSOCIATION**
500 Linden Street
Seaford, Delaware 19973
Phone: (302) 629-9097

Membership Fees: $15 (includes NFAA membership)
Approximate Membership: 110
Contact: Carol LeGates, Secretary

**PANHANDLE BOWHUNTER'S ASSOCIATION**
310 Muscogee Road
Cantonment, Florida 32533

**FLORIDA ARCHERY ASSOCIATION**
3029 Northwest 38th Street
Gainesville, Florida 32601
Membership Fees: $22 adult; $5 youth; $36 family maximum
Approximate Membership: 575
Contact: Timothy O. Austin

**GEORGIA BOWHUNTERS ASSOCIATION**
Route 1, Box 112
Mansfield, Georgia 30255

**HAWAII STATE ARCHERY ASSOCIATION**
91-506 Onelua Street
Ewa Beach, Hawaii 96706

**IDAHO FIELD ARCHERY ASSOCIATION, INC.**
Route 3
Jerome, Idaho 83338

**IDAHO STATE BOWHUNTERS**
Route 1, Box 245
Blackfoot, Idaho 83221
Membership Fees: $5
Approximate Membership: 1000
Contact: Blaine Lyon, Secretary/Treasurer

**ILLINOIS ARCHERY ASSOCIATION**
506 East Locust
Chatham, Illinois 62629
Phone: (217) 483-2092
Membership Fee: $23 (includes NFAA membership)
Approximate Membership: 1000
Contact: Joyce Christensen, Business Manager

**INDIANA BOWHUNTERS ASSOCIATION**
3829 South LaSalle
Indianapolis, Indiana 46227
Membership Fee: $10

**INDIANA FIELD ARCHERY ASSOCIATION**
Box 42
Brownsville, Indiana 47325
Phone: (317) 458-6927
Membership Fee: $16 (includes NFAA membership)
Contact: Harold Carlton

**IOWA BOWHUNTERS ASSOCIATION, INC.**
Box 872
Waterloo, Iowa 50704
Phone: (319) 234-1685
Membership Fees: $7
Approximate Membership: 450
Contact: Mike Judas, Secretary

**KANSAS BOWHUNTERS ASSOCIATION**
Box 234A, Route 5
Manhattan, Kansas 66502
Membership Fee: $10
Approximate Membership: 350
Contact: Dave Easton, Secretary/Treasurer

**KANSAS STATE ARCHERY ASSOCIATION**
P.O. Box 475

Bonner Springs, Kansas 66012

**KENTUCKY BOWHUNTERS ASSOCIATION, INC.**
1429 Longfield Avenue
Louisville, Kentucky 40215
Phone: (502) 368-4991
Membership Fee: $6
Approximate Membership: 1000
Contact: Marvin Almon, Executive Secretary

**LOUISIANA BOWHUNTERS ASSOCIATION**
P.O. Box 4180
Shreveport, Louisiana 71104
Phone: (318) 221-0851
Membership Fee: $5
Approximate Membership: 500
Contact: Henry Miller, Jr., Membership Director

**LOUISIANA FIELD ARCHERY ASSOCIATION**
5111 Green Ridge
Baton Rouge, Louisiana 70814

**MAINE BOWHUNTERS ASSOCIATION**
North Palermo Road
Palermo, Maine 04354
Phone: (207) 993-2366
Membership Fee: $10
Approximate Membership: 226
Contact: Norman L. Leeman

**MICHIGAN BOWHUNTERS ASSOCIATION**
1650 Avondale
Ann Arbor, Michigan 48103
Membership Fees: $10 adult; $15 family
Approximate Membership: 4973
Contact: Ronald Spring, President

**MINNESOTA STATE ARCHERY ASSOCIATION**
6941 Zane Avenue North
Brooklyn Park, Minnesota 55429

**MISSISSIPPI BOWHUNTER'S ASSOCIATION**
108 Ray Street
Cleveland, Mississippi 38732
Phone: (601) 846-6910
Membership Fees: $6
Approximate Membership: 800
Contact: William "Bunky" Wienke

**MISSISSIPPI STATE ARCHERY ASSOCIATION**
312 Cameron Street
Jackson, Mississippi 39212
Phone: (601) 372-4864
Membership Fees: $16, single (includes NFAA membership. Special family rates)
Approximate Membership: 130
Contact: Sheila Williams, Secretary

**MISSOURI BOWHUNTERS**
8709 Booth
Kansas City, Missouri 64138
Phone: (816) 763-2699
Membership Fees: $5, single; $7.50, family
Approximate Membership: 1000
Contact: Earl or Millie Foster

**MONTANA BOWHUNTERS ASSOCIATION**
P.O. Box 837
Three Forks, Montana 59752
Phone: (406) 285-3236

organization not only asks that bowhunters practice these ethics, but that landowners who might experience problems with a specific bowhunter on their lands contact the organization to make them aware of the problem.

A major topic for Bowhunters Who Care since its inception has been the struggle to prevent Either/Or laws from being initiated in American states. The Either/Or laws refer to regulations through which a hunter might be permitted to hunt with a gun or with a bow, but could not hunt with both tools. Representatives of the corporation have met with local organizations and town councils throughout the nation in an effort to explain the impact archery has on hunting, and the unfairness of such laws. Their efforts have met with some success, although the struggle is far from over.

Archers seeking additional information can write to them at P.O. Box 511, Squaw Valley, California 93646.

## STATE ORGANIZATIONS

Aside from these there are many smaller, specialized organizations designed to promote individual areas of archers such as the Fred Bear Sports Club, Professional Archers Association, and Pope and Young Club. Each state also has at least one state organization. Below are listed the names and addresses of these organizations as they are currently known. Through your active support and participation in them you guarantee that archery has a voice in the future of sports development in the United States and that you have an opportunity to contribute to that future.

Membership Fee: $5
Approximate Membership: 825
Contact: Scott Koelzer

**MONTANA BOWMEN, INC.**
Box 282
Havre, Montana 59501

**NEBRASKA PRAIRIE BOWMAN STATE ARCHERY ASSOCIATION**
Walt Hall, Nebraska 68067

**NEBRASKA BOWHUNTERS ASSOCIATION**
647 Eldora Lane
Lincoln, Nebraska 68505

**GRANITE STATE BOWHUNTERS**
103 Woodland Avenue
Manchester, New Hampshire 03103
Phone: (603) 624-4737
Membership Fees: $3
Approximate Membership: 390
Contact: Donald W. Merrill

**NEW JERSEY ARCHERY ASSOCIATION**
Route 1, Box 294
Cape May, New Jersey 08204

**NEW JERSEY STATE FIELD ARCHERY ASSOCIATION**
509 East Main Street
Somerville, New Jersey 08876
Phone: (201) 759-2691
Membership Fee: $15
Contact: William Sobolewski

**UNITED BOWHUNTERS OF NEW JERSEY**
P.O. Box 337
Belleville, New Jersey 07109
Phone: 201) 759-2691
Membership Fee: $5; Bowhunter, $10;
    Sponsoring, $25
Approximate Membership: 1000
Contact: Izzy Donatiello

**NEW MEXICO ABC BOWMEN**
P.O. Box 4525
Albuquerque, New Mexico 87106
Phone: (505) 265-5226
Membership Fee: $7
Contact: Vic Boyer, Chairman

**NEW MEXICO BOWHUNTERS ASSOCIATION**
1213 Indiana
Alamogordo, New Mexico 88310

**NEW YORK FIELD ARCHERY & BOWHUNTERS ASSOCIATION, INC.**
Box 149, Overlook Road
Pleasant Valley, New York 12569
Phone: (914) 635-3153
Membership Fees: $16
Approximate Membership: 2100
Contact: Joyce Lang, Corresponding Secretary

**NEW YORK STATE ARCHERY ASSOCIATION**
79 Martin Court
Jerico, New York 11753
Phone: (716) 549-2307; (315) 689-9076;
    (516) 931-3662
Membership Fee: $3; Student, $1.50;
    Family, $5
Contact: Syril B. Farber, Secretary

**NORTH CAROLINA ARCHERY ASSOCIATION**
5928 Lebanon Road
Charlotte, North Carolina 28212

**NORTH CAROLINA BOWHUNTERS ASSOCIATION**
6354 Rannock Drive
Fayetteville, North Carolina 28304
Phone: (919) 424-4446
Membership Fee: $8
Approximate Membership: 700
Contact: Lin Webb, Secretary/Treasurer

**NORTH DAKOTA BOWHUNTERS ASSOCIATION**
Box 1413
Fargo, North Dakota 58107
Membership Fees: $5
Approximate Membership: 350
Contact: Paul Speral

**OHIO ARCHERS, INC.**
P.O. Box 391
Norwalk, Ohio 44857
Phone: (419) 668-3257
Membership Fee: Archers, $10; Bowhunter, $10; Both, $13; Family, $12
Approximate Membership: 1500
Contact: Marjorie Naylor, Secretary

**OKLAHOMA STATE ARCHERY ASSOCIATION**
434 Highland Drive
Bartlesville, Oklahoma

**OREGON BOWHUNTERS**
1365 Franklin Street
Lebanon, Oregon 97355
Phone: (503) 258-7595
Membership Fees: Adult, $9; Second Adult, $2.50; Family, $12
Approximate Membership: 1000
Contact: Phyllis Stalcup, Secretary/Treasurer

**PENNSYLVANIA PROFESSIONAL BOWHUNTERS SOCIETY**
Route 2, Box 89
Middlebury Center, Pennsylvania 16935
Phone: (717) 376-4026
Membership Fee: $12, Annual; $150, Life; $3, Big Buddy
Approximate Membership: 450
Contact: Terry Peavler

**PENNSYLVANIA STATE ARCHERY ASSOCIATION, INC.**
102 Dewey Avenue Ext.
Pittsburgh, Pennsylvania 15223
Phone: (412) 822-7505
Membership Fee: $10
Approximate Membership: 2000
Contact: Albert C. Oswald, Executive Secretary

**SASKATCHEWAN PROVINCIAL BOWHUNTERS**
6 Lorimer Crescent
Regina, Saskatchewan, Canada

**SOUTH CAROLINA ARCHERY ASSOCIATION**
Box 509
Clemson, South Carolina 29631

**SOUTH DAKOTA ARCHERY ASSOCIATION**
720 East 4th Street
Sioux Falls, South Dakota 57103

**TENNESSEE ARCHERY ASSOCIATION**
P.O. Box 621
Church Hill, Tennessee 37642
Phone: (615) 357-4851
Membership Fee: $15, first member; $4 each additional member
Approximate Membership: 350
Contact: Tommy Lea

**TEXAS FIELD ARCHERY ASSOCIATION**
5725 Sunset Road
Fort Worth, Texas 76114
Phone: (817) 738-7426
Membership Fees: $10; State & National, $20
Contact: Nelle Butts, Secretary

**LONE STAR BOWHUNTERS ASSOCIATION**
P.O. Box 675
Angleton, Texas 77515
Phone: (713) 849-9517
Membership Fee: $5
Approximate Membership: 700
Contact: Peggy Barcak, Secretary/Treasurer

**UTAH BOWMEN'S ASSOCIATION**
276 East 200 North
Lindon, Utah 84062
Phone: (801) 785-4891
Membership Fees: $5; Family, $8; Independent Youth, $1.50
Approximate Membership: 700
Contact: James C. Jensen, President

**VERMONT BOWMEN**
28 Highland Street
Brattleboro, Vermont 05301

**VIRGINIA BOWHUNTERS ASSOCIATION**
Route 2, Dogwood Lane
Vinton, Virginia 24179
Phone: (703) 890-3072
Membership Fee: $5, Adult; $4, Youth; Maximum, $12
Approximate Membership: 1025
Contact: Nancy L. Western, Corresponding Secretary

**WASHINGTON STATE ARCHERY ASSOCIATION**
14135 Highway 99, Space 90
Lynwood, Washington 98036
Phone: (206) 745-8291
Membership Fees: $10, family head; $3, each additional adult
Approximate Membership: 900
Contact: Dot Doescher, President

**WEST VIRGINIA ARCHERY ASSOCIATION**
Sandy Heights
Pt. Pleasant, West Virginia 25550
Phone: (304) 675-3387
Membership Fee: $15.50
Approximate Membership: 400
Contact: Gene Brown

**WISCONSIN BOWHUNTERS ASSOCIATION**
Route 2
Crivitz, Wisconsin 54114
Phone: (715) 757-3871
Membership Fees: $5
Approximate Membership: 7850
Contact: Anne Fancher, Executive Secretary

**BOWHUNTERS OF WYOMING, INC.**
208 Jensen Street
Green River, Wyoming 82935
Phone: (307) 875-3948
Membership Fee: $10
Approximate Membership: 350
Contact: Mark Peterson

# GLOSSARY OF TERMS

**ACTUAL WEIGHT** — The difference between holding and maximum weight of a compound bow.

**ANCHOR POINT** — The position of the string hand against the face when at full draw. For field archers, normally considered the corner of the mouth. For tournament archers, the center point of the chin.

**ARM GUARD** — Section of leather held in place over inside of forearm on the bow arm to protect against string slap. Also made of plastic.

**ARROMETER** — Chronograph for measuring arrow speed, adjustable for individual arrow lengths.

**ARROW** — A completed arrow shaft with nock, fletching and point.

**ARROW REST** — Accessory finger added to riser section of bow to hold and guide the arrow during release.

**ARROW SHAFT** — The wood, fiberglass or aluminum dowel on which fletching and arrow points are added to produce a completed arrow.

**ARROW SIZE** — The thickness and stiffness of an arrow shaft.

**BACK** — The surface of the bow furthest from the archer when held in a shooting position.

**BARB** — A steel finger extending from a fish point and functioning as the hook section of the point.

**BELLY** — The surface of the bow closest to the archer during draw.

**BLUNTS** — Small-game points with characteristic flat faces.

**BOLTS** — Arrows for crossbows, usually measuring fourteen to sixteen inches.

**BOW ARM** — The arm that holds the bow during shooting.

**BOWHUNTERS WHO CARE** — A professional organization created to advance the image of the archer and bowhunter.

**BOW SQUARE** — Clamp-on measuring device used to position the nock locators.

**BOW SIGHT** — A mechanical device used for sighting including a mounting plate that extends alongside the riser with sight pins to guide the archer to the target.

**BOWYER** — An individual craftsman who makes bows.

**BROADHEADS** — Big-game arrowheads, extremely sharp, designed to kill by bleeding.

**BULL'S-EYE** — Most central ring of a target, normally gold in color.

**BUTT** — Backstop for arrows, normally supporting a target.

**CAST** — The arc of an arrow when released.

**COCK FEATHER** — The lead or hen feather of an arrow, normally a different color than the remaining feathers, placed at right angle to the bowstring.

**CLOTH-YARD ARROW** — An arrow used by English longbowmen measuring exactly one yard in length.

**CRESTING** — The addition of bands of color to an arrow to identify or decorate the shaft.

**CROSSBOW** — The marriage of a rifle and bow into one shooting instrument.

**CUT-OFF TOOL** — A machine that cuts full-length arrows to individual archer draw lengths.

**DIPPING** — The technique of immersing an arrow shaft into enamel paint to color and protect the shaft from moisture.

**DOMINANT EYE** — The stronger eye, which tends to take over when shooting or aiming.

**DRAW** — To pull the bowstring back toward the archer.

**DRAW LENGTH** — The length between the arrow rest or front of the bow and the anchor point of the archer, the bow arm fully extended.

**DRAW WEIGHT** — The amount of pull required to draw a bow to full draw.

**DRY FIRE** — To shoot a bow without an arrow; considered extremely harmful to bow limbs.

**EASTERN COUNT** — The counting of all tines measuring one inch or more, on both antlers, to obtain a total point count.

**END** — A round of arrows shot in a regulation tournament, normally containing six arrows.

**FEATHERS** — The oldest form of fletching, turkey feathers are favored for archery.

**FIELD POINT** — Rocket-shaped point used for small game.

**FISHTAILING** — The left/right swishing movement of an arrow in flight.

**FLETCHING** — The guidance system of arrows, either plastic vanes or turkey feathers.

**FOLLOW-THROUGH** — The technique of holding shooting position until the arrow has hit the target.

**GRIP** — The handle section of the bow.

**GROUPING** — The placement of several arrows in one general area.

**HAIRLINES** — Fine, extremely thin lines used to frame a crest.

**HOLDING WEIGHT** — The draw weight of a bow when at full draw.

**HOT MELT** — A solid stick glue heated to melting point when used to secure inserts to arrow shafts.

**HUNTING BOW** — More subtle in color than the tournament bow, but otherwise identical. Finish will be non-reflective or require the use of bow socks to camouflage it.

**INSERTS** — Lightweight aluminum plugs sized to match the inside diameter of aluminum and fiberglass shafts, tapped to accept screw-in points.

**INSTINCTIVE AIM** — Spontaneous aiming, without specific effort to lock on to the target.

**JIGS** — Fletching tools used to hold fletching in place against the arrow shaft until the glue dries.

**JOAD** — Junior Olympic Archery Development, an NAA archery program designed to foster the practice of archery among young archers.

**JUDO POINT** — A specialized small-game point featuring spring-loaded arms which fan out to grab the target.

**LET-OFF** — The percentage of weight reduction effected by the eccentric design of compound bows. Normally thirty or fifty percent.

**MATCHING** — Pairing of arrows to bow weight to produce the best arrow flight.

**MAXIMUM WEIGHT** — The greatest draw weight of a bow.

**NAA** — National Archery Association

**NFAA** — National Field Archery Association

**NOCK** — Plastic finger on end of arrow which grabs the bowstring to hold the arrow in place.

**NOCK LOCATOR** — A string accessory positioned to provide a constant nocking position for the arrow shaft.

**NOVELTY SHOOT** — An archery tournament in which traditional ringed targets are replaced by unique targets, frequently of cartoon design.

**OVER-BOWED** — Attempting to shoot a bow of excessive weight or draw.

**PENETRATION** — The depth an arrow will enter a target.

**PLUNGER** — A mechanical finger running through the width of the riser and projecting out at the arrow rest, intended to adjust the left/right movement of the arrow shaft.

**POINT** — The business end of an arrow; may be a field, target, small-game or big-game hunting point.

**POINT OF AIM** — Specific spot on a target on which the archer aims.

**POINT-ON AIMING** — The use of the point of the arrow as a guidance device for aiming. Also called the gap method of aim.

**PORPOISING** — The up-and-down fluttering of an arrow in flight.

**PRO SHOP** — A sporting goods store specializing in archery equipment.

**PUNCH POWER** — Kinetic energy of an arrow.

**QUIVER** — A holder for arrows available in various styles, either worn by the archer, attached to the bow or placed in the ground.

**RANGE** — An area set aside for archery shooting.

**RECURVE BOW** — Similar to the longbow with the ends curved back, away from the normal curve of the bow.

**RELEASE** — Mechanical aid for releasing the bowstring, intended to release the bowstring smoothly and consistently. Also, the letting go of the bowstring.

**RISER** — Handle section of the bow.

**SERVING** — Wrapping around the center of the bowstring at the nocking point, intended to protect the string from wear.

**SHAFT** — Dowel section of the arrow — aluminum, fiberglass or wood — to which the nock, fletching and points are added.

**SHELF** — The natural ledge of a bow providing a resting place for the arrow during draw.

**SHOOT-IN** — To position your bowsight by a series of shooting and adjustment.

**SIX-GOLD** — All six arrows of an NAA regulation end in the bull's-eye.

**SMALL-GAME HEAD** — A blunt head intended to kill by shock.

**SPEED** — The rate at which an arrow will cover a given distance, normally given as feet per second.

**SPINE** — The bending and spring-back capability of an arrow.

**STRAIGHTENER** — A mechanical device for realigning aluminum arrow shafts.

**STRING HAND** — The hand that draws the bowstring back.

**STRING SLAP** — The unintentional slapping of the bowstring against the bow arm.

**TACKLE** — Archery equipment including bow, arrows and all accessories.

**TAPER** — The angling of an arrow shaft to accept a point or nock.

**TARGET POINT** — A lightweight, pyramid-shaped point for tournament shooting.

**TOURNAMENT BOW** — Often bright, ornate in finish, a finely tuned compound or recurve bow, drilled and tapped to accept sights and stabilizers.

**TRADITIONAL DRAW LENGTH** — The draw length of an archer measured from the anchor point to the back, far side of the bow.

**TRUE DRAW** — Draw-length measurement from the anchor point to the arrow rest.

**TUNING** — The adjustment of the bow to the arrows to provide the best arrow flight, accomplished by positioning the nock locator and rests.

**TURN BOLTS** — The adjustable center bolts of each limb on a compound bow that hold the bow limbs in place and are adjustable to change the draw weight of the bow.

# Directory Of The ARCHERY TRADE

## BOW MANUFACTURERS

Allen Archery, 200 Washington St., Billings, MO 65610 (bows, accessories)

American Archery, P.O. Box 100 Indus. Park, Oconto Falls, WI 54154 (bows, accessories)

Bear Archery, RR 4, 4600 Southwest 41st Blvd., Gainesville, FL 32601

Bingham Archery, Box 3013, Ogden, UT 84403 (bows, accessories)

Browning, Rt. 1, Morgan, UT 84050 (bows, accessories)

Carroll's Archery Products, 59½ South Main, Moab, UT 84532 (bows, accessories)

Cravotta Brothers, Inc., Third St., E. McKeesport, PA 15132 (bows)

Darton, Inc., Archery Division, 3261 Flushing Rd., Flint, MI 48504 (bows)

East Side Archery Ltd., 3711 E. 106th St., Chicago, IL 60617 (longbows, accessories)

Golden Eagle Archery Co., Inc., P.O. Box 310, 104 S. Mill St., Creswell, OR 97426 (bows)

Graham's Custom Bows, P.O. Box 1312, Fontana, CA 92335 (bows, accessories)

Herter's Inc., RR1, Waseca, MN 56093 (bows, accessories)

Howard Hill Archery, Rt. 1, Box 1397, Hamilton, MT 59840 (longbows, accessories)

Damon Howatt (Martin Archery), Rt. 5, Box 127, Walla Walla, WA 99362 (bows)

Jack Howard, Washington Star Rt., Nevada City, CA 95959 (bows, accessories)

Hoyt Archery Co., 11510 Natural Bridge Rd., Bridgeton, MO 63044 (bows, accessories)

Indian Archery, 817 Maxwell Ave., Evansville, IN 47717 (bows, accessories)

Jeffery Enterprises, Inc., 821 Pepper St., Columbia, SC 29209 (bows)

Jennings Compound Bow Inc., 28756 N. Castaic Cyn. Rd., Valencia, CA 91355 (bows, accessories)

Kittredge Bow Hut, P.O. Box 598, Mammoth Lakes, CA 93546 (bows, accessories)

Martin Archery, Rt. 5, Box 127, Walla Walla, WA 99362 (bows, accessories)

Mohawk Archery, 228 Bridge St., E. Syracuse, NY 13057 (bows, accessories)

Dick Palmer Archery, 932 N. College, Fayetteville, AR 72702-1632 (longbows, accessories)

Ben Pearson Archery, P.O. Box 7465, Pine Bluff, AR 71611

Plas/Steel Products, Inc., Walkerton, IN 46574

Precision Shooting Equipment, 2550 N. 14th Ave., Tucson, AZ 85705 (bows, accessories)

Pro-Line Co., 1843 Gun Lake Rd., Box 370, Hastings, MI 49058 (bows, accessories)

Stemmler Archery, 984 Southford Rd., Middleburg, CT 06762 (bows, accessories)

Total Shooting Systems, Inc., 419 Van Dyne Rd., N. Fond du Lac, WI 54935

Woodcraft Equip. Co./York Archery, P.O. Box 110, Independence, MO 64051

Yamaha International Corp., 6600 Orangethorpe Ave., Buena Park, CA 90620 (bows)

Zebra Long Bow Mfg. Co., 231 E. Meuse St., Blue Grass, IA 52756 (longbows)

## ARROW SUPPLIES

Acme Wood Products Co., P.O. Box 101, Myrtle Point, OR 97458 (cedar)

American Archery, P.O. Box 100, Industrial Park, Oconto Falls, WI 54154 (arrows ready-made)

Anderson Archery Corp., Grand Ledge, MI 48837 (arrows ready-made, components)

Archery Headquarters, 4591 N. Peck Road, El Monte, CA 91732 (made-to-order, ready-made, components)

Arrow Manufacturing, Inc., 1365 Logan Ave., Costa Mesa, CA 92626 (made-to-order, ready-made, components)

Arrow Mart, 1670 Babcock, Costa Mesa, CA 92627 (ready-made)

Bear Archery, RR 4, 4600 Southwest 41st Blvd., Gainesville, FL 32601 (ready-made, Bear Metrics, components)

Bohning Adhesive Co., Ltd., Rt. 2, Lake City, MI 49651 (components, arrow repair kits)

Bowhunters Discount Warehouse, Inc., Box 158-R, Wellsville, PA 17365 (ready-made, components)

Cabela's, P.O. Box 199, Sidney, NE 69162 (graphite)

Custom Archery Equipment, 1645 W. Sepulveda, Torrance, CA 90501 (ready-made)

Darton, Inc., Archery Division, 3261 Flushing Rd., Flint, MI 48504 (ready-made)

Easton Aluminum Inc., 7800 Haskell Ave., Van Nuys, CA 91406 (aluminum, components)

Vic Erickson, 1295 Ada Ave., Idaho Falls, ID 83401 (arrows)

F/S Arrows, Box 8094, Fountain Valley, CA 92708 (ready-made)

Gordon Plastics, Inc., 2872 S. Santa Fe Ave., Vista, CA 92083 (fiberglass, graphite)

Herters, Inc., Waseca, MN 56093 (ready-made, accessories)

Jack Howard Archery Co., Washington Star Rt., Box 220, Nevada City, CA 95959 (ready-made, components)

Hunter Arrows, 177-F Riverside Ave., Newport Beach, CA 92663 (ready-made, components)

Indian Archery, P.O. Box 889, 817 Maxwell Ave., Evansville, IN 47706 (ready-made)

Doug Kittredge Bow Hut, P.O. Box 598, Mammoth Lakes, CA 93546 (ready-made, components)

Lamiglass, Inc., Box 148, Woodland, WA 98674 (arrows)

Martin Archery, Inc., Rt. 5, Box 127, Walla Walla, WA 99362 (ready-made, made-to-order, components)

McKinney Arrow Shafts, Oakland, OR 97462 (arrows)

Northeast Archery, P.O. Box 552, Brewer, ME 04412 (ready-made, components)

Norway Archery, Norway, OR 97460 (cedar)

Ben Pearson Archery, Inc., P.O. Box 7465, Pine Bluff, AR 71611 (ready-made)

Precision Shooting Equipment, Inc., 2550 N. 14th Ave., Tucson, AZ 85705 (ready-made, components, PSE Pro-Fletch vanes)

Rose City Archery, Inc., Box 342, Powers, OR 97458 (cedar)

Seattle Archery, Inc., Box 120, Lynwood, WA 98036 (ready-made)

Shaw Custom Arrows, Julie Dr., RD 4, Hopewell Jct., NY 12533 (custom-made)

Stemmler Archery Inc., Southford Rd., Middlebury, CT 06762 (ready-made)
Sweetland Products, 1010 Arrowsmith St., Eugene, OR 97402 (components)
Texas Feathers, Inc., Box 1118, Brownwood, TX 76801 (feathers)
Trueflight Mfg. Co., Inc., Manitowish Waters, WI 54545 (feathers)
Ultra Products Ltd., Box 100, Fairfield, IL 62837 (vanes)
Utah Feathers, Box 396, Orem, UT 84057 (feathers)

## BOW-SHOOTING ACCESSORIES

Accra Mfg. Co., 9724 E. 55th Place, Tulsa, OK 74145 (sights, other accessories)
Altier Archery Mfg., Honesdale, PA 18431 (sights)
Archer's Arm, Payne St., Elmsford, NY 10523 (armguards, accessories)
Barner Release, P.O. Box 382, Bozeman, MT 59715 (release)
Joe Bender, Stoddard, WI 54658 (bowstring attachment)
Bigame Products, 20551 Sunset, Detroit, MI 48234 (broadhead)
Bobkat Archery, 2312 N. 400 E., Ogden, UT 84404 (peepsight)
Bonnie Bowman, 1619 Abram Ct., San Leandro, CA 94577 (accessories)
C/J Enterprises, 410 S. Citrus Ave., Covina, CA 91722 (release)
Cajun Archery, Inc., Rt. 3, Box 88, New Iberia, LA 70560 (accessories)
Cobra Bow Sight, 6737 E. 5th Pl., Tulsa, OK 74112 (sights)
J. Dye Enterprises, 1707 Childerlee Ln., NE, Atlanta, GA 30329 (arrow guide)
Dyn-O-Mite Archery, 225 SW Western Ave., Grants Pass, OR 97526 (releases, other accessories)
Evans Archery Products, Box 40453, Cincinnati, OH 45240 (accessories)
Fine-Line, Inc., 6922 N. Meridian, Puyallup, WA 98371 (sights)
Frontier Archery Co., 3440 La Grande Blvd., Sacramento, CA 95823 (accessories)
Full Adjust Products, 915 N. Ann St., Lancaster, PA 17602 (accessories)
M.R. Gazzara Mfg. Co., 345 White Horse Pike, Hammonton, NJ 08037 (release)
Golden Key Futura Archery, 1851 S. Orange Ave., Monterey Park, CA 91754 (sights, other accessories)
Gorman's Design, Box 21102, Minneapolis, MN 55421 (sights)
Granpa Specialty, 10801 Ridgecrest Dr., St. Ann, MO 63074 (broadhead)
Interstate Archery Co., Inc., 7179 W. Grand Ave., Chicago, IL 60635 (target mat)
Hi-Precision Co., Orange City, IA 51041
J.C. Mfg. Co., 6435 W. 55th Ave., Arvada, CO 80002 (accessories)
Kolpin Mfg. Inc., P.O. Box 231, 119 S. Pearl St., Berlin, WI 54923 (gloves, tabs, other accessories)
Kwikee Kwiver Co., 7292 Peaceful Valley Rd., Acme, MI 49610 (quivers)
Lee's Archery Mfg., Rt. 2, Box 269, Sedalia, MO 65301 (slings, other accessories)
Lewis & Lewis, Rt. 1, Box 4, Nekoosa, WI 54457 (release)
Moto Miter Co., Prairie du Chien, WI 53821 (release)
Make-All Tool & Die Co., 1924 S. 74th St., W. Allis, WI 53219 (broadhead)
National Archery Co., Rt. 1, Princeton, MN 55371 (accessories)
New Archery Products, Inc., 6415 Stanley Ave., Berwyn, IL 60402 (broadheads, other accessories)
Nirk Archery Co., Potlatch, ID 83855 (accessories)
Nock Rite Co., 3720 Crestview Circle, Brookfield, WI 53005 (bowstring attachment)
Old West Leathercraft, Inc., 2244-2 Main St., Chula Vista, CA 92011 (leather quivers, accessories)
Papoose Arrow Quiver, P.O. Box 5056, Kofa Station, Yuma, AZ 85364 (quiver)
Precision Shooter Co., P.O. Box 201, Flushing, MI 48433 (release)
RC Mfg., 3465 Woodward Ave., Santa Clara, CA 95050 (accessories)
Rancho Safari, Box 691, Ramona, CA 92065 (quiver, other accessories)
Range-O-Matic Archery Co., 35572 Strathcona Dr., Mt. Clemens, MI 48043 (sight, other accessories)
Ranging, Inc., 90 Lincoln Rd. North, East Rochester, NY 14445 (rangefinders)
Razorback Sporting Goods Mfg., Box 367, Flippin, AR 72634
Renson Sport Supply, 6307 Long Lk. Rd., Sterling Hts., MI 48037 (broadhead)
Richmond Sports, 56 Spartan Ave., Graniteville, NY 10303 (clicker)
S&K Mfg., 11320 East Mill Plain Blvd., Vancouver, WA 98664 (release)
Safariland Archery, Box 579, McLean, VA 22101 (accessories)
Saunders Archery Co., P.O. Box 476, Columbus, NE 68601
Savora Archery, Inc., Box 465, Kirkland, WA 98033 (broadheads)
Saxon Archery, Inc., P.O. Box 1277, Bellaire, TX 77401 (broadheads)
Sherwin Industries, P.O. Box 849, Port Richey, FL 33568 (broadheads)

Sportronics, P.O. Box 09045, Detroit, MI 48209 (sight)
Stanislawski Archery Products, 7135 SE Cora St., Portland, OR 97206 (accessories)
Stuart Mfg. Co., P.O. Box 718, Rockwall, TX 75087 (release)
Sure Shot, P.O. Box 486-B, Parowan, UT 84761 (release)
Tomar Corp., Indus. Pk. Dr., Harbor Springs, MI 49740 (accessories)
Toxonics, Inc., P.O. Box 1303, St. Charles, MO 63301 (sight)
Trueflight Mfg. Co., Inc., Manitowish Waters, WI 54545 (accessories)
WASP Archery Products, P.O. Box 760, Bristol, CT 06010 (broadheads)
L.C. Whiffen Co., Inc., 923 S. 16th St., Milwaukee, WI 53204 (accessories)
Wilson Allen Corp., Box 302, Windsor, MO 65360 (accessories)
Zwickey Archery Co., 257 E. 12th Ave., No. St. Paul, MN 55109 (broadheads, points)

## MISCELLANEOUS SHOOTING EQUIPMENT

A.J.'s Targets, 267 Highland Ave., Downington, PA 19335 (targets)
Don Adams Marine, Rt. 2, Box 241, Veneta, OR 97487 (bow wood)
Henry A. Bitzenburger, Rt. 2, Box M1, Sherwood, OR 97140 (jigs)
Bohning Adhesives Co., Ltd., Rt. 2, Box 140, Lake City, MI 49651 (lacquers, epoxy, other materials and accessories)
Calmont Compound Archery Target, Box 207, Inverness, MS 38753 (targets)
Freeman's Archery, RR 3, Box 536, Plainfield, IN 46168 (targets)
Jim Dougherty Archery, 4304 E. Pine Place, Tulsa, OK 74115 (bows, arrows)
Dave Miller, Rare Woods, 3180 Bandini Blvd., Vernon, CA 90023 (bow wood)
Old Master Crafters Co., 130 Lebaron St., Waukegan, IL 60085 (bow making materials)
Papi, P.O. Box 55184, Fort Washington, MD 20022 (trophy system for bowhunters)
San Angelo, Box 984, San Angelo, TX 76901 (bow racks, other accessories)
Earl Ullrich, Box 862, Roseburg, OR 97470 (bow wood)
Van's Archery Supplies, P.O. Box 929, St. George, UT 84470 (arrow puller)
Zonkers, P.O. Box 4304, Auburn Heights, MI 48057

## BOW & ARROW CASES
Alco Carrying Cases, Inc., 601 W. 26th St., New York, NY 10001
The Allen Co., Inc., 2330 W. Midway Blvd., Broomfield, CO 80020
Gun-Ho, 110 E. Tenth Street, St. Paul, MN 55101
Paul-Reed, Incorporated, P.O. Box 227, Charlevoix, MI 49720
Penguin Industries, P.O. Box 97, Parkesburg, PA 19365
Protecto Plastics, Incorporated, 201 Alpha Road, Wind Gap, PA 18091
Sloane Products, P.O. Box 56, Saugus, CA 91350
Sylvester's Archery Supplies, 212 Hawthorne Circle, Creve Coeur, IL 61611

## VARMINT & GAME CALLS
Burnham Brothers, Box 110, Marble Falls, TX 78654
Faulk's Game Call Company, Incorporated, 616 18th Street, Lake Charles, LA 70601
P.S. Olt Company, Pekin, IL 61554
Penn's Woods Products, Incorporated, 19 W. Pittsburgh Street, Delmont, PA 15625
Scotch Game Call Company, Incorporated, 60 Main Street, Oakfield, NY 14125
Johnny Stewart Game Calls, Incorporated, 5100 Fort Avenue, P.O. Box 1909, Waco, TX 76703
Thomas Game Calls, P.O. Box 336, Winnsboro, TX 75494
Western Call & Decoy, P.O. Box 425, Portland, OR 97207

## MISCELLANEOUS HUNTING EQUIPMENT

A&W Archer, Box 1219, Garden Grove, CA 92640 (bow quivers)
Avery Corporation, P.O. Box 99, 221 N. Main Street, Electra, TX 76360 (varmint calling lights)
Baker Manufacturing Company, Box 1003, Valdosta, GA 31601 (tree stands)
Belke Company, 2308 Pleasant, New Holstein, WI 53061 (saw-knife)
Joe Bender, Stoddard, WI 54658 (No-Glove finger protectors)
Vic Berger, 1019 Garfield Avenue, Springfield, OH 45504 (Berger button)
Brownell, Incorporated, Moodus, CT 06469 (bowstring material)
Buck Knives, 1717 N. Magnolia Avenue, El Cajon, CA 92022 (hunting knives)
Buck Stop Lure Company, 3015 Grow Road, Stanton, MI 48888 (insect repellent, deer lure)
C/J Enterprises, 410 S. Citrus Avenue, Covina, CA 91722 (one-piece aluminum release)
Camillus Cutlery Company, Camillus, NY 13031 (hunting knives)

Camp Trails, P.O. Box 14500, Phoenix, AZ 95031 (backpacking and camping equipment)

The Coleman Company, Inc., 250 N. St. Francis, Wichita, KS 67201 (camping equipment)

Cutter Laboratories, Incorporated, Fourth and Parker Streets, Berkeley, CA 94619 (insect repellents, snake bite kits, first aid kits)

Deer Me Products, Box 34, Anoka, MN 55303 (tree steps, tree stands, deer drags)

Dolch Enterprises, Incorporated, Box 606, Westlake, LA 70669 (telescopic bowstringer)

General Recreation Industries, Fayette, AL 35555 (sleeping bags)

Gordon Plastics, Incorporated, 2872, S. Santa Fe, Vista, CA 92083 (giberglass shafts)

Gutmann Cutlery Company, Incorporated, 900 S. Columbus Ave., Mt. Vernon, NY 10550 (hunting knives)

Jet-Aer Corporation, 100 Sixth Ave., Paterson, NJ 07524 (insect repellents, game lures, fabric and leather treatments and water-proofings)

Jim Dougherty Archery, 4304 E. Pine Place, Tulsa, OK 74115 (all archery equipment)

Kelty Pack, Incorporated, P.O. Box 639, 10909 Tuxford St., Sun Valley, CA 91352 (pack bags, pack frames, soft packs)

Killian Chek-It, 12350 S.E. Stevens Rd., Portland, OR 97226 (com-petition string release)

Kwikee Kwiver Company, 7292 Peaceful Valley Rd., Acme, MI 49610 (bow quivers)

Len Company, BT-101, Brooklyn, NY 11214 (survival knives)

Magna-Flight, 212 Hawthorne Circle, Creve Coeur, IL 61611 (bow-string releases)

Mac's Archery Supplies, Incorporated, 6336 W. Fond du Lac Ave., Milwaukee, WI 53218 (bowfishing reels, arrows, points)

Marco's Enterprises, 2120 Ludington St., Escanaba, MI 49829 (deer soap)

Mountain Products Corporation, 123 S. Wanatchee Ave., Wenatchee, WA 98801 (lightweight camping gear)

Natural Scent Company, 1170 Elgin Ave., Salt Lake City, UT 84106 (animal scents)

New Archery Products, 107 Berrywood Dr., Marietta, GA 30060 (flipper rests)

Nock Rite Company, 3720 Crestview Circle, Brookfield, WI 53005 (bowstring attachments)

Old Master Crafters Company, 130 Lebaron St., Waukegan, IL 60085 (bow laminations)

W.C. Phillips, 2515 Magnolia, Texarkana, TX 75501 (tree stands)

R&D Products, P.O. Box 154, Euless, TX 76039 (arrow holders and bowfishing points)

Ranger Manufacturing Company, P.O. Box 3386, Augusta, GA 30904 (camouflage clothing)

Ranging, Incorporated, 90 N. Lincoln Rd., East Rochester, NY 14445 (range-determining devices)

Ron's Porta-Pak Manufacturing Company, P.O. Box 141, Greenbrier, AR 72058 (tree stands)

Rorco, Box 1007, State College, PA 16801 (shaft spiders)

S&K Manufacturing, 1707 S.E. 136th Avenue, Vancouver, WA 98664 (hunting release)

San Angelo Die Casting Company, Box 984, San Angelo, TX 76901 (bow racks and holders)

Saunders Archery Company, P.O. Box 476, Industrial Site, Columbus, NE 68601 (complete line of archery accessories)

Schrade Walden Cutlery Corporation, New York, NY 12428 (hunting knives)

Shockalator, 12122 Monter, Bridgeton, MO 63044 (mercury bow stabilizers)

Smiths Sports Products, 925 Hillcrest Place, Pasadena, CA 91106 (bow slings)

Trophyland USA, Incorporated, 7001 West 20th Avenue, P.O. Box 4606, Hialeah, FL 33014 (trophies)

Trueflight Manufacturing Company, Incorporated, Manitowish Waters, WI 54545 (string silencers, nock locators and assorted accessories)

Wilson-Allen Corporation, Box 104, Windsor, MO 65360 (brush nock)

L.C. Whiffen Company, Incorporated, 923 S. 16th Street, Milwaukee, WI 53204 (bow quivers)

R.C. Young Company, Incorporated, Manitowoc, WI 54220 (feather trimmers)

## NATIONAL BOWHUNTING ORGANIZATIONS

American Archery Council (AAC), 200 Castlewood Rd., N. Palm Beach, FL 33408

Archery Manufacturers Organization (AMO), 200 Castlewood Rd., N. Palm Beach, FL 33408

The Fred Bear Sports Club, RR4, 4600 S.W. 41st Blvd., Gainesville, FL 32601

Bowhunters Who Care, P.O. Box 476, Columbus, NE 68601

National Archery Association (NAA), 1951 Geraldson Dr., Lancaster, PA 17601

National Bowfishing Association, 1895 N. McCart, Stephenville, TX 76401

National Field Archery Association (NFAA), Rt. 2, Box 514, Red-lands, CA 92373

Pope & Young Club, Rt. 1, Box 147, Salmon, ID 83467

Professional Bowhunters Society, P.O. Box 13, New Concord, OH 43762

## MAIL ORDER DEALERS
(not listed elsewhere)

Al's Sports Inc., 195 E. State St., Iola, WI 54945

Anderson Archery, Box 130, Grand Ledge, MI 48837

Archery Discount Co., P.O. Box 324, Youngwood, PA 15697

Archery Distributors, Box 488, Holmen, WI 54636

Arrowhead Archery, 1454 Velp Ave., Green Bay, WI 54636

Barefoot Archery, Inc., 5501 Wilkinson Blvd., Charlotte, NC 28202

Bowhunters Discount Warehouse, Inc., Zeigler Rd., Wellsville, PA 17365

Bowhunters Supply, Rt. 6, Box 1158, Parkerburg, WV 26101

Butler's Archery, 100 8th St., No. 1, Evanston, WY 82930

Cabela's Inc., Sidney, NE 69162

Deercliff Archery Supply, 2852 Lavista Rd., Decatur, GA 30033

Feline Archery, 220 Willow Crossing Rd., Greensburg, PA 15601

Glenn's Bow Benders' Supplies, 204 W. Main, Morganfield, KY 42437

Graham Archery Sales, 425 Faith Rd., Salisbury, SC 28144

S. Meltzer & Sons, 118-120 Outwater Lane, Garfield, NJ 07026

North American Archery Distributors, Box 248, Rouzerville, PA 17250

PGS Archery, 46 Almond St., Vineland, NJ 08360

Robert's Archery Co., P.O. Box 7, Palmer, MA 01069

Sayne's Archery, Inc., P.O. Box 328, 6766 St. Rd. 128, Miamitown, OH 45041

Seattle Archery, Box 120, Lynwood, WA 98036

Southeastern Archery, 101 Gatlin Shopping Center, Orlando, FL 32806

TJS Distributors, 110 2nd Ave., Pelham, NY 10803

West Virginia Archery Supply, 616 Chestnut St., S. Charleston, WV 25309

Western Archery Sales, 3505 E. 39th Ave., Denver, CO 80205

Western-Direct Sales, Box 1270, Moab, UT 84532